KILLER
NURSE

KILLER NURSE

JOHN FOXJOHN

BERKLEY BOOKS, NEW YORK

THE BERKLEY PUBLISHING GROUP
Published by the Penguin Group
Penguin Group (USA) Inc.
375 Hudson Street, New York, New York 10014, USA

USA | Canada | UK | Ireland | Australia | New Zealand | India | South Africa | China

Penguin Books Ltd., Registered Offices: 80 Strand, London WC2R 0RL, England
For more information about the Penguin Group, visit penguin.com.

KILLER NURSE

A Berkley Book / published by arrangement with the author

Berkley Books are published by The Berkley Publishing Group.
BERKLEY® is a registered trademark of Penguin Group (USA) Inc.
The "B" design is a trademark of Penguin Group (USA) Inc.

For information, address: The Berkley Publishing Group,
a division of Penguin Group (USA) Inc.,
375 Hudson Street, New York, New York 10014.

ISBN: 978-0-425-26365-5

PUBLISHING HISTORY
Berkley premium edition / August 2013

PRINTED IN THE UNITED STATES OF AMERICA

10 9 8 7 6 5 4 3 2

Cover design by Jane Hammer.
Cover photos: *Hospital Hallway* © Randall Schwanke; *Biohazard Sign* © mtkang.
Interior text design by Laura K. Corless.

Most Berkley Books are available at special quantity discounts for bulk purchases for sales,
promotions, premiums, fund-raising, or educational use. Special books, or book excerpts, can
also be created to fit specific needs. For details, write: Special.Markets@us.penguingroup.com.

ALWAYS LEARNING   PEARSON

I'd like to dedicate this book to the victims: Ms. Thelma Metcalf, Ms. Clara Strange, Mr. Garlin Kelley Jr., Ms. Cora Bryant, Ms. Opal Few, Ms. Marva Rhone, Ms. Carolyn Risinger, Ms. Debra Oates, Ms. Graciela Castaneda, and Ms. Marie Bradley, and all of their family members—especially Linda Few James and Donald Young.

ACKNOWLEDGMENTS

I am sure that there are authors who can go through the process of writing a book of this nature with little or no help—I'm not one of those. Because of the vast number of people who have helped and contributed to this book, my biggest fear in writing this acknowledgment is leaving out people who were important to me in this process. Please, if I do, it wasn't intentional. First, I'd like to thank my agent, Jill Marsal; Catherine Knepper; Laury Frieber; and Berkley editor Shannon Jamieson Vazquez. Also, I'd like to thank someone who helped more than he knows: Kevin Flynn.

Along these same lines, I interviewed 237 people, and quite a few of them asked me not to mention their names, and of course, I kept my word on that. But still, you know who you are. Please know that my gratitude is just as great for you as those whose names are mentioned in this acknowledgment.

I would like to thank Clyde Herrington, not only for his cooperation, but his service to Angelina County.

Also from the Angelina County Court House: Art Bauereiss, Katrina Carswell, Layne Thompson, Judge Barry Bryan, Candace Parke, Deborah Lee, Charlotte Griffith, Paul Love, and Johnny Purvis.

Thanks to Chris Tortorice, Assistant U.S. Attorney.

Also the people I spent a lot of time with dealing with open records, release of information, and freedom of information requests: the ladies from Angelina County and district clerk's office—especially Kathy Claunch. Also, Health and Human Services, Texas Department of State Health Services, the Centers for Disease Control, Texas Attorney General's Office, Texas Department of Public Safety, Houston Police Department, and Texas Department of Corrections.

From the Lufkin Police Department: Sergeant Stephen Abbott, Sergeant Mike Shurley, and Christy Pate.

I'd also like to thank Joe Reikers, federal investigator, Office of Inspector General; Bill Horton, investigator, Texas Attorney General's Office; and several others who wished for their names not to be mentioned.

I'd like to thank Merry Bright for the medical knowledge.

For some of the insight into the defense: Steve Taylor, Cheryl Pettry, and LinMarie Garsee. And others from the defense team who didn't want their names used.

Thanks also to the twelve jurors and two alternates in the Saenz trial: Martha Moffett, Caren Brooks, Gail Brasuell, Brenda Gibson, David Bradford, Kimberly Flores, Daniel Phipps, Laura Bush, Karla Myers, Yolanda Bell, Larry Walker, Regina McAvoy, Willie Wigley, and Kristine Bailey.

Special thanks go to several DaVita employees—past and present—as well as those friends, family, and former schoolmates of Kimberly Saenz who wished to remain anonymous.

CONTENTS

PART I

RISING RIVER

The quality of mercy is not strained.
It droppeth as the gentle rain from heaven . . .
It is enthroned in the hearts of kings;
It is an attribute to God himself;
And earthly power doth then show likest God's
When mercy seasons justice.

—WILLIAM SHAKESPEARE

CHAPTER 1

THE OWL

Lightning flashed and thunder filled the sky as citizens of Angelina County, Texas, somberly rushed to the courthouse on Thursday morning, March 29, 2012. In addition to the county's residents, the horde included newspaper and TV journalists—local, state, and national—plus family and friends of the victims, as well as of the defendant, and of the lead defense attorney. The previous day, both sides of the trial had rested. All that was left in this historic case were closing arguments and jury deliberation to see if Kimberly Clark Saenz would become the county's first serial killer, and if so, would the jury elect to send a woman to Texas's infamous death row?

The trial had begun almost four weeks earlier, when Saenz (pronounced "signs"), an East Texas nurse, was charged with five counts of aggravated assault and one count of capital murder. Saenz, a former nurse at the DaVita Lufkin Dialysis Center, was accused of having harmed or killed many of the dialysis patients under her care. There were two things that made this case unique and garnered national attention: First, that one count of capital murder (a very serious charge that can carry the death penalty) actually included *five* murders. Second, the method Saenz was accused of using to injure and kill her alleged victims (by injecting the patients with bleach) had never been heard of before.

As the rain poured down, drivers circled the courthouse looking for parking places that didn't exist. If they were hoping someone would move, they were wasting their time—no one was leaving. The lucky ones who'd found parking spots earlier hurried through the downpour, anxious to get out of the rain and into the courtroom.

Prior to the Saenz trial, the Angelina County Courthouse had employed no security. But now sheriff's deputies patrolled the floor, and two stood before the locked courtroom doors with metal detectors. In addition to the media firestorm that would be sure to erupt no matter what the verdict was, a recent courtroom shooting in nearby Beaumont, Texas, had everyone's nerves on edge. Then there was the young man who'd called the DA's office on the second day of trial and informed authorities that he was coming from Louisiana to "get" Kimberly Saenz. He eventually showed up in Lufkin, but Deputy Sheriff Johnny Purvis and others were waiting. After patting the man down for weapons and not finding any, he eventually told them that he had heard about the trial on the news and he believed Kimberly Saenz had once tried to kill him. As it turned out, he had her confused with someone else. Although the threat didn't amount to anything, he'd been drawn by news reports of the trial, and in such a high-profile case, officials were acutely aware that there were plenty of other chances for trouble.

Cryptic comments and vague threats had also appeared on KTRE-TV's website from anonymous posters, apparently looking for vengeance against Saenz. Law enforcement took these comments and potential threats seriously, and Sergeant Luna with the Angelina County Sheriff's Department confirmed that they had a lot to do with the extra security. Tensions were high even before the comments emerged, and the last thing this sensational trial needed was a violent incident in the courtroom.

The strain of the trial had worn down everyone involved. As the weeks slipped past, the attorneys and their assistants' attitudes had withered from friendly to a hard-jawed exhaustion. They now seemed to slump where they'd stood tall before.

On that rainy Thursday morning, the courtroom was full. Sitting behind the prosecution were the families of the victims—and given the number of victims, there were a *lot* of family members, most of whom believed that Saenz had killed or injured their loved ones. A smoldering rage seemed to burn under the surface, just waiting for a crack to escape.

On the other side of the courtroom sat Saenz's supporters, her family and the members of her church, who were fervent believers in Saenz's innocence and whose attitudes seemed to say that they would brook no disagreement.

The combustible atmosphere spilled out beyond the courtroom doors, as did the rampant speculation about Saenz's guilt or innocence. People gathered in groups in the hallways to discuss what was happening inside, or rushed out during breaks to find a quiet place to make calls and send texts. In the coffee shops, restaurants, barbershops and beauty salons, and even churches, everywhere people gathered, the debate raged whether Saenz was guilty or not, and whether the jury would actually convict her.

Citizens with no more experience of the law than what they'd seen on *Law and Order* were saying things like, "The preponderance of evidence doesn't measure up to a conviction." In truth, the citizens of Angelina County overwhelmingly believed that Saenz was guilty but would walk out of the courtroom a free woman. According to a jailer who heard the remark, one inmate in the county jail awaiting transport to prison for embezzlement of six figures from her employer said, "I got thirteen years for stealing money, and she killed five people and she's going to get away with it."

But of course, Kimberly Clark Saenz's destiny wasn't in her hands. That would be up to twelve of her peers.

———

Angelina County has two district courts, and both of them are located on the second floor of the courthouse. The 159th district courtroom, the older, rundown one, sits in the front at the landing of the stairs. The 217th district courtroom, the new, modernized one, is in the back of the second floor.

Originally, the trial was scheduled to take place in the newer courtroom, but during *voir dire*, Judge Barry Bryan changed the location. The older one was three times the size of the newer one, and he correctly assumed that they would need all the space they had available.

As it turned out, not even the older courtroom was large enough to accommodate all the spectators. Two small windows in the doors allowed people to peek in, but during the trial, the only peeking done was from TV cameras; film crews were barred from the courtroom and had to make do with filming through the windows. Inside were two sections with a rail and a small swinging gate that separated the court from the large spectator section. Besides a hint of stale sweat and urine, the two sections of pew-like seats with dirty, stained cushions, scratched and scarred from decades of use, dominated the back part of the courtroom. The walls on two sides were mostly comprised of dark paneling, and the wall to the east had large windows covered by dark venetian blinds that allowed shards of light through.

However, on this morning, with the rain and overcast sky, little light bled through—just enough to reflect eerily off the large marble slab on the wall behind the judge's bench. Sirens from the fire station a block away cut through the silence. Instead of dampening the mood of the spectators packed into the room, the noise heightened the tension.

The strain inside the courtroom dialed up several notches when thirty-eight-year-old Kimberly Clark Saenz strolled in. Although facing a possible death sentence, her mood, either by design or temperament, didn't match the weather or that of the spectators. At approximately five-feet-four and weighing in the neighborhood of one-seventy, she had shoulder-length dark hair, parted on the side and held in place with a barrette. Heavy makeup helped hide acne scars.

On this morning she wore black slacks, a teal-colored blouse with a flowery embellished neckline under a dove gray blazer, and a three-strand necklace of large turquoise, olive, jasper, and pink stones.

Waiting on Saenz and the finish of the trial was fifty-three-year-old Clyde Herrington, the district attorney for Angelina County. Herrington could best be described as pudgy, and when he walked, his feet pointed out at forty-five-degree angles. He wore glasses and his brown hair was thin, disappearing slightly at the back of the crown, with only a spattering of gray mixed in.

The veteran district attorney, who was prosecuting his last big case before intending to retire at the end of the year, led off with his closing arguments. In contrast to everyone else in the courtroom, his demeanor was soft and seemingly unaffected by the circumstances and the extreme anxiety and responsibility he shouldered. His words and body language had remained even-tempered throughout the trial, except when he'd caught a witness lying. Only then had he shown anger.

For thirty minutes, Herrington reminded the jury about the two eyewitnesses, what they'd seen and said, and how everything they'd told the police and had later testified to had proven correct.

Herrington also showed sections of Kimberly Saenz's taped interview with the police—including the part where, unprompted, she told them she'd never researched bleach poisoning. The jury again got to see that she'd said this on her own, not as an answer to a police question.

This interview had also revealed several things that were in direct contradiction to what Saenz would later testify to the grand jury—including an acknowledgment that she'd used a 10cc syringe to measure bleach even though she knew she wasn't supposed to.

Herrington next showed the interview with the grand jury, where Saenz contradicted what she'd told the police, but did tell them that she thought that DaVita, her employer, was using her as a scapegoat. Herrington pointed out that in her first interview with the police, Saenz didn't have an attorney to tell her what to say. He called the grand jury testimony "the birth of the scapegoat theory."

The DA also submitted pictures of all the victims. While the jury had heard the names a thousand times, the pictures connected the dots for them—they literally gave faces to the victims, making them human, not just statistics.

It wasn't until Herrington finished the first part of his closing argument and turned the podium over to the defense attorney that he seemed to become tense. Ryan Deaton's reputation among his adversaries on the prosecution side was that he might misrepresent facts, and Herrington was bracing himself for it.

Deaton's athletic physical appearance and young age contrasted sharply with Herrington. Deaton had a fashionable three-day growth of hair on his face, and stood a few inches over six feet with wide shoulders. There was a permanent scrape mark on his forehead, just above the bridge of his nose. His shaved head, an apparent attempt to conceal early male pattern baldness, stood out especially in the afternoons with a five o'clock shadow. Deaton's shaved head did more than hide his lack of hair. When he got angry or upset, a bright red splotch about four to five inches in diameter appeared on the left side of the back of his head, a dead giveaway that things weren't going his way.

As Deaton began his closing arguments, something occurred that left an indelible impression: an owl hooted a couple of times just outside the courthouse window. Deep East Texas is steeped in traditions and in some cases superstitions—one of which is that hearing the hoot of an owl during the day means imminent death. It's a superstition not only confined to East Texas; many other cultures also look on the owl as an omen of death or disaster. For instance, the Romans believed that the deaths of people such as Julius Caesar, Augustus, and several other famous leaders were predicted by the hoot of an owl.

To those who believed in such things, it seemed ominous. But if Deaton heard the owl or knew about its significance, he didn't show it. He went on to speak for almost two hours with his closing, reiterating his main argument in support of Saenz's innocence: he blamed DaVita and accused them of a cover-up—of using his client as a scapegoat. He reminded the jury that DaVita was a huge Fortune 500 company. He told the jury and the spectators about Biblical goats, and how the Jews would cast all their sins on the goat and send it out to die as a sacrifice to rid themselves of all their own sins. He compared this to what DaVita had done to his client.

He begged the jury not to let this big company come into East Texas and snatch one of their own away from her home—they couldn't let a corporate giant blame this poor East Texas girl for their sins.

Deaton also blamed the water in the dialysis center for the deaths and injuries to the patients. He pointed out that Saenz was "only one of three employees that were giving meds, and that was how she was connected to all the patients." He told the jury that one of the witnesses had claimed that Saenz injected 20cc of bleach, but that wasn't true—the witness never said how much bleach was in the syringe. What she'd actually said was that Saenz had used two syringes.

Deaton reminded the jury of how another witness had changed her testimony. In fact, he told the jury, she had been told how to testify in the trial. He left out how she'd testified that the instructions she'd received had been simply to tell the truth.

The more Deaton spoke, the redder Herrington's face got and the madder he became.

Still Deaton wasn't done. He told the jury that the doctor overseeing the DaVita clinic hadn't cared enough about his patients to make them go to the hospital after it was reported that two patients had been injected with bleach. Deaton played his sympathy card—pointing out that his client was a daughter, wife, and the mother of two children. He told the jury about how the police had unfairly snatched Saenz from her trailer home, took her to the police station, and grilled her.

When Deaton finished, so did Herrington's calm demeanor. He shot out of his seat like someone had hit his rear with a cattle prod. His first words set the tone for the remainder of his closing: "That has to be the biggest case of misrepresented facts I have ever heard in my life!"

Indeed, Deaton's spin had been so egregious that Kristine Bailey, the first alternate on the jury, later said she'd "wanted to stand up and cheer" when Herrington took issue with Deaton's untruths. She wasn't alone. Quite a few people who had followed all of the trial agreed with her assessment.

The more the angered Herrington spoke, the lower Deaton slumped in his seat. This was also noted by the jury. "One thing I noticed when Clyde got up and started talking, I noticed Ryan just kept going farther and farther down in his chair—you know, that kind of stuck," said jury member Willie Wigley. "Not so much what Clyde was saying, but Ryan's reaction to it."

As Herrington talked, his seething anger turned into raw emotion, and the court saw another side to him, one that had not previously shown itself. It was obvious to all that the DA believed with every fiber of his body that Kimberly Saenz was guilty, and he wanted her to pay for what she'd taken away from the families of the victims. With tears running down his face and his voice trembling, Herrington said something else that stuck with jurors and spectators alike, something that spoke directly to the question of motive. "Why do mothers scald their babies? You don't need to know what evil is to recognize it." In other words, even if everyone knew all the reasons why Saenz had killed and injured the patients, they'd never understand them.

When Herrington finished and sat, emotionally spent, not a single person in the courtroom breathed—not even the judge. Many attempted to choke back their own emotions. It was like a giant vacuum had sucked all the air out of the packed room. Moments passed before the judge was finally able to speak.

Many who were in the courtroom that day, including other local attorneys who'd shown up just to watch the finish, said that Herrington's closing was one of the greatest they'd ever heard. Five days later, *The Lufkin News*, in their "Toast and Roast" editorial, toasted Clyde Herrington "for his impassioned plea to the jury just before it retired to deliberate its verdict." The article observed that "[y]ou could tell as he choked up that he was determined to get justice for the victims' families, and not just because it was his last big case as district attorney."

The newspaper then "roasted" defense attorney Ryan Deaton for his "in-your-face closing arguments on Saenz's behalf. . . . he crossed the line by berating the state's witnesses as 'crazy' and 'liars.'"

However, if Deaton had raised doubts about the prosecutor's evidence, and if his scapegoat theory about Fortune 500 DaVita held sway in the minds of the jury of working-class East Texans, then how he'd come across in closing arguments was moot. His job was to get his client off, and if he accomplished that, he would be a hero, at least to some.

The jury began deliberations at one thirty and the hours dragged. Little clusters of people—prosecutors, investigators, family members of the victims, and friends of the defense attorney there to support him—gathered all around the second floor of the courthouse.

Close to five in the afternoon, the normal time that

the jury left, a note came from the Saenz jury that they planned to deliberate until seven that night, but when seven came, the jurors left without having yet reached a verdict. Family members and friends of Saenz said this was the longest night in their lives.

At nine the next morning, the jury reconvened, but the morning dragged by with no verdict. The same conversations as the day before swept through the groups: "Do you think she's guilty?" "Will the jury let her go?" But most of all, "How long do you think the jury will take?"

Although no one had an answer to this question, most believed that the jury would have a verdict by that evening, but this was more of a desire than outright knowledge.

After lunch on Friday, word passed from one group to another that the jury had taken care of three of the six charges. This seemed to revive the spirits of those waiting, until someone mentioned that it may not mean anything— it depended on which charges they'd done. The person pointed out that one of those charges contained five murders. In order to convict Saenz of the capital murder charge, the jury would have to find her guilty of at least two of the five murders.

Time passed like watching a turtle race. Some people attempted to work or read, but they, too, didn't fare well with their tasks. People's nerves were tottering on the edge, and those emotions weren't conducive to anything that required concentration.

Finally, at three thirty, word swept through the second floor that the jury was almost done, which sparked a mass of cell phone calls to pass on the news. Still, it wasn't until Saenz, her family, and attorney showed shortly thereafter that real hope began to thread its way through the gathering.

Anticipation rose even higher when a long line began to form outside the courthouse doors. TV reporters with camera crews crowded close, or stood on the steps out of the way, where they had a better view of the people waiting to get into the courtroom. Sheriff's deputies were again on hand blocking the doors with their handheld metal detectors.

Anticipation crackled up and down the line that reached all the way to the end of the second floor. The news began to leap from mouth to mouth. The jury had reached a verdict.

Suddenly, the courtroom doors opened, and the noise in the hallway vanished.

As the line inched forward, the only noise became the loud beeps from the metal detectors, which had been turned to their most sensitive settings.

Saenz's immediate family took up their stations in the first two rows behind the defense table on the left; just behind them sat Lesa and Vann Kelley, the husband and wife investigative team hired by the defense. Along with them were friends of the defense attorney and friends and supporters from Saenz's church.

The right-hand side, behind the prosecution table, filled with spectators and people who had assisted in the prosecution, but most of the seats were taken by the true victims in this case—family members of the people Saenz was accused of killing. Their faces showed the strain they'd been through, and the families sat close together, bodies touching, black and white alike—maybe to garner some strength from the person next to them. Many of the family members of the victims sat with their arms wrapped around themselves almost in a protective cocoon, while others visibly trembled.

Several of these family members said that going in, they didn't know if Kimberly Saenz was guilty or innocent—they just wanted the truth of what happened to their loved one to come out. Some said that if she was found guilty, they hoped that she wouldn't get the death penalty. Two family members pointed out that the rest of her life in prison would be much better because she'd have all that time to think about it—death was too easy. Other family members said that only God had the right to put someone to death. Several said that, either way, they would leave the verdict in the hands of God. He was the final judge, and He would impart unto the jury what they should do.

With the family that Friday was Ms. Marie Bradley, one of the surviving victims. Alongside Ms. Bradley sat several ex-DaVita employees who'd also testified in the trial. Their attitude seemed to be, "We cared for your loved ones and we'll stand by you now."

The tension inside the courtroom was as thick as the East Texas humidity. People sat rigid in their seats, most leaning forward—some rocking slightly. Every pair of eyes in the courtroom went to Kimberly Saenz as she entered, slumped slightly, her eyes red and swollen from crying—in stark contrast to her earlier appearance and demeanor throughout the trial. Most pictures taken by the paper or TV as the trial progressed had showed a woman laughing or smiling who appeared to be supremely confident she was about to be found not guilty.

After Saenz collapsed in her seat, everyone rose when Judge Barry Bryan entered. With silver hair and beard with traces of gray showing through, the judge looked exactly as someone might picture a district judge to look like. The judge had the ability to be stern when needed, and even funny when appropriate. He took care of the jury, and the people who worked for him loved him. Everyone, even people who weren't that fond of him, agreed on one thing—Judge Bryan was fair. What better recommendation can a judge receive?

As Herrington said later, "I don't always agree with his decisions, but I know that when he makes one, he has thought about it a lot."

However, on this day, moments before the jury was to enter and deliver the verdict, Judge Bryan was neither stern nor funny, but solemn. After a warning to the spectators on how to behave themselves when the six verdicts were read, he indicated for the bailiff to bring in the jury.

It was easy to tell the newcomers to the courtroom—mostly media from out of town—because the ones who'd followed the trial knew to rise when the jury entered. In the Angelina County Courthouse, the spectators rose out of respect for the jury just as they did for the judge.

As the twelve jurors and three alternates filed in, some were visibly shaking. The women had scared looks on their faces, and the men were somber. Two closed their eyes while the others stared at the judge—all avoided looking at the spectators in the court or the defendant. When the judge asked if the jury had come to a unanimous verdict, foreman Larry Walker's voice cracked when he answered, "Yes, sir." Once the bailiff handed the verdict sheet to the judge, most of the jurors turned their heads and faced Saenz, as if they wanted to show their solidarity in the verdict.

The judge asked Saenz to rise, and she got to her feet on wobbly legs. At her side were defense attorney Ryan Deaton on one side and Steve Taylor, Saenz's court-appointed defense attorney, on the other.

What Kimberly Saenz's life would be like after this, no one could say at that moment. Even if the jury pronounced her not guilty, the mother of two as well as her family would always have to live with the lingering stigma that she was a serial killer who got away with it.

However, the alternative would be what the owl was hooting about. Life in prison without a chance for parole, which meant Saenz would leave prison in a box—her life as she knew it would end. In what would perhaps be a grim case of poetic justice, if Saenz received the death penalty, she'd die by lethal injection—the same fate she'd allegedly given her victims.

Seconds that felt like hours passed as Judge Bryan looked at the charge sheet and the verdicts—all six of them. Five of the charges were for aggravated assault with a deadly weapon. Those were the only charges for which the jury would actually impose the sentence. The sixth charge was for all the murders.

The judge looked at Kimberly Saenz and began to read the jury's verdict.

CHAPTER 2

RÉSUMÉ

On March 7, 2012, not long after Kimberly Clark Saenz's trial began, Nancy Grace featured Lufkin, Texas, on her CNN show. She began by calling Lufkin a suburb of Houston. This statement tells people two things about Nancy Grace—she has obviously never been to Lufkin, nor consulted a map either.

In Grace's defense, Lufkin had no reason to be on the world's radar before Kimberly Clark Saenz put it there. Cut deep into the piney woods of East Texas, 120 miles north of Houston and 150 miles southwest of Dallas, Lufkin is in Angelina County, named for a Hainai Native American woman who reportedly assisted early missionaries and so was named Angelina by the Spanish. Lufkin is the county seat.

The relative size of the town depends on whom you ask. To Nancy Grace and others outside of East Texas, Lufkin is a small town. In 2008, it had a population of around 30,000. However, the heart of East Texas is made up of a lot of truly small towns and communities— Huntington, Zavalla, Diboll, and Hudson surround Lufkin, each with its own government, school, stores, and post office, and not a one of them with a population over 5,000. Unincorporated communities such as Pollok—the area where Saenz was raised—also dot the landscape around Lufkin and make up the rest of Angelina County. Residents of these little towns and communities consider Lufkin a big town, maybe even a city. After all, Lufkin is where they travel for entertainment, shopping, eating out, and in many cases, work.

Geography has a tendency to mold people, and the citizens of Angelina County are no different. Most people in the county are descendants from East Texans—people who moved to the area and remained not only because of the forests, rivers, lakes, and abundance of fish and wildlife but also because of the lifestyle. For the most part, East Texans don't like or want a fast-paced, large-city atmosphere with its problems and crime. They are happy right where they are.

A vast majority of Angelina County's blue-collar residents wake up and throw on jeans to go to work rather than dress pants. The largest employer in the county is Lufkin Industries, a manufacturing plant that makes oilfield pumping units and equipment and power transmission products. It's not hard to find ranches and chicken houses in the East Texas landscape, with trucks carrying poultry to Pilgrim's Pride, Lufkin's chicken processing plant. It's even easier to find log trucks on the roads taking advantage of one of the true resources of East Texas, the pine forests. Between those industries, the paper mills and wood processing plants, is where the majority of the people work. Seventy-eight percent of the population are high school graduates, and only 16 percent have a bachelor's degree or higher. Considering that Lufkin's second biggest employer is the Lufkin Independent School District and there's a community college in town, that doesn't average out to much post-high-school education for the rest of the people of Angelina County. But this doesn't bother most folks. You don't need a Ph.D. to process wood or poultry.

Kimberly Clark Saenz's parents were typical East Texans with stalwart East Texas values. William Kent Fowler, who goes by Kent, was born August 24, 1952, and hails from the Redland area, an unincorporated area just north of Lufkin. Saenz's mother, Benjamin Frances Thigpen—known as Bennie—was born on September 8, 1954, in Pollok, in Angelina County. Nineteen-year-old Kent and seventeen-year-old Bennie were married in Angelina County on October 1, 1971. Two years later, on November 3, 1973, the couple had their first child, a daughter they named Kimberly Clark Fowler. In an almost improbable occurrence, their second child, a son they named William Cody Fowler, was born exactly three years after Kimberly, on November 3, 1976.

Like most of their neighbors, Kent and Bennie Fowler epitomized the term "blue-collar." Kent Fowler worked at Rush Truck Center in Lufkin, and Bennie Fowler worked at Lufkin's Walmart, starting in 1980 and working her way up to department manager. Kent, like most East Texans, loved NASCAR and football—especially the

Dallas Cowboys. Friends and acquaintances said that to get this quiet and unassuming man to talk, just mention the Cowboys. Several people described Kent as just a good ol' country boy, and they meant it as a compliment. Both Kent and Bennie Fowler loved country music and performers such as the Sons of the Pioneers, one of America's earliest country and western singing groups. They also liked to gamble—in person at the casinos in Louisiana or on-line. They were members of the Clawson Assembly of God Church, and Bennie especially took her church and her religion very seriously.

This was the culture in which they brought up their daughter and son. The parents' beliefs in many ways echoed those of most parents in East Texas and other working-class communities—seldom can anyone find fault in parents who teach patriotism, God's graces, honesty, family values, and hard work.

But plenty of East Texans said that these teachings didn't seem to take in either of the Fowlers' children. As adults, both Kimberly and Cody got to know law enforcement well.

William Cody Fowler, known to most as Cody, officially began his acquaintance with the police and the court system at the age of seventeen. (If there were earlier incidents, they remain sealed in juvenile records.) On September 16, 1994, a little less than two months before his eighteenth birthday, he was charged with driving while his license was suspended and failure to give information—both misdemeanors.

On October 18, 1997, Cody Fowler married Christiane Hayes. Marriage often has a tendency to make men mature, but from the continuation of his minor problems with the legal system, this doesn't seem to have been the case with Cody. On March 4, 1998, he was cited for failure to maintain financial responsibility. In other words, he didn't have insurance on his vehicle as required by law. He followed that up on March 10 with driving while intoxicated. Then in June, he was again cited, this time for no safety belt.

Somehow he lay low until 2002. On April 15, 2002, he was pulled over for doing 95 in a 55 mph zone. Of course when police pulled him over, they also found that his driver's license had expired.

Christine filed for divorce on May 1, 2002. A week later, on May 8, 2002, Cody was arrested for public intoxication. And if that wasn't enough, Cody followed that up with another arrest for public intoxication on June 14, 2002.

After the divorce became final on July 9, 2002, Cody went almost ten years before he slipped again, but slip he did. He was again arrested for public intoxication on February 22, 2012.

Cody Fowler had a long arrest record, but mainly for minor infractions that either called for fines or a few days in jail. Although driving while drinking was serious, he managed not to get into any accidents, and his later alcohol charges did not involve driving. There's a huge distinction between minor traffic infractions or misdemeanor drinking, and murder.

Although he and his sister, Kimberly, were raised the same way and in the same place, by the same parents, their history would be different.

From the time Kimberly Fowler entered school, people

said that she didn't work as hard as the other students. She participated in sports, especially softball, but she didn't put in the effort to excel.

The longer she stayed in school, the more activities she dropped. In the eighth grade she was a cheerleader and participated in University Interscholastic League events, but by her sophomore year she was no longer a cheerleader and participating halfheartedly in the Central Junior Varsity softball team, which lost all four of the games it played that year.

Most of the students who talked about Saenz during her formative years described her as overly quiet—even morose at times. Small and marked with an acne problem, she didn't quite seem to fit in. A classmate said of her, "She was there, but in ways she wasn't." He couldn't explain his sentiments further—perhaps evidence that Kim didn't leave much of an impression on people. In fact, very few people she grew up going to school with professed to know her all that well, even the ones with whom she'd played sports.

Some of that changed for Saenz in 1990, her sophomore year, when she became involved with a Central senior by the name of Chris Dion Hopper. Chris was everything at Central High School that Saenz wasn't. In 1990, his senior year, he was voted most likely to succeed and most spirited by his class. Not only that, he played basketball and baseball all four years of high school, and was honorable mention all-district in basketball in the 1988–89 school year, and topped that off with second team all-district in 1990.

Chris Hopper had a long and distinguished list of

accolades that included the student council, yearbook staff, and later yearbook editor, and won a Tops in Texas award in 1988 for his work on the yearbook. Besides being Who's Who in computers and Who's Who in journalism, he also won awards for English, and was not only a member of the National Honor Society, but its vice president. As an active member of the Fellowship of Christian Athletes, he helped unite the school's two Christian groups to form one group called Students for Christ.

After Chris Hopper graduated in 1990, Saenz's extracurricular activities stopped. One former fellow student said that Saenz was only into Chris. Evidence seems to back up that statement: on July 26, 1991, before the beginning of Saenz's senior year, she gave birth to a son she named Jacob Hopper. Two months later, in September, the time most of her Central classmates were settling down into their senior year, the new mother was marrying Chris Dion Hopper.

Speculation at the time, whether true or not, was that Saenz had gotten pregnant on purpose in order to "trap" the boy she thought of as Mr. Right. Many of the students agreed that Chris Hopper was Mr. Right but had married Ms. Wrong, for him anyway, and few thought the marriage would last.

The marriage actually lasted six years, until October 1997. After the divorce and with a six-year-old child, Saenz went to work for Fleetwood Transportation Services in Diboll, ten miles south of Lufkin.

At what point Kimberly Fowler Hopper's life began its downward spiral is a matter of opinion. But the fact that her life became like a vortex is not up for debate.

Kimberly Hopper was still working at Fleetwood on September 9, 1999, when she became extremely ill. Her family rushed her to Memorial Hospital in Lufkin with pneumonia. Her condition was so bad the hospital couldn't handle it, and they sent her on an emergency trip to the Methodist Hospital in Houston, where her illness was treated aggressively. Friends said she later referred to September 9, 1999, as a near-death experience. Kim later told others that this was the time she became a Christian. "I felt my ride would be downhill from that time," she said. By "downhill" she meant coasting—as a Christian who'd put her faith in the Lord, she assumed it would be easy streets from here.

But another significant event in her life marked an entirely different kind of downhill slide. At Fleetwood Transportation, she met an employee by the name of Mark Kevin Saenz, who went by Kevin.

Kevin was a recent resident of the county. Previously, he'd lived in Harris County, Houston, but evidence suggests that he didn't agree with Harris County or vice versa. On August 13, 1994, the Houston Police Department had arrested Mark Kevin Saenz for theft greater than $750 but less than $20,000—a third-degree felony. Records of this arrest show him to be a white male, five-feet-seven and a hundred and thirty pounds, with a date of birth of January 28, 1969.

This wasn't the last of his problems with law enforcement in Houston. On November 14, 1996, the Houston Police Department arrested him on another felony: possession of more than five but less than fifty pounds of marijuana. Yes, more than five *pounds*. (To put that into

perspective, average recreational users buy their pot in
Ziploc baggies. Five pounds is like a standard-size metal
office wastebasket stuffed to overflowing with marijuana.)
Quantities that large usually mean the person is dealing.

Records indicate that Kevin Saenz pleaded guilty to
this charge on February 3, 1997, and was sentenced to
four years in the Department of Criminal Justice at Hunts-
ville (the Texas prison system). He began his sentence on
March 5, 1997, and was paroled to Angelina County,
where his mother lived, on August 14, 1998.

While on parole in Angelina County, Saenz was also
pulled over for a traffic violation on October 13, 1999, in
Wickenburg, Arizona (in clear violation of his parole). At
the time, he listed his address as Green Sanders Road in
Pollok, Texas. As it happened, that was the address Kim
C. Hopper listed as her own, too. The ticket would have
been minor and the last he heard of it if he'd paid it, but
he didn't, and the state of Arizona issued a warrant for
his arrest on failure to appear.

None of this dissuaded Kimberly Fowler Hopper, who
married Kevin Saenz on June 10, 2000, six months pregnant with his child. Saenz was finally released from parole
on November 14, 2000. (Whether or not Texas authorities knew that he had a warrant out for his arrest from
Arizona is unclear, but Arizona finally got their pound
of flesh—almost twelve years later. On August 22, 2011,
they collected the money Saenz owed for his traffic violation and failure to appear.)

With a young son and a baby on the way, Kimberly
Clark Fowler Hopper Saenz quit Fleetwood Transportation on June 23, 2000, less than two weeks after marrying

Kevin Saenz. She'd held the job for almost three years, and when she left, they would have hired her back. As things turned out, this distinction made them unique among Kim's employers.

Saenz gave birth to a daughter, Madison Grace, on December 22, 2000, and for the next year and a half, life seemed to have quieted down for the Saenzes.

On July 24, 2002, Kimberly Saenz's parents paid $14,000 to Angelina Savings Bank in Lufkin to pay off the loan on their property. The property then played Ping-Pong. They sold it to Kimberly Saenz for a $20 token fee. However, less than a month later, Kimberly Saenz sold them back that same property for the same fee.

Then one month and three days after paying the loan off, Saenz's family used that same property to borrow $24,225 from the same bank. That loan coincided with their daughter's start at Angelina Community College in the nursing program.

Saenz graduated in December 2004 as an LVN (licensed vocational nurse) in Texas. Naturally her parents and other members of the family were proud of her. In an E! Program interview, her father, Kent, talked about how hard she'd worked to become a nurse. He said, "It was a full-time job just to become a nurse." He also said his daughter hadn't pursued nursing for the money. "It was about helping people," he said. "She just liked to help people."

Her son, Jacob Hopper, told the same program, "I always got to go to school knowing my mom was out there saving lives."

Fate, however, had other plans.

The same month she graduated from nursing school, Saenz went to work for Memorial Hospital, one of the two hospitals in Lufkin, but she worked there only five months. Exactly one month after leaving Memorial, Saenz went to work for Woodland Heights, the other hospital in Lufkin. There's no official indication as to why she left Memorial Hospital, but in August 2005, two months after going to work for Woodland Heights, she was fired for stealing Demerol—a highly controlled narcotic. Records also indicated that she supposedly gave Demerol to patients who were not in pain.

As the whirlpool swirled around her and with a bad work record for the two nursing jobs she'd held in less than a year since earning her degree, complete with the charges against her at the last one, one might assume that Saenz would not get another nursing job anytime soon. However, federal employment laws only allow employers to disclose if they would hire that person back or not. Although Saenz had a serious charge against her nursing license, the Texas State Board of Nursing only lists the allegation against a nurse's license after they have investigated the charges. At that point, the board hadn't yet investigated the Woodland Heights charges about the stolen Demerol. At the time Saenz was looking for another job after Woodland Heights, potential employers only had a clear nursing record to look at. Despite her two no-rehires, nurses were hard to find and in high demand.

Saenz's next job was at Wright Choice Home Health. She worked for them under two months. Employees said that, in the beginning, she was pleasant and on time, and seemed to enjoy the job. However, her mood and work record quickly changed drastically. She became morose when she was there, and often arrived late. Finally, Wright Choice let her go because she was constantly late and didn't call in—and sometimes just simply didn't show up for work.

Kevin Saenz told people at this point that his wife was so depressed that she couldn't get out of bed and he was taking her to Brentwood Hospital in Shreveport, Louisiana, for treatment. She was, in fact, admitted there for depression and suicidal thoughts. While there, she also complained about how Kevin treated her.

After the Brentwood stay, Kimberly applied for employment with the Lufkin State School, a state-supported living facility for people with developmental and mental disabilities. She began work there on October 1, 2006, as a probationary employee. Thirty days later on October 31, 2006, they terminated her employment because she was not suited for her assigned position.

At this point, she'd been a nurse for less than a year and had been fired from four nursing jobs—and had four no-rehires on her record. Then before she celebrated her first year as a nurse, she got her fifth job. On November 27, 2006, she went to work for the Children's Clinic of Lufkin.

The fact was, Kimberly Saenz was having some real problems in her life—problems that people she'd gone to school with, gone to church with, or who knew her socially had no idea about. In addition to her depression, she and Kevin were experiencing serious financial difficulties, which was putting incredible strain on the marriage and surely exacerbating her depression.

The family got some welcome good news when Kevin found a job as an appraiser with the Angelina County Appraisal District, a job that paid well for the area. Whether or not they knew about his criminal history and time in prison is unknown. As an indicator of what he might have made in 2005, in 2012, Chief Appraiser Tim Chambers asked the appraisal board for permission to hire two additional appraisers. The two new employees would cost the county approximately $130,000, which included salary, benefits, equipment, and car allowance. That's roughly $65,000 a year apiece. Considering that a policeman earns in the low $30,000s, and a teacher with a college degree begins in the mid-$30,000 range, $65,000 is a good salary, especially for Angelina County.

Kevin Saenz's annual salary was likely more than many families in Angelina County lived on per year. However, the couple was supporting their eight-year-old daughter as well as Saenz's teenage son, Jacob, from her previous marriage, for whom she hadn't received financial help until on January 23, 2006, when the Texas Attorney General filed a motion to make Chris D. Hopper pay child support.

However, the extra income didn't seem to help. On Friday, December 15, 2006, Green Tree Servicing and Conseco Finance Corporation filed a lawsuit in Angelina County against the accounts, contracts, and notes of one Kim C. Hopper; in other words, she was being sued for nonpayment. With all of these financial strains in play, the family had a hard time making it, even with Kevin's relatively generous paycheck.

And just when Saenz really needed job stability, she

wouldn't find it at the Children's Clinic. On March 20, 2007, the clinic reprimanded her for missing eight and a half days of work without calling in. But the reprimand didn't help, and after working there for six months, her last day there was May 29, 2007.

That wouldn't be the last the Children's Clinic heard from Kimberly Saenz. After they fired her for basically not showing up for work, she filed for unemployment compensation. Some people said she was actually surprised when it was denied.

At this point in Kimberly Saenz's life, the question was not if she'd go down, but how far, and the trip continued. Whether financial troubles were the tipping point or not, on June 7, 2007, Kevin and Kimberly Saenz split up. This in itself wasn't all that unusual, but the police don't usually get involved when a couple separates.

Lufkin police officer Sterling Glawson responded to a disturbance call on Tulane Drive in Lufkin. When he arrived, he was told that an argument had begun between Kimberly and Kevin Saenz at their home in Pollok. Kevin had fled from the home to his mother's boyfriend's home on Tulane Drive, but Kimberly had followed him. In a scuffle, he was injured.

Glawson arrested Kimberly Saenz for assault causing bodily injury and issued her a criminal trespass citation. She spent the night in jail and was released the next day on a $1,500 attorney bond, but once out, she discovered that her husband had gotten an Emergency Magistrate's Protective Order against her. Between June and August 2007, Kim and Kevin worked things out, temporarily at least.

With her employment record as a nurse in Angelina County showing that her longest stint was the six months at the Children's Clinic—and showing her five no-rehires—it seemed a long shot that anyone would hire her again. However, the State Board of Nursing still hadn't investigated that charge from Woodland Heights in Lufkin. A check of Saenz's nursing license didn't show those charges.

Against the odds, Saenz was hired in August 2007 as an LVN, or licensed vocational nurse, working for the DaVita Lufkin Dialysis Center. Kevin Saenz told the E! Program, "She was ecstatic and excited to go to work for DaVita. . . . Her exact words were, 'This job has to be a Godsend.'"

But as events would play out, the "Godsend" turned out to be anything but.

CHAPTER 3

DAVITA

Upon entering the DaVita Lufkin Dialysis Center, visitors and patients alike sat in a waiting room dominated by a "wall of fame" board that covered most of the wall. The board consisted of photos of patients in the middle of a red heart. Large words next to the pictures proclaimed, "Concentrating on compassionate care the DaVita way." The wall of fame board, a point of pride for DaVita, was where patients and staff shared a little about their lives outside of the clinic. DaVita was so proud of this board that each of their 1,300 clinics had to have one.

On most days, the center was full of mature to elderly people waiting to begin their treatments. The patients' ages, physical characteristics, and backgrounds varied, but all had one thing in common: they were there because their kidneys were failing them. Human kidneys help sustain life in many ways. The kidneys maintain blood pressure, convert vitamin D to calcitriol, a form of vitamin D that treats and prevents low levels of calcium in the blood. They also regulate calcium, and secrete the hormone erythropoietin, which triggers red blood cell production. They also act as a filtering system to get rid of impurities in the blood and discharge waste through the urinary tract. People with renal failure need dialysis because the treatment does what the kidneys no longer can. Without dialysis, the patients would die.

Inside the treatment area, the DaVita Lufkin Center had an atmosphere of cleanliness and, like most medical facilities, an antiseptic feeling. In addition, a hint of bleach lingered in the air. Bleach was the predominant disinfectant and sterilizer at DaVita, and other dialysis clinics. In April 2008, the staff at DaVita ran a bleach solution through all the dialysis machines once a week, on Thursdays. After they did that, they then rinsed all the bleach out of the machines. They also used bleach on the floor, where occasionally nurses or PCTs spilled blood. After every patient left a chair where treatments took place, the caregiver wiped the chair, machine, and area down with a bleach solution.

DaVita Lufkin had two bays for patients. Each bay had a nursing station that overlooked the open end of a large horseshoe-shaped arrangement around three walls of the bay, and in the center of the horseshoe, two rows of patient stations that sat back to back.

With the computers at the nursing station, the nurse could monitor how well the dialysis machines were functioning, the time patients had remaining to receive treatment, and when they needed to have their vitals checked again. DaVita required patients' vitals to be checked every thirty minutes.

Dialysis is a lengthy process—taking hours at a time—because the body's entire blood system must be pumped through the dialyzer, filtered and cleaned, and returned to the body. Most patients spent between three and four hours a day, three days a week doing the treatments. They were confined to sitting in the chair as their blood was drained from their body, cleansed of impurities, and put back. The comfortable patient chairs were padded and had white laminate butterfly trays on both sides that could be flipped up or down. Nurses and technicians used the trays to help hold the medicine vials, syringes, and other equipment, and they also doubled as patient armrests.

The patients passed the time differently. Some watched TV, other patients listened to music. Some talked on cell phones, while others balanced checkbooks or read, things the patients could do with one hand.

Because the same people spent the same three days a week with one another at the clinic for the same three to five hours a day, many of them became extremely astute observers of what was going on with their own treatment as well as others'. These patients often discussed their treatment with one another and noticed any variations in protocol, such as a change in medication. In many instances, some even gave one another medical advice.

Some patients didn't care which nurse or technician administered their treatments; they'd take whoever was available. But others asked for or even demanded to have their favorite nurses and technicians hook them up to the machine. They had a preferred time and favorite chair, too, much like they probably did at home. Although some patients could be difficult, irritable, and unpleasant to be around, most were easy to get along with, friendly, and trusted their care providers.

Ms. Clara Strange and Ms. Thelma Metcalf were two of those friendly, trusting patients. They both had appointments at DaVita Lufkin on Tuesday, April 1, 2008. With light winds, a seventy-one-degree temperature, and no rain, it was a typical spring day in East Texas. April Fools' jokes played out in Lufkin as they would all over the world.

But unlike those who could look forward to pranks and practical jokes, Ms. Strange and Ms. Metcalf would be spending about half of their April Fools' Day hooked up to dialysis machines. One of the nurses on duty was Kimberly Saenz.

Ms. Clara Strange was born Clara Jones on November 6, 1930, in nearby Pollok, Texas, the same place as Kimberly Saenz. Although she grew up in the country, she didn't have to worry about company—her five sisters and four brothers along with her parents provided plenty. Later, she married A. C. Strange, and they settled down and raised a family of their own.

Eventually, Ms. Strange went to work for the Lufkin State School, and she worked there until her retirement. Not that Ms. Strange sat back and took it easy—when her daughter Betty Fernandez died, Ms. Strange also raised her grandchildren.

On that Tuesday morning, Ms. Strange was put on the dialysis machine at 11:34 by patient care technician (PCT) Werlan Guillory. She had some shortness of breath when she was hooked up, but as the treatments progressed, she improved quite a bit. That afternoon when Guillory went on break, Ms. Strange was tolerating treatments well, and her blood flow rate was set at 400 cc/min as prescribed by her doctor. When Guillory returned approximately thirty minutes later, however, he was shocked to discover Ms. Strange unconscious, unresponsive, and without a heartbeat. Her blood flow rate had been changed to 300 without doctor approval or any documented reason to turn it down. Blood flow rate (BFR) is an important component of dialysis, and the nephrologist calculates the rate based on each individual patient, his or her health, as well as other factors. Basically it is the rate that the patient's blood is removed and put back in the body. A normal slowdown of the rate might, depending on the patient, be from 400 cc/min to 390 cc/min. Normally, even when the blood flow rate is turned down, it is done in small increments because this rate affects the patient's blood pressure.

After yelling for help, Guillory said he asked Saenz, "Kim, what is going on?" But she didn't answer or even seem to care, he later reported.

Although the clinic wasn't an emergency room and not equipped as such, they did have nurses and doctors there as well as a crash cart, and they constantly monitored the patients' vital signs. Besides that, they were only a minute away from both Lufkin hospitals. Seldom did life-threatening medical situations develop without any symptoms. Nurses and doctors converged on Ms. Strange, and a PCT by the name of Cory Smith rushed the crash cart out in an attempt to save her. But nothing helped. Ms. Clara Strange died while attached to the dialysis machine at DaVita.

Ms. Strange's death affected most of the DaVita employees deeply because she was well liked—one of those patients who was kindhearted and affable, and not a bother or trouble to the staff. They sincerely enjoyed treating her. However, they didn't have time to grieve at that moment.

Ms. Thelma Metcalf, another of the well-liked patients who happened to be in the same patient bay as Ms. Strange, was also in trouble.

Known to her many friends as Fran, Ms. Metcalf had lived the majority of her life in Zavalla, a small town in Angelina County twenty miles east of Lufkin. Though she was born in Houston, after marrying Walter Metcalf, the couple eventually settled deep in the piney woods of East Texas. There Ms. Metcalf went about raising her family. She was a loving, caring mother who'd instilled discipline in her four children, provided support to her husband, and made time for friends and her church.

In the latter part of 2007, her health began to fail and she was admitted to Memorial Hospital in Lufkin with renal problems. In August, with her condition improving, Ms. Metcalf was released from the hospital and began outpatient kidney dialysis treatments at DaVita Lufkin Dialysis Center. However, within a few days of beginning treatments, Ms. Metcalf's condition worsened and she was unable to walk. After an interview with Mr. Metcalf, *The Lufkin News* reported, "Her condition not only shocked her husband of forty-eight years, but also her family doctor. He told the family that he didn't understand why she went downhill so fast."

Although the sixty-eight-year-old Ms. Metcalf was a

type 2 diabetic, not in good health, and had to be helped out of her wheelchair for treatment, on that April morning she was in a good mood, talkative, and her vital signs were great. Then she began her dialysis treatment.

Ms. Metcalf's blood pressure dropped from 105/82 to 93/68 in thirty-one minutes. At 3:05 in the afternoon, just like Ms. Strange, she became unresponsive and her heart stopped beating.

Cory Smith, the PCT who had rushed the crash cart to Ms. Strange in that unsuccessful attempt to save her, had not even gotten it put away before Ms. Metcalf coded. After grabbing another breathing device—he'd just used the one on the cart on Ms. Strange—he rushed the crash cart back to try to help Ms. Metcalf.

He handed Saenz the breathing device and she placed the mask on Ms. Metcalf and started operating the breathing pump while another nurse did chest compressions. As they did CPR, Smith noticed that there was no rise and fall of Ms. Metcalf's chest, which indicated that no oxygen was getting into her lungs.

Smith told Saenz that she had to open Ms. Metcalf's airway, but Saenz didn't respond.

He told her two or three more times, but Guillory said Saenz not only never responded, but never even acknowledged that he was talking to her. Finally, Smith said, "Let me do it." He took the breathing bag from Saenz and attempted to clear Ms. Metcalf's airway and then put the mask back on, but it didn't do any good. Ms. Metcalf was rushed to the hospital, where EMTs administered three doses of epinephrine, a drug used with cardiac arrest patients to attempt to revive them, but it was too late.

Ms. Metcalf became the second patient to die on the dialysis machine at DaVita Lufkin—and within five minutes of Ms. Strange.

After Ms. Metcalf was rushed to the hospital, employees discovered that her blood flow rate had also been turned down from 300 to 200, and again without doctor approval.

The correct blood flow rate is crucial for every dialysis patient. Obviously, too much blood cannot be removed from the body at once, so usually no more than a pint of blood is outside the patient's body at one time. An alarm system is triggered if the blood flow rate falls too low.

An air detector also triggers an alarm in the event that air enters the bloodlines, which can be deadly. Yet another alarm system checks for foreign substances that shouldn't get into the patients' bloodlines and be brought into the body. If these or any other problems occur with the machine, the alarm is set to go off and stop the blood flow of that patient—therefore eliminating the harmful things from entering the patient's blood.

However, if a foreign substance were introduced into the lines in any way, slowing the blood flow rate gave that substance time to be diluted with the blood, and therefore reduced the chance of the alarm going off. If the alarm didn't go off, the blood continued to flow, carrying the substance throughout the patient, and the staff would not be alerted to the problem.

Neither Ms. Strange nor Ms. Metcalf's alarm systems went off that day—and both were found with lowered blood flow rates.

Dr. Imran Nazeer, a nephrologist and the medical

administrator of DaVita Lufkin, later said that in all of his twenty-three years as a kidney doctor, he'd never before seen a patient die of a heart attack while receiving dialysis, and he'd only ever even heard of two such cases. The chances of one patient dying of cardiac arrest while on a dialysis machine are something in the neighborhood of 7 in 100,000. The odds of two patients at the same facility dying of cardiac arrest within five minutes of each other while on a dialysis machine are beyond astronomical. What's more, neither Ms. Strange nor Ms. Metcalf had exhibited any sign of heart problems before they suddenly both died of cardiac arrest.

Ms. Metcalf's family had her cremated. After a service in Zavalla, they took her ashes to a creek in Arkansas where she'd played as a child and spread them there. Seldom does a cremation play a vital role in a trial, but four years later, this cremation did.

CHAPTER 4

INQUIRY

The truly anomalous circumstances of Ms. Strange's and Ms. Metcalf's deaths on April 1, 2008—two cardiac arrests within five minutes of each other while on dialysis machines in the same facility—spurred DaVita officials to take immediate action. They brought in independent investigators and monitors led by DaVita's regional director, a registered nurse named Amy Clinton. Although DaVita Lufkin had a facility administrator, an RN named Sandy Lawrence, as of April 2, 2008, Clinton assumed all responsibility for the operation of DaVita Lufkin. Clinton's team specialized in problems dealing with dialysis centers, and their mission was quite simple: find the problems affecting the patients and stop them.

Unfortunately for Clinton, she stepped into a mess. DaVita Lufkin was not known as a model dialysis facility, and the problems went back as far as 2003.

In order for dialysis centers to operate, they have to

receive what is called a CMS reimbursement. The Department of State Health Services, who oversees dialysis clinics in Texas, is required by federal law to conduct a surveyed inspection of each dialysis center every three years. This is how the facilities receive the reimbursement.

On April 8, 2003, one of the survey inspectors toured DaVita Lufkin and, while observing the process, determined that the reuse technician did not properly process used dialyzers according to standards set by AAMI or, for that matter, DaVita's own procedure. This is vitally important. The dialyzer is what the patient's blood goes through to purify it.

At the same time, the inspector found that DaVita had not properly trained its staff.

On June 2, 2003, the Department of State Health Services conducted a follow-up survey of DaVita Lufkin, and after that return trip, they reported that DaVita Lufkin had not corrected infection control problems that they'd found in the inspection two months before.

After DaVita corrected these problems, the Department of State Health Services returned on May 23, 2006. Again they found problems. This time the inspectors found that DaVita Lufkin was not properly documenting its test results on the water or on discharge summaries on patients who'd died, or their cause of death.

The Department of State Health Services had let three years pass from 2003 to 2006, but then they were back in July 18, 2007. This time the state inspectors found that DaVita Lufkin did not have the required number of properly trained personnel present to meet the needs of patients.

Not only that, but the inspectors found that, at times,

the facility had not given patients the correct treatments as ordered by the doctor. While there, two employees came forward and told the inspectors that they were administering treatments against a physician's orders because the facility administrator told them to.

Another problem the inspector found in 2007—which would also be a headache for Amy Clinton in 2008—was that DaVita Lufkin had a part-time biomedical technician, commonly referred to as bio-med. He spent part of his working time in the clinic in Lufkin, and the other part of the time in Livingston, Texas, a small town 70 miles to the south.

In 2007, the inspector at DaVita Lufkin observed that the center ran out of a mix used to treat the water. The problem: the only person who knew how to mix the chemicals was in Livingston that day.

No one can or will say that these problems contributed to a higher death toll for DaVita Lufkin patients than other clinics. It also must be noted that dialysis patients tend to have a higher death rate than other patients. However, from January 1 to December 31, 2007, twenty-seven DaVita Lufkin patients died. This is 7.1 percent higher than the state average.

The results were no better in 2008. From December 2007 to April 28, 2008, some of this on Amy Clinton's watch, DaVita Lufkin had nineteen patients die—including Ms. Metcalf and Ms. Strange, the ones whose deaths threw DaVita officials into a panic.

Even with Amy Clinton and all of her monitors at the clinic from April 2 until April 28, DaVita Lufkin rushed thirty-four patients to local hospitals by ambulance.

These were the problems Clinton faced as she assumed the responsibility of the clinic. However, before she could fix the problems, she first had to identify what they were.

First, Clinton and the monitors examined all aspects of the biggest part of a dialysis clinic, the water used in the dialysis process. Purified water plays a vital role in dialysis, and the Lufkin clinic had a water treatment room where they purified their own water.

Because the purification process was so complex, the investigators checked every aspect of the system, from the water itself to the equipment. There was an alarm on the water system designed to alert everyone throughout the clinic if something went wrong with any aspect of the water purification. However, like all the other equipment in the purification area, the investigators found nothing wrong with the alarm system, the purification system, or with the water itself.

Next, the investigators looked at the biomedical technicians who maintained the water system. They checked the techs' qualifications, work history, as well as all the paperwork that went along with the job. Like the equipment, the techs and their records weren't the problem.

Next, the investigators checked the reuse technicians and their on-site reprocessing area. This was where the patients' hemodialyzer—basically the filter that removed the impurities in a patient's blood—was cleaned, sterilized, and made ready for that patient's next treatment. DaVita Lufkin used both new and reuse dialyzers, but there were strict guidelines on the cleaning and maintenance of the reuse dialyzers and the patients had to agree to use them. Although the survey inspection team had found problems in this area in 2007, DaVita had corrected them, and Clinton's team could find no problems in this area in April 2008.

After not finding the problem in the reuse area, the DaVita officials checked all the dialysis machines themselves, but again failed to find a problem.

Everyone at the clinic, and that included the investigators, believed that something on-site was causing the problems, but they'd checked the trouble-prone areas and had determined that those weren't responsible. Next they checked the clinic's policies and procedures to see if it was anything the technicians and nurses were doing that could be killing and harming the patients. The investigators looked at every procedure and could find nothing that could contribute to the fatalities and complications if the employees followed all procedures as prescribed.

Last, they checked the patients themselves. Like all dialysis facilities, DaVita took the patients' vital signs before treatment, several times during treatment, and after treatment. If the patient had a serious medical problem before or during treatment, their vital signs should so indicate, and the DaVita staff could get them medical help. This was one of the reasons that it was so unusual for a patient to die while hooked up to the machine. The patient had constant monitoring from medical professionals.

However, according to their recorded vital signs, none of the patients who died at DaVita or suffered serious health complications while undergoing treatment began with problems. The problems began after they started their treatment, and they happened suddenly.

The officials checked three areas where dialysis patients commonly had problems: blood pressure during treatment, heart rate, and edema, aka swelling—usually from a buildup of fluids.

One thing that gave them some pause was the heparin that the DaVita clinic was using. Heparin is a common drug used in dialysis to prevent blood clots in veins, arteries, and lungs. Given that the patients' blood was being removed and put back in their bodies after traveling through a filter, the chances of clots were high. There had been a manufacturer recall of one brand of heparin, however, and even though it wasn't for the brand DaVita was using, the investigators gathered up all their heparin, and brought in another batch from a different facility. In the end, this didn't help either.

The stumped investigators and administrators didn't have a clue as to what was causing the problem. In a last-ditch effort to find anything that explained it, they even looked at the possibility of simple chance, but like everything else, they eventually ruled this out, too. The odds of the two deaths simply didn't allow for it to be a chance occurrence.

During this time, two of the nurses made the same comment: "The only thing they didn't check was the employees." Indeed, they hadn't. They didn't think they needed to; they believed that medical professionals wouldn't intentionally harm their patients.

After Clinton's arrival, the problems at DaVita ceased for a short time. But that moment of calm turned out to be merely the eye of the storm—a temporary respite before a horror that no one had seen before, or even imagined, fell upon DaVita.

————

Wednesday, April 16, 2008, was a gorgeous East Texas day. Temperatures were in the sixties, skies were clear, and there was just enough of a breeze to cool off those who were working outside, as Mr. Garlin Kelley Jr. was that morning. Neighbors walking or driving by his home routinely saw him outside doing yard work, and honked at him or waved and yelled hello. Most of them knew that he wasn't in great health—one of his legs had been amputated and he was learning to use a walker to get around.

Just the sight of a man with one leg doing yard work drew some attention. But this wasn't just any man. A ring of respect jingled in everyone's voices when they said Mr. Kelley's name.

Mr. Garlin Kelley Jr. was born and grew up in segregated Lufkin, and he'd lived in segregated neighborhoods and attended segregated schools all the way up through college in the late 1960s and early 1970s. It had taken East Texas a long while to get on board with integration. In fact, Dunbar High, Mr. Kelley's alma mater, did not integrate until 1970, and only then because the school district was forced to do so by a federal court order. These experiences could have had a negative effect on anyone—caused feelings of prejudice or harbored anger—but not with Mr. Kelley. Even early on, his friends said that he recognized that it wasn't up to him to judge others, and that as he had no control over how other people felt, it did him no good to worry about it. He would let the Lord judge him on who he was, and others on who they were.

As a boy, young Garlin and his friends would go to watch the Dunbar Tigers play every Friday night in football season. Dunbar High School had hired a coach by the name of Elmer Redd, who became a legend not only in Lufkin, but in the entire state of Texas. Dunbar had an abundance of talented athletes, but it was Coach Redd who molded that talent into state championship winners. Growing up in this environment, Garlin Kelley dreamed of playing football for the coach. He watched Tiger players like future NFL hall of famer Ken Houston receive college scholarships, and dreamed that he could, too, someday.

As Garlin entered junior high, he was smaller than many of the other boys, but that only meant that he had to work harder. From his parents and coaches, he learned the value of hard work, honesty, education, and the Good Lord. With encouragement and teaching from the coaches, and his own willingness to work and push himself, he progressed, and by the time he reached high school, Garlin Kelley was a force to be reckoned with on the football field.

Owing to hard work, desire, and plain old heart, Garlin Kelley first became an all-district player, and then was voted as an all-state player. He was instrumental in helping Dunbar High bring home three more state championships in his four years of high school. He was offered a college scholarship to Prairie View A&M University to play football. He would be following in the footsteps of not only one of his heroes, Dunbar star Kenny Houston, but also his mentor. Coach Redd had also attended the school.

Garlin Kelley never gained the stardom that Houston did in college or in the National Football League, and he wasn't a first ballot Hall of Famer like Houston. But in 1966, Garlin Kelley won a whole lot more than football games—he also won the heart of a young lady named LaFrancis. Infatuation turned to puppy love, and continued to grow into a deep friendship and a lifelong love affair. After graduating from college, Mr. Kelley soon accomplished his greatest feat—he married LaFrancis.

Mr. Kelley first worked as an insurance agent and later for the Lufkin Independent School District. However, his love for football never ended. Through most of his adult life until his health failed him, he refereed high school football games.

Over the years, the Kelleys had three daughters: Ulrica, Angela, and LaTonya, and Mr. Kelley couldn't have been any prouder of them. He instilled in them the same values he'd learned from his parents and coaches, and all three girls graduated from college.

Then at the age of fifty-three, Mr. Kelley was diagnosed with renal failure. It took a while, but he finally had a successful kidney transplant. For a while, things looked good, but three years later, the kidney gave out and Mr. Kelley had to start dialysis. He began treatment at the DaVita Lufkin Dialysis Center. The doctors later said that he was in excellent health considering the problems he had; in addition to his kidney problems, Mr. Kelley had type 2 diabetes, COPD, and hypertension.

With all these health problems going on at the same time, Mr. Kelley developed gangrene in one leg. The doctors had no choice but to amputate it.

One longtime friend of Garlin Kelley's said, "Even after he lost his leg, there was never a time when he felt sorry for himself. There was never a time when he didn't attempt to lift people up around him. It just wasn't in Garlin's nature to focus on his problems."

This was what set Mr. Kelley apart from many others. Not only DaVita employees, but his family, friends, and even casual acquaintances all said that if you weren't already aware of Mr. Kelley's health problems, there was no way of knowing from his actions or demeanor. La-Francis said of her husband, "He never met a stranger. You never knew what he had gone through the way he carried himself."

No one ever had an unkind thing to say about Mr. Kelley. The other DaVita patients also liked him. Carolyn Risinger, who'd spent hours with Mr. Kelley while they received treatments, told KTRE-TV, "I knew Mr. Kelley. He came in early with me. He was a sweet man."

As it turned out, "He was a sweet man" was the worst thing anyone had to say about Mr. Kelley.

Early on the morning of April 16, 2008, Mr. Kelley woke early as he usually did. He took a boiled egg and a grilled cheese sandwich to eat as snacks at DaVita—he was known as much for his boiled egg as he was for his warm personality. LaFrancis dropped him off at DaVita's front door, where Mr. Kelley walked himself in using his walker. He'd spent many an hour with a therapist to get in shape and learn to use the walker because he didn't want to be a burden on anyone.

As the med nurse that day prepared the patient's medication, Mr. Kelley's PCT, Sharon Dearmon, hooked him up to the machine. Dearmon said that he was his normal joking self, and ate his boiled egg while he watched ESPN on TV. There weren't any problems with his vitals or anything else when they hooked him up at 5:36 A.M. His flow chart showed that he was fine between 5:36 and 7:30 that morning. In fact, a notation in his flow sheet said he was resting comfortably at 7:30.

Half past seven was break time for the employees, and Dearmon said that a lot of employees were off the floor then, including shift supervisor Sharon Smith. Dearmon was monitoring her own patients as well as another PCT's while that person was on break. At 7:35, she had her back to Mr. Kelley as she was taking care of another patient when the alarm on Mr. Kelley's dialysis machine went off. She turned and found Kimberly Saenz, the med nurse, by Mr. Kelley's machine trying to reset the alarm. After running over, Dearmon also found Mr. Kelley unresponsive, and called for help. After clamping off his lines, she started CPR, and someone called for an ambulance.

One of the people who responded to that call for help was RN Sharon Smith, charge nurse for that bay, who'd just returned from break. Smith later noted that she saw something in the bloodline that she'd never seen before. It looked to be a very unusual blood clot. It was fibrous, almost like hair. She said, "I've never seen it before and I've never seen it since."

Dearmon echoed Smith's description of the strange clot.

The DaVita employees did everything in their power to save LaFrancis's husband, but he was still unconscious when paramedics arrived to transport him to the hospital.

Once at the hospital, Garlin Kelley remained in a coma for months until on August 15, almost four months to the day that he lost consciousness at DaVita, he died without ever waking.

After Mr. Kelley died, LaFrancis told a reporter, "He was the love of my life. But I know he's happy where he is. He's whole again."

One question lingered in everyone's mind: How could he go from resting comfortably at 7:30 to massive cardiac arrest in five minutes with no symptoms?

DaVita investigators had found no problems with either the new or the reuse dialyzers. However, after the incident with Mr. Kelley (who was using a reuse dialyzer), DaVita Lufkin immediately suspended the use of reuse dialyzers on April 16. As they would soon learn, it wouldn't help.

As far back as September 2007—one month after Kimberly Saenz was hired—DaVita had instituted a new policy. They were to collect all the bloodlines and other instruments used on patients who experienced cardiac problems while undergoing treatment, put these items in biohazard bags, put the patient's name on the bag, and put the bags in a freezer to preserve them. But they'd never followed this policy until Ms. Strange and Ms. Metcalf died on April 1, 2008. On April 16, they followed protocol and preserved Mr. Kelley's bloodline, and that included a syringe still attached to that bloodline. This would not be the last anyone heard about that bloodline and syringe.

CHAPTER 5

WHAT IF

The same morning that Mr. Garlin Kelley arrived at the clinic, on April 16, 2008, so did Ms. Graciela Castaneda. She was an elderly Hispanic woman who didn't speak English. She'd been married for forty years and had three daughters. Prior to April 2008, she'd been a dialysis patient for ten years, and felt fine that morning—no different than any other day.

Yet at 8:00 that morning, after Mr. Kelley's incident, Ms. Castaneda went into cardiac arrest. Just before she passed out, Ms. Castaneda remembers, she was talking to a woman doing something to her lines, but didn't remember anything else. The DaVita staff, maybe because of all the recent practice, reacted immediately with the crash cart and gave her a shot of epinephrine at 8:08.

Ms. Castaneda was a lucky woman—at the hospital she recovered and survived that day.

Several months later, she saw a picture of a woman in

the newspaper, and pointed it out to her daughter. Ms. Castaneda identified the woman in the photo as the nurse who had been talking to her right before she lost consciousness. The picture was of Kimberly Clark Saenz.

Two days before her heart attack, Ms. Castaneda's LDH level had been measured at 219, well within normal range. LDH, which stands for lactic acid dehydrogenase, is an enzyme that helps produce energy. It is also present in almost all of the tissues in the body and becomes elevated in response to cell damage. Twenty minutes after Ms. Castaneda's cardiac arrest, her LDH level was 2150.

Besides being an indicator of hemolysis, or cell damage, an elevated LDH level is also a marker for bleach poisoning.

Unfortunately for DaVita and especially the patients, instead of calming down, the storm plaguing DaVita was gathering strength, and it focused on Ms. Marie Bradley next.

Ms. Bradley was a Lufkin native who'd graduated from Lufkin High School in 1948. She later went to work for Jim Walter Homes in Lufkin where she remained for twenty-five years, advancing to upper management. In 2000, she began having heart and kidney problems, and started dialysis at Woodland Heights Hospital.

On May 7, 2007, Ms. Bradley began her treatments at the DaVita Lufkin Dialysis Center. From the time the news first broke about Saenz, and all through her trial, many people referred to Saenz as "an angel of mercy." It was just so difficult to accept the idea that a medical professional could have been intentionally harming or killing her patients in the first place; if she really were doing so, it was far easier for people to believe that perhaps Saenz had had noble motivations, such as ending unnecessary suffering. However, Ms. Bradley was one of the patients who knocked down the "angel of mercy" theory. Although ill and in need of dialysis, Marie Bradley was notably robust and energetic. Her doctor said of her, "She was one of the exceptional patients as far as health went." Unlike many dialysis patients, Ms. Bradley drove herself to and from her treatments.

April 23, 2008, was her regularly scheduled appointment. After all the preliminaries, she was hooked up to the machine at 11:00 A.M. As she neared completion at about 3:30 that afternoon, her blood pressure took a surprising drop, from 145/66 to 97/50, and her oxygen levels also fell drastically.

A few days earlier, her LDH levels had been 169. After she was rushed to the hospital on April 23, they were 1372. At the time, however, Ms. Bradley had no idea what had actually happened to her. She woke up in the hospital two and a half days later. She didn't know about the DaVita employees who'd frantically worked to save her life or the mad dash to Memorial Hospital in the ambulance. Nor was she aware of the Memorial emergency doctors and nurses who'd revived her and then closely monitored her condition in the intensive care unit.

As Ms. Bradley herself later said, it was clear that during her treatment on the twenty-third, "Something went horribly wrong."

What would a patient in the dialysis center feel like as she watched EMTs rush two other patients before her to the hospital? What could she have been thinking when her turn for treatment arrived, and the nurse who had helped her pass the long dreary hours by telling her jokes hooked her up to the machine?

Imagine the patient's horror as her arm, at the point where she was attached to the machine, began to bleed and wouldn't stop. As the blood flowed out of her, she started throwing up, and pain shot through her entire body. Then, agonizing pain made her believe her chest would explode. Imagine her terror as DaVita employees loaded her into another ambulance and whisked her off to the same hospital where others before her had gone—others who hadn't survived the trip.

This terrible experience was what happened to Ms. Debra Oates, another patient at the DaVita Lufkin Dialysis Center, on April 26—one of the worst days of the storm. Ms. Oates, like Ms. Bradley, was a Lufkin resident. Also like Ms. Bradley, she was healthy enough to drive herself back and forth to dialysis for treatments.

On April 26, she had been watching TV and her treatments were going well—no problems at all. Then LVN Kimberly Saenz came over to give her medication, and that's when she started to feel bad. At 9:13 A.M. Debra Oates's blood pressure was 147/73, but at 10:39 it dropped to 83/56. During this interval Ms. Oates experienced nausea and vomiting and trouble breathing. She said she "hurt all over." Her heart was beating faster and she was sweating, and the access in her arm where they hooked the dialysis lines up started bleeding and wouldn't stop.

She also had a funny taste in her mouth. She'd been a dialysis patient since February 2005 and was familiar with the process, and knew that each medication given through the blood while on dialysis had a different taste. This taste was unfamiliar.

Ms. Oates asked Saenz, "What did you give me?"

Sharon Smith, the nurse supervisor, overheard this question from Debra Oates and she said that she'd never heard her ask that before. However, Ms. Oates didn't get an answer to her question. Kim Saenz just walked off.

And then Ms. Oates's condition worsened.

PCT Werlan Guillory was again on duty that day, and said that Ms. Oates had been doing well until 9:43 A.M. and then she became sick to her stomach and started throwing up. They immediately got her into an ambulance, where the technicians gave Ms. Oates some nitro and more of it at the hospital. Like Ms. Bradley, Ms. Oates was one of the exceptional patients, and she somehow survived the storm.

However, neither of the patients Ms. Oates and Werlan Guillory had watched them carry out earlier that day was as lucky as Ms. Oates was. The first was ninety-one-year-old Ms. Opal Few, and the other was Ms. Cora Bryant.

Ms. Bryant was born on May 10, 1943, in San Augustine, a small town east of Lufkin. She settled down in Lufkin and raised four daughters and one son. People said that Ms. Bryant loved her kids and family and could always make people laugh.

The family talked about the values their mother taught them, and how their mother inspired them. Angela Scott told the newspaper, "Our mama passed on a will to never give up. She refused to give up. And she has given me the strength to carry on."

The day before Ms. Bryant went for her appointment at DaVita for the last time, she took a walk with her granddaughter, Jamina Agnew. Ms. Agnew related how Ms. Bryant was feeling that day, telling her granddaughter, "I feel good. Come on, keep up."

On the morning of April 26, Candace Lackey, an LVN at DaVita Lufkin, hooked up Ms. Bryant to the machine. She said that Ms. Bryant was in a good mood that day. She'd had some clotting problems early in the treatment, but they'd changed out her lines and that took care of it.

When Lackey went on break, everything was fine with Ms. Bryant—she tested well. But when she came back from break, Lackey found Kim Saenz trying to reset the alarm on Ms. Bryant's dialysis machine, even though she was assigned to a different bay. Ms. Bryant, however, seemed okay and was watching TV. Lackey hadn't expected Ms. Bryant to start clotting again, but because of the earlier incident, this was the first thing she checked. There was no appearance of clotting in the bloodlines.

Lackey explained that "a number of things can make the alarm go off, including clotting, or pushing medication into a port too fast. When the alarm goes off, the machine shuts down the blood from entering or leaving the patient. The machine has to be reset before the patient can continue to receive treatment."

After Lackey checked the machine and reset it, she

returned Ms. Bryant's blood to her. Like Ms. Oates, Ms. Bryant was familiar with the tastes and sensations of her medications, and detecting something unusual, she asked, "What are you giving me?" She then turned her head and her heart stopped.

As Ms. Bryant coded, employees rushed to save her, all but one. Martha Mann, a PCT on duty that day, said, "Kim was just standing there watching. She never attempted to help give CPR to save the patient."

Four years later, Candace Lackey was asked if she knew then what she did now, would she have returned Ms. Bryant's blood to her. A tearful Lackey responded that she would not have returned the blood.

After Ms. Bryant coded at DaVita, she was also rushed to the hospital in a coma—one that she never awoke from.

Angela Scott, one of Ms. Bryant's daughters, told *The Lufkin News* in 2009, "We knew my mother was going to die eventually of kidney failure, but not this way. Not by the hands of someone else."

People confronted with disappointment or tragedy often become fixated on the "What if?" questions. What if I had stopped sooner? What if I hadn't gone there? What if I'd never agreed to do this, or not do that? We can never know, of course, but everyone's said it at some time in their lives. Would certain things be different if I had or hadn't acted a certain way?

April 26, 2008, was a day rife with "What if?" questions, and it wasn't over yet. While horror unfolded within the DaVita clinic, outside it was another perfect spring day in Lufkin. The temperature was in the mid-sixties with little wind and no rain. Many of the East Texas residents would be heading to the lakes for fishing or other activities.

Ms. Opal Few's usual dialysis appointment was scheduled at the DaVita Lufkin Dialysis Center in the afternoon, but that morning she had received a call from DaVita asking her if she would like to come in early. A couple of patients had canceled their appointments.

Ms. Few was a little silver-haired woman—short and small, but with a feisty and large personality. When she came into a room, people knew she was there. DaVita employees who knew her referred to her as a dream patient—always cheerful and full of life. One employee said she was the kind of patient who made employees happy to take care of her.

When hearing friends, family, and acquaintances speak of ninety-one-year-old Ms. Few, regret spirals through the listeners. She sounded like the type of person whom anyone would have really liked to have known.

Opal Mae Jordan Few was born in Pollok on October 13, 1916, and graduated from high school at Central ISD, a small school in Pollok. She married, and for many years ran a boardinghouse in Lufkin. The family lived downstairs and the boarders lived upstairs.

Linda James, one of Ms. Few's daughters, stated, "My mother was a family person who loved her family above all else except God. She devoted her entire life to her children, grandchildren, and great-grandchildren." Above all else, Ms. Few's children, Linda Few James, Selena Lynch, and Donald Young, remember that their mother believed in doing what was right. Ms. Few instilled these virtues in her children, and lived the moral values she taught them.

One story about Ms. Few epitomized the way she led her life. Ms. Few's income was based on the number of boarders she had and the money they paid her. One time in particular, her children remember that the house was totally empty of boarders. Their mother had gone to church on Sunday morning with just enough money to either pay the light bill or give a tithe to the church. They said that their mother prayed and asked what the right thing to do was.

Ms. Few left the church with no money. That very afternoon there was a knock on the door, a man looking for a room. By Monday afternoon, the boardinghouse was completely filled.

Linda James, a drug and alcohol abuse counselor, told this story about how her mother instilled values in her: When she was about five or six years old, she went with her mother to the Big Chief convenience store. She wanted a piece of bubble gum, but because she had bad teeth, her mother wouldn't get her any. So Linda swiped a piece.

On their way home, Linda turned her head so her mother couldn't see her plop the gum in her mouth, but she didn't fool her mother, who said, "Linda, look at me." Her mother figured out she'd stolen the gum, turned around, and made her go back in the store, spit it out into a Kleenex in front of the manager, apologize, pay for the gum, and when they got home, she made Linda iron sheets as punishment. Linda said she still got punished after all that, and she didn't even get to chew the gum.

For years Ms. Opal Few went up and down, changing sheets, cleaning and cooking meals for her family and boarders. Maybe it was all those trips up and down those stairs, the exercise Ms. Few did to make a living for her family, or just genetics; whatever the reason, Ms. Few reached the age of ninety-one in pretty good shape—a lot better than most of the other dialysis patients. Ms. Few had hip replacement surgery when she was eighty-eight years old, but the surgery was because her hip had simply worn out—not from a fall. She'd worked hard all her life. She eventually moved in with her daughter Linda, who said it was her mother's arthritis, not illness, that prompted the move.

When Ms. Few was eighty-seven years old, she went into the hospital very ill with a virus. She was admitted on a Monday, and on Wednesday, Linda said she got a call from a nurse. The nurse was whispering, and told her that she needed to get up there right away because her mom was dying. Linda learned that for three days the hospital had been giving her mother Lasix—a drug that treated fluid retention in patients. Linda recalls that the nurse said that the drug was shutting down her kidneys.

Linda James rushed to the hospital. Later, in explaining what had happened, the doctor told her that it was really hard when someone is older to know what is wrong with them. Ms. Few's life was saved, but the damage was done. When Ms. Few went into the hospital, she had 40 percent kidney function. When she came out, she had 10 percent.

Most people would have filed a lawsuit immediately,

especially when the doctor admitted that he'd made a mistake, but Ms. Few said she knew it was an accident. They were trying to do what was best for her and the thought of a lawsuit never occurred to her. When it was brought up, she wouldn't hear of it.

The doctor's mistake was one of the chief causes she had to start dialysis to begin with. Ms. Few had wanted to stop dialysis and stay at home—she had things to do and didn't want to be tied to a chair for so long—but of course, her doctors and family told her she couldn't.

Right up until April 26, 2008, Ms. Few led a very independent life. She still did all her own cooking and cleaning, and took care of Linda's ten- and twelve-year-old kids after they got out of school while Linda worked. The ten-year-old was autistic and had to be monitored closely because of his special needs. Every day when the children got home, Ms. Few had pizza and a cold Dr Pepper waiting on them. She even babysat her two-year-old great-grandchild whose mother was attending the Academy of Hair Design, a beauty school.

On that "What if?" Saturday morning, Ms. Few answered the phone when DaVita called. She was glad to be able to get in for her treatment early and get it over with.

Ms. Few walked into DaVita that morning on her own with the use of a walker. Dr. Imran Nazeer, the DaVita director and Ms. Few's doctor, said that, as always, she was lively, full of energy and spirit. It wasn't just her doctor who said this; everyone described Ms. Few this way, but especially on the morning of April 26. Donnya Heartsfield, now an RN but an LVN in April 2008, said

Ms. Few was just a sweet little lady; happy and cheerful, excited to be able to get in early.

After Ms. Few was called back to begin her treatment, Heartsfield hooked her to the machine. The older woman had no problems, her vitals were good, and she was progressing well with her treatment. The nurse made her rounds of the patients, and then checked on Ms. Few again and found her doing well. Before leaving to go on her break, Heartsfield asked her teammate to look after her patients until she returned.

Approximately thirty minutes later, the length of breaks at DaVita, Donnya Heartsfield returned to her patients. She found Ms. Few unresponsive and with no pulse. She yelled for help, and the staff attempted to save Ms. Few, but to no avail. She became the fifth patient in twenty-six days to die on the dialysis machine.

After Ms. Few was transported away from DaVita, Dr. Nazeer asked RN Sharon Smith what meds Ms. Few had been given. When Smith checked the computer, she didn't see where the meds were documented. Smith asked Saenz if she'd given Ms. Few her meds, and when Saenz said yes, Smith told her to document it. Saenz then went to the computer and put in a time she'd given the meds.

Just one week later, the syringe that Saenz had used to administer Ms. Few's meds would become a key piece of evidence in leading investigators to the true cause of so many unanswered what-ifs.

CHAPTER 6

IN PLAIN SIGHT

When Kimberly Clark Saenz awoke around 4 A.M. on April 28, 2008, it was to a cool, windy Monday morning. Chances are that, like most of the other days she'd worked as a nurse for DaVita Lufkin, she didn't want to go in, but felt she didn't have a choice. They needed the money and she'd already missed a lot of days that month.

She probably had no inkling that by the end of the day she would become the subject of an investigation, or that news stories carrying her name would soon bounce all across the United States.

After dressing in regulation nursing scrubs and putting her hair in its usual ponytail, she would've made her way down the steps of her double-wide trailer (which sat next door to Saenz's parents, Bennie and Kent Fowler). A large sign in front of a huge pine tree at the edge of the road announced the family's affiliation with the Clawson Assembly of God Church.

Deep in the woods of East Texas, the early-morning darkness would be complete—no lights anywhere as Saenz eased her way through a heavy dew that blanketed the driveway. The moisture, combined with the layer of fine red dirt that accumulated on the windshield, meant that her wipers smeared across the glass before eventually clearing enough for her to see.

With her lights on bright, she would be able to see some of the wildlife that flourished in the dense forest that lined the edges of the rough, pothole-laden blacktop. The twisting road mostly held dense trees and under-brush, but was occasionally interrupted with pockets of human habitation—from run-down trailers, to wood and brick houses, and even a scattering of mansions sitting off the road on hilltops.

Because of the darkness and the rough condition of the road, it took Saenz almost fifteen minutes to travel the four miles from her home to Highway 69, the main thor-oughfare through Pollok, an unincorporated community in the northwest corner of Angelina County.

After turning right on the highway, she could speed up, passing Central High School on the left and a couple of churches on the right—one of them her own. Her quick trek took her past a Polk Pick-It-Up, a convenience store and meat market. At that hour everything was closed except the convenience store.

Minutes after turning on the highway, she came to the loop around Lufkin. She turned right, traveled through two traffic lights, and arrived at the DaVita Lufkin Dialysis Center. A fellow DaVita employee said she saw Saenz sitting in her car with her eyes closed and her head back for several minutes. She said she was about to go back and check on Saenz, when her coworker's car door finally opened.

The atmosphere Saenz encountered at DaVita on April 28 was extremely tense, as it had been for some time. All throughout April 2008, the clinic had existed in what is called a comorbid state. There were simply too many unexplained patient deaths at DaVita Lufkin and too many patients suffering serious health complications.

From April 1 to April 28, the facility had had to transport thirty-four patients by ambulance to hospital emergency rooms. This number was three times the amount of patients taken to the hospital in March. Even more disturbing to DaVita officials were the nineteen patients who'd died in a five-month span from December 2007 to April 2008.

This was the atmosphere of the clinic that Kimberly Clark Saenz walked into on the twenty-eighth of April 2008. Anxiety was already high, and things began to go wrong immediately. One of the patient care technicians had to call in sick, so Amy Clinton, the head investigator who had taken over the operations of the clinic, called an off-duty RN by the name of Dale Stockwell to come to work.

Clinton never thought calling Stockwell in would cause any problems. But looking back, it may have only highlighted a problem that already existed.

Amy Clinton was a professional, smart, and vivacious woman in her early thirties, with a classic beauty. Not the beauty queen type of looks, but the kind that proclaims breeding and class—the type that makes men look twice, and then a wistful third time.

Clinton earned her bachelor of science degree at Stephen F. Austin State University in Nacogdoches, Texas (pronounced Nak-uh-DOE-chez), and became a registered nurse. She worked in a busy hospital emergency room for a year before starting to work as a dialysis nurse in 1997.

Owing to her intelligence, hard work, and ability to lead and interact with her coworkers and subordinates, she soon climbed the corporate ladder. People who worked with and under Clinton were quick to point out that she knew how to listen—even to the people under her—and was receptive to implementing advice if it made sense and fit what was best for the patients.

People who talked about Amy Clinton described her as kind and caring. Nursing wasn't an occupation to her, but a calling. She honestly cared about the patients, their suffering, and their problems. Several commented that it wasn't only her aptitude and professionalism, but her compassion that was much of the reason behind her quick ascent in the company.

When Clinton arrived at the DaVita Lufkin Dialysis Clinic, she didn't know that location's employees, their specific problems or issues, but she knew how DaVita was structured and how each clinic was supposed to be run. DaVita basically had three tiers of employees who dealt with patients. The lowest tier was the patient care technicians (PCTs). These employees weren't nurses, but people hired and trained to care for patients as they underwent the dialysis process.

The second tier of employees were the licensed vocational nurses (LVNs) like Kimberly Clark Saenz. Unlike the techs, the LVNs were nurses who went to two years of college to earn their licenses. For the most part, LVNs and PCTs performed the exact same job; despite the extra education, the only practical difference between the two at DaVita was that the LVNs could give shots but the techs couldn't.

The top tier of employees were the RNs—registered nurses. Like Clinton, RNs had attended four years of college and had progressed beyond LVNs. These nurses held supervisory roles, responsible for all the other employees caring for patients. In most circumstances, DaVita Lufkin had three RNs on duty per shift. One acted as the med nurse, responsible for drawing up and administering the meds to the patients, and the other two as charge nurses, one for each of the two bays of patients in the facility.

Except in emergencies or when there was a shortage of people to work on a given day, the RN usually didn't have direct involvement with patient care. This job fell to the techs and the LVNs. Because she was new to the facility and didn't know the staff, Clinton was unaware that this was a huge point of contention with Kimberly Saenz. Saenz constantly voiced her displeasure to other DaVita employees about caring for patients. She thought patient care was beneath her as a nurse. The only job she cared about doing was that of med nurse.

Because of illness, vacation, time off, and other such issues, there wasn't always an RN available to do the med job, and even when there was, the staff sometimes got behind and the LVNs had to act as med nurses and pull their own meds.

On the morning of April 28, when Amy Clinton had to find a replacement for the PCT who'd called in, she didn't think anything about it when Dale Stockwell agreed to come in. However, Stockwell was an RN, so Clinton had to change the schedule around. Stockwell became the med nurse for that day, and the LVN scheduled to do that job was relegated back to patient care. With most that wouldn't have been a problem, but on that day, Kimberly Saenz was scheduled to be the med nurse.

When Clinton informed Saenz that she'd been switched, Saenz got teary-eyed and upset, which surprised Clinton. She didn't understand what the problem was. After all, nurses were supposed to take care of patients. That's why most went into the field, and that's why most stayed with it. After talking to her for a few minutes, Clinton thought Saenz would be okay.

It wasn't until later, when another employee came to Clinton and told her that she needed to talk to Saenz, that Clinton realized that the LVN hadn't gotten over it. Clinton found Saenz not at her station but out back on the loading dock smoking a cigarette and still very upset about the assignment change.

After several minutes, Clinton was finally able to calm Saenz down enough to get her to return to work.

On this day, Saenz had four patients to care for. Like all the other PCTs and LVNs at DaVita, the employees who cared for patients did so in teams of two. While one team member was on break or lunch, the other team member watched the other's four patients, and vice versa.

On April 28, Saenz's team member was a PCT named Angie Rodriguez, who'd arrived at work that morning at 4 A.M. to get ready for patient arrival at 5:30. After clocking in, Rodriguez began her usual job of preparing everything for the patients' arrivals. This included getting the "bleach buckets" (actually small pails) set up.

Each patient care station had two of these buckets, which were approximately six inches deep, ten inches long, and six inches wide. In one of the buckets Rodriguez poured a 1:100 ratio of bleach to water. She measured the bleach using a small measuring cup. At each patient care station were boxes of one-use cleaning cloths. To clean a surface, the technician or nurse pulled out one of the cloths, dipped it in the bleach bucket, wrung it out, and wiped the patient chairs before and after use—simply a sanitation procedure.

The procedure for the second bucket was the same, except the ratio of bleach to water was 1:10. The PCTs and LVNs used this solution to wipe up blood off the floor or any other surface. After the ten-hour shift was over, they were supposed to throw the solution out and draw a new one up for the next shift. These two buckets were enough to get them through an entire shift.

When both bleach buckets were set up, the tech placed them on top of the dialysis machine to give the PCT or nurse easy access, but at the same time keeping them off the floor. In a sterilized health care facility, nothing involving patient care is ever placed on the floor.

Like every other day, as patients arrived, Angie Rodriguez brought them in and weighed them. It was imperative to do this with each patient because their weight showed how much fluid they'd retained from the previous treatment and told the nurse how much fluid needed to be drained. The last thing the patient did before leaving when the treatments were over was to get weighed again.

Next the patient was led to a sink to thoroughly wash the arm where their access port was. The patients waiting on Rodriguez had surgically implanted arterio/venous grafts inside their nondominant arm.

After the washing, Rodriguez took the patients to the treatment station and began an in-depth but important process. It was critical for the employees who treated patients to keep accurate records of the patients' vital signs and all procedures that took place. Nursing schools hammered it into the students' heads, it was on their licensing test to become a nurse, and each medical facility emphasized it—especially DaVita.

First Rodriguez took the patient's standing blood pressure, followed by the patient's sitting blood pressure. After she recorded her findings on the flow chart, she checked all of the vital signs—pulse, temperature, lungs, heart rate—and recorded those on the chart, too.

Next, Rodriguez placed two large, IV-type needles through the patient's skin and into both ports. Each needle had a tube connected to it; one tube took the patient's blood out and through a filter in the machine that acted as the kidney, and the other tube brought the filtered blood back into the patient's body.

Rodriguez's patients sat on the opposite side of the bay from her teammate that day: Kimberly Clark Saenz. Two of the four patients under Rodriguez's care were Ms. Carolyn Risinger and Ms. Marva Rhone.

Rodriguez hooked Ms. Rhone up at 5:52 A.M. Records indicate that her blood pressure dropped that morning, but it wasn't anything to be worried about. Rodriguez kept a careful check on all of her patients, including Ms. Rhone, and they were all okay when she told Saenz that she was going on break at about 8:00.

Rodriguez had no way of knowing that during the approximately fifteen minutes that she was away, the unspeakable would occur.

One of Kim Saenz's own patients that morning was Ms. Lurlene Hamilton, a sixty-two-year-old black woman who was a veteran of the dialysis process—by 2008, she had been undergoing dialysis for eight years, the last three at the DaVita Lufkin Dialysis Center. Ms. Hamilton had been born and raised in Chireno, Texas, a small community in Nacogdoches County just north of Angelina County, though in April 2008, she lived in Zavalla, a small community in Angelina County. Before she became ill, Ms. Hamilton had worked at a nursing home and at the Mental Health Mental Retardation Center, taking care of the elderly.

On the morning of April 28, Saenz hooked Ms. Hamilton up to the machine. As she progressed through her treatment, Ms. Hamilton—an especially observant patient, and with medical training besides—saw Saenz across the bay with Rodriguez's patients. This in itself wasn't unusual; the veteran dialysis patient had seen this scenario carried out a thousand times. What drew Ms. Hamilton's attention on this occasion, however, was that Saenz wasn't acting normal. As she later said, "Saenz was just looking around at her coworkers like, 'Do anyone see me?'"

What Saenz did next shocked the elderly patient. Ms. Hamilton saw Saenz kneel and place the bleach bucket on the floor. Ms. Hamilton asked herself, "What is she doing?" In her eight years of dialysis and all the time she'd worked in a medical setting, she'd never seen a medical professional place something used in patient treatment on the floor.

As Saenz poured the bleach, Ms. Hamilton could smell it. She witnessed the LVN draw bleach into four syringes and place them in her bosom, then look around again to see if anyone had noticed. She didn't spot Ms. Hamilton watching her.

Ms. Hamilton then watched in horror as Saenz injected both Ms. Rhone's and Ms. Risinger's dialysis lines with the syringes.

Ms. Hamilton wasn't the only one to have witnessed this macabre scene. In the chair next to Ms. Hamilton that day was Ms. Linda Hall, a sixty-eight-year-old black woman also from Angelina County, and also with a medical background. Ms. Hall had worked at Memorial Hospital in Lufkin as a nurse's assistant until her failing health caused her to quit. She'd been in dialysis for a year, and all of that with DaVita.

Ms. Hall had been reading on the morning of April 28, but as she glanced up from her book, she witnessed an event as scary as any horror story.

Ms. Hall watched Saenz open a drawer, remove a syringe, stick it in her shirt pocket, then look around very carefully as if she was checking to see if anyone had noticed her.

Moments later, Ms. Hall saw Saenz set a bleach pail, the

kind they used to wipe the chairs and machines with, on the floor. Like Ms. Hamilton, this alarmed Ms. Hall, who had also never seen any medical personnel set anything on the floor. She continued to watch as Saenz looked around again, squatted beside the bleach pail, inserted the syringe, and filled it with the bleach.

Ms. Hall asked herself, "Lord, what is she fixing to do with that?"

Transfixed, Ms. Hall watched Saenz as she rose and walked back to the nurses' station, where the LVN stood for a couple of minutes, before walking over to Ms. Rhone's station. Saenz looked around again . . . and then injected one of the syringes into Ms. Rhones's saline port.

Ms. Hall asked herself, "Lord, did I see what I saw? Am I dreaming?"

Surely she was mistaken, Ms. Hall thought—something so unthinkable couldn't be occurring right in front of her. And the nightmare didn't stop there. Ms. Hall continued to watch as Saenz walked over and also made an injection into Ms. Risinger's lines.

Her book totally forgotten, Ms. Hall was at a loss for what to do. She knew what she'd seen, but didn't want to believe it. Not only had she just seen a nurse injecting patients with bleach—it was the same nurse taking care of *her*.

When PCT Angie Rodriguez returned from break at approximately 8:15, she found several unanticipated problems. Ms. Rhone's blood pressure had risen and her actions were unusual. She seemed agitated, and when Rodriguez asked her how she was, Ms. Rhone said she felt "uncomfortable." Ms. Risinger was also complaining,

of pressure in her chest and stomach pain. In a later interview with KTRE-TV, Ms. Risinger described the sensa-
tion: "It started out with a pressure on my chest," she
said. "It felt like somebody was pushing on me and then
my stomach started a severe hurt." That morning, she was
left drifting in and out of consciousness. "It turned into
a nightmare, and so many had died I thought, well, this
is my turn."

Dr. Nazeer, who had been at another dialysis center
tending to other patients, made his way back to DaVita
after learning of Ms. Risinger's chest pains. Before he
arrived, though, Rodriguez and others were able to sta-
bilize Ms. Rhone and Ms. Risinger. The women's mysterious and sudden symptoms passed almost as quickly as
they'd arrived. But Ms. Risinger, at least, was still suffering
some ill effects. When her husband, Jim, arrived to pick
up his wife, DaVita employees said he demanded, "What's
wrong with my wife? Who did something to my wife?"

Meanwhile, Ms. Hamilton, normally a quiet person,
was not only scared but extremely agitated. She looked
around for someone she felt she could trust, spotted Yazmin Santana, a PCT, and frantically waved her over. After
telling Santana the story, Ms. Hamilton begged her not
to let "Kim" touch her.

On the other side of the machine, Ms. Hall heard Ms.
Hamilton tell Santana that she'd seen something. She
spoke up. "Lord, I did, too!" Ms. Hall also begged a
nurse who'd walked by not to let "Kim" touch her.

Santana now had two terrified patients, and she related
that what Ms. Hamilton told her scared her, too. Santana
had no idea what to do, so she went to Amy Clinton.

When Santana told Clinton what the two women had claimed to see, Clinton couldn't believe it. She went over to talk to them herself. The witnesses' stories were almost identical. They also both said that after Saenz injected the bleach into the patients, she had dropped the syringes into two sharps containers, and they told Clinton exactly which containers the syringes were put in.

After hearing their stories in person, Clinton still had trouble believing them—the idea of a nurse injecting bleach into her own patients' lines just seemed too far-fetched, too inconceivable—but she knew she had to do something. First, she called Saenz off to the side and asked her if she'd put the bleach bucket on the floor, and something turned inside her when Saenz admitted that she had. Clinton shook her head and informed Saenz, "We don't do that."

Clinton then asked her if she'd given Angie Rodriguez's patients any medication. Kim told her that she hadn't. All she'd done, she said, was give them saline because the patients' venous chambers were clotting. She also told Clinton that she'd charted what she'd done on the patients' flow charts.

Clinton was astonished when Saenz told her that she'd injected the patients with saline. DaVita Lufkin and all other dialysis facilities did indeed use saline to prevent the blood from clotting in the lines. However, at DaVita Lufkin, every dialysis machine had a bag of saline hanging from an IV rack attached to the machine. The saline bag had a clip attached to the line coming from the bag. If the patient needed saline, the care provider simply opened the clamp. Also on the line was a port for injections. This was where the care provider injected the patient's medicine. The oddity of Saenz's statement was that she'd need to inject the saline into the bag that already contained saline.

Clinton now had a huge dilemma on her hands. She didn't fully believe the story—the patients had to be mistaken somehow—but clearly *something* had happened, and she had two extremely upset patients on her hands who were scared to death. She had to do something to defuse the situation, and the only way she could think of at the time was to get Saenz out of the clinic. She hoped that her absence would calm down Ms. Hamilton and Ms. Hall enough to finish their treatments.

She told Saenz, "You've had a bad day. Go home, relax, and we'll start fresh in the morning."

Saenz was upset but left, and Santana took over her patients.

With Saenz out of the building, the patients calmed down, but Clinton was left with an even bigger problem: what to do now? She began by checking Ms. Risinger's and Ms. Rhone's flow charts, a simple process, but became even more alarmed when she discovered that, despite her claim, Saenz had not, in fact, documented anything.

Clinton then went to Dr. Imran Nazeer, the clinic medical administrator. She told him what she'd learned, and like everyone else who heard this story, Dr. Nazeer was shocked. He'd never heard of anything like this. In a way, though, he was relieved—if the story was true, at least they finally had an explanation for what had been happening at the clinic over the past month, a cause for all the deaths and injuries to the patients.

The situation placed Dr. Nazeer in an unusual situation, one which later became very controversial. Since both patients who had allegedly been injected with the bleach were in the final stages of their treatments, and about ready to go home, Dr. Nazeer had opted to advise Ms. Rhone and Ms. Risinger to go to the hospital for blood work, but he didn't tell them why. When neither patient heeded his advice, however, he called them at home, told them about the possible bleach injections, and again asked them to go to the hospital for blood tests. This time they listened to him and went.

Dr. Nazeer's hesitation, though ill-advised, was understandable. There were no contingency plans for a scenario like this at DaVita Lufkin. Nothing like this had ever happened, not to them, or to anyone else for that matter.

Dr. Nazeer and Amy Clinton did two important things that morning after Saenz left, though: they took both sharps containers that the witnesses claimed Saenz had dropped the syringes in and saved them, and they also bagged Ms. Rhone's bloodlines to preserve as evidence.

However, for reasons unknown, they neglected one vital piece of evidence: they didn't preserve Ms. Risinger's bloodlines.

CHAPTER 7

THE INVESTIGATOR

Sergeant Stephen Abbott of the Lufkin Police Department had no idea that at about the same time he was walking into the back door of the Lufkin Police Department on Monday morning, April 28, 2008, two dialysis patients were in the process of telling a DaVita employee a horrifying story of something they'd witnessed.

He had no instinct warning him that by the time the day ended, he'd be involved in an investigation that placed him in a worldwide spotlight.

At six-four and around two hundred and fifty pounds, Sergeant Abbott was an imposing sight. With a Nordic appearance, short white hair that didn't quite make it to blond, and black-rimmed glasses that emphasized his milky coloring, he stood out in a crowd like a lumbering giant. He tended to move slowly, but was capable of moving very quickly if he had to.

That Monday morning he was second in command of

the department's criminal investigation division (CID). Like most police departments the size of Lufkin, which had a population of around 28,000 in 2008, they didn't have specialized investigative divisions; the detectives basically handled whatever came their way. Sergeant Abbott usually supervised the eight detectives on staff, but as in most small departments, he also had several other jobs to oversee—namely, he was in charge of the evidence room and the crime scene unit, both vital parts of any criminal investigation.

Born and raised in Huntington, a small community nine miles east of Lufkin, Sergeant Abbott went into the Army after high school, and became a military policeman. Little if any information is available of his high school or Army days mainly because he wouldn't tell anyone. All he'd tell a person in a soft voice that never seemed to rise or fall was that he was a private person and he wished to stay that way.

Although Abbott declined to speak much of his days in the Army, it's known that he was assigned to a military police unit attached to Fort Dix in the mid- to late eighties, and that that unit was deployed to Nicaragua in Central America during the infamous Iran-Contra affair. More than that is a mystery. The sergeant also didn't tell war stories.

After being honorably discharged in 1988, Sergeant Abbott returned home to East Texas and attended Angelina Community College, a local community college. He worked as a security guard at a chicken processing plant and at a pizza place to help pay his way through school.

In 1993, he was hired by the Lufkin Police Department.

After graduating from the police academy, he did a long stint in patrol, broken up with some time in the drug enforcement unit.

By 2008, Sergeant Abbott had been with the department for fifteen years, and the fact that he rose to the rank of sergeant in that time, with little investigative experience, spoke to the kind of officer he was and to the higher-ups' belief in his abilities. His fellow officers described Abbott as extremely intelligent, honest, and as dedicated to his job as anyone, though never willing to take credit for anything. He always attempted to deflect credit to others.

Almost all police investigative units have someone with the ability to go into any situation and deal with any sort of person or problem—be it a board meeting with suits, politicians with an agenda, or a ditch digger in ripped jeans—and be able to relate to the people and handle whatever situation comes up. In April 2008, Sergeant Abbott was that person in the Lufkin CID whom higher-ups sought out to handle delicate or unusual cases.

Around four thirty that Monday afternoon, Sergeant Abbott was sitting in his office—a room with bare white walls except for two prints that were there when he moved in, and a wooden plaque in the shape of a military police badge with the words "Military Police" on it—getting ready to leave for the day when his two bosses sought him out. They had what they thought might become a sensitive situation. In other words, the proverbial mess had hit the fan, and Sergeant Abbott was going to have to clean it up.

Initially, all Sergeant Abbott was told was that there

was an issue that might involve possible tampering with medicine at the DaVita Lufkin Dialysis Center, and he needed to go there and find out what was going on. This in itself issued a major challenge. He had no background whatsoever in the medical field, had never investigated anything in the medical field, and didn't know anyone who had.

Since he didn't have a clue as to what he was about to walk into, Sergeant Abbott went looking for another detective to take with him. By that time of day, most of the detectives were out of the office, but as luck would have it, he found Corporal Mike Shurley, another supervisor. Like Sergeant Abbott, Corporal Shurley also had additional duties other than investigations; he'd spent the day at SWAT practice and was still in his SWAT uniform. He'd just dropped by the office for a moment to check his messages when Sergeant Abbott stuck his head in and asked him to come along to DaVita.

On the five-minute drive from the police department to DaVita, Sergeant Abbott filled Corporal Shurley in on what he knew, which wasn't much. Shurley wasn't as large as Abbott, but he looked imposing in his SWAT uniform. As the two detectives walked into the dialysis center (still full of patients) that evening, they still had no real idea why they were there.

Jerry McNeill, DaVita divisional vice president, met the detectives and explained the horrific situation to them. McNeill told them that two patients had claimed to see a DaVita nurse purposefully inject bleach into the lines of two other patients and then dispose of the syringes in two sharps containers. He told them that after Saenz was dismissed for the day, Amy Clinton and Giselle Frenette, another RN whom Clinton had brought in to help her monitor DaVita, went into the reuse room and used a screwdriver to pry the lids off the two sharps containers. They dumped all of the syringes from one container on a piece of paper and from the other container on a different piece of paper to ensure that they didn't get the contents of one container mixed with the other.

Now Clinton used the same test strips they used on the dialysis machines to check the syringes.

Clinton soon found a syringe that wasn't labeled but appeared to have a little clear liquid inside. She pulled the syringe apart and used the strip to test the inside of the syringe. When the strip turned purple—an indicator of bleach, her heart sank. "Oh, my goodness," Clinton said.

As the two RNs continued to test, they found four syringes in the two containers that tested positive for bleach. That just happened to be the exact number of syringes the two witnesses claimed Kim had used and put in the containers.

Frenette said that she was shocked when the syringes tested positive—so much so that she uttered a "bad word," which was something she just didn't do.

Even with the test results now in front of them, both detectives were still doubtful. Sergeant Abbott said later, "I was skeptical. Witnesses don't always know what they saw." Corporal Shurley echoed those thoughts.

In truth, no one really wanted to believe that a medical professional would do something to deliberately harm patients. As Jessica Cooley, *The Lufkin News* crime reporter, later told E!, "It seemed like such a wild accusation. A nurse would inject someone with something that was used for cleaning. It just didn't make any sense."

Despite his doubts, however, Sergeant Abbott called for the crime scene unit to come to DaVita, while McNeill filled the two detectives in on some back story. He gave them a list of patients who had died while on the dialysis machines, but stressed that it was extremely rare for patients to die suddenly on the machines while doing dialysis—however, as April 2008 drew to a close, the DaVita Lufkin Dialysis Center had experienced an unusually large number of deaths and injuries to patients, totally perplexing the company. After a thorough investigation that had focused on four areas—the water, the machines, the policies and procedures, and the patients themselves, all of which had come back clean—the company had been left as confused as ever. DaVita's investigators simply could not find anything to explain what was causing the fatal issues, yet clearly, the deaths and injuries had continued.

But, McNeill told them, two patients had come forward that very day with disturbing information. Both claimed to have seen Kimberly Clark Saenz, a nurse, fill a syringe with bleach from a container used to sterilize the equipment and inject the fluid into the IV port of Carolyn Risinger, and then Marva Rhone. Thankfully those patients had both survived, but now DaVita had a full-blown criminal investigation on its hands.

Sergeant Abbott said later that DaVita had only one request: to let the rest of the patients finish their treatments and leave the clinic before the police began the main part of their investigation. Although defense attorney Ryan Deaton later claimed that DaVita had its hooks into everyone, including the police department, Sergeant Abbott said, "In my experience, there was never any interference in the investigation from DaVita or their attorneys." He added, "Besides that, I'm not the type to allow interference in my investigations." Coming from Sergeant Abbott, it was a simple statement of truth.

As the detectives waited for the crime scene unit to arrive and the patients to leave, DaVita gave them a crash course on how dialysis worked, and the procedures that the PCTs and nurses had to follow. Like most police officers, other than basic lifesaving skills—CPR and things like that—Abbott and Shurley knew little about medical procedures, and absolutely nothing about the dialysis process.

As the nurses took the detectives through the medical procedures and patient care, Sergeant Abbott asked questions and had them go through things again and again. As a colleague said of Abbott, "He always goes the extra mile to prepare himself for the investigation." That proved to be an understatement.

Once the crime scene unit arrived, they were directed to the reuse room to examine the evidence that Amy Clinton and Giselle Frenette had found. In the room were two sharps containers in biohazard bags, and Corporal Shurley, still dressed for battle, guarded the door to make sure no one could tamper with any evidence as the crime scene techs began to do their jobs.

Although the DaVita inquiry later turned into a murder investigation—the first one Sergeant Abbott had ever headed—that night, all they were looking at was the injection of two patients with bleach. Since both patients had lived, the most anyone could be charged with in Texas was aggravated assault with a deadly weapon—bleach, if it proved true—and at that point, both detectives had entertained some healthy skepticism about what the witnesses had said.

One important thing the detectives learned was that DaVita had been keeping all the bloodlines used for the patients who suffered cardiac arrests while undergoing treatment on a dialysis machine. They kept the individual lines in marked biohazard bags in a freezer. Sergeant Abbott didn't have a clue what to do with the bloodlines, but he instructed CSU to collect all of them and take them in as evidence. These later became the most important evidence in the entire case.

In addition to the two sharps containers from the reuse room that Corporal Shurley was guarding, the two investigators also confiscated *every* sharps container in the clinic as evidence. Sergeant Abbott had the crime scene unit number and label every container based on the patient station numbers that were on the walls. They also made a chart of where each container had been before they took it into custody. Corporal Shurley said later that this was hugely important in the long run and defused a defense theory that DaVita was merely trying to cover up their own negligence by blaming a single employee. There was no way DaVita could have known in advance that the investigators would take all of the sharps containers.

Next to the bloodlines, these sharps containers proved the most important evidence collected. They didn't point to aggravated assault. They pointed to murder.

PART II

SEARCH FOR JUSTICE

Neither evil tongues, rash judgements,
nor the sneers of selfish men, nor greetings
where no kindness is, nor all the dreary
intercourse of daily life, shall
e'er prevail against us.

—WILLIAM WORDSWORTH

CHAPTER 8

---⋀---

THE HAND GRENADE

Sergeant Steve Abbott, Corporal Mike Shurley, and the crime scene techs stayed at DaVita until around ten thirty that night collecting all the evidence, taking pictures, and speaking with members of DaVita's hierarchy—namely, Jerry McNeill and Amy Clinton.

After hearing what DaVita had to say, Sergeant Abbott called his immediate supervisor, a lieutenant who was off that day, and then the assistant and chief of police to inform them of what he had. His supervisors didn't offer him any advice or tell him how to proceed. After all, he was the one who cleaned up the messes, not them, and this kind of situation had never come up before. Sergeant Abbott said later, "That first day we didn't know enough to know what made sense or what didn't."

But meanwhile at DaVita, Sergeant Abbott was still finding out plenty.

Sergeant Abbott had the CSU sit in Ms. Hall's and

Ms. Hamilton's chairs and take pictures of people sitting in the alleged victims' chairs. These pictures along with the measurements offered valuable insight into what kind of sight lines the witnesses could have had.

While the CSU was taking the containers and making the chart, Sergeant Abbott decided to test what he'd been told about procedures by Clinton and McNeill. He stopped an employee at random to question about the process of getting the two pails of bleach water, and policies they had to follow. The employee, who turned out to be Yazmin Santana, a PCT, told him the same thing the DaVita administrators had. Abbott specifically asked her about the practice of using a syringe to measure bleach, and Santana responded that they always used a cup to measure the bleach. She was emphatic that it was never acceptable to use a syringe to measure bleach—though she did tell him that a week earlier in a meeting, a teammate, she couldn't remember who, had suggested using a syringe. However, no one agreed that this was a proper method, and they had all agreed to continue using the measuring cups.

Santana also emphasized using a syringe to measure bleach would require one to pour the bleach into something first before drawing it into a syringe. The best thing they had for that was the measuring cup they were supposed to use to start with. So what would be the point of using a syringe?

Before Sergeant Abbott left that night, state health officials gave him a report on the blood samples taken from Ms. Risinger and Ms. Rhone—the two patients whom the witnesses claimed Saenz had injected with bleach. The report confirmed that both patients had been exposed to bleach poisoning.

Sergeant Abbott also learned that Clinton had arrived on April 2 and brought several specialists with her to inspect all aspects of the clinic. In April, Clinton spent 90 percent of her time at the clinic. After the two patients died on April 1, DaVita didn't have another documented occurrence, one they kept bloodlines on, until April 16, when Mr. Kelley coded while on the machine—likely because of all the monitors and Clinton's near constant presence. At that point, even though DaVita investigators didn't believe reuse dialyzers were causing the problems, they stopped using reuse dialyzers.

Then Clinton passed along what two employees had said to Sandy Lawrence, who was the facility administrator prior to Clinton's arrival, that it had to be an employee who was harming the patients. As badly as Clinton didn't want to believe Ms. Hall's and Ms. Hamilton's stories, in the back of her mind, she realized they now had the answer they'd been searching for.

Before the detectives left that Monday night, Clinton confirmed what Yazmin Santana had already told them: at no time were the employees—or anyone else, for that matter—supposed to use a syringe to measure bleach. There was no reason for the syringes to come in contact with bleach at all. The bleach solutions DaVita used for cleaning and disinfecting were mixed in the back, not at the patient care stations, and with abundantly available measuring cups. It didn't make any sense to try to use a syringe.

———————

The next morning, Tuesday, April 29, Sergeant Abbott and Corporal Shurley received a call from an unexpected source, an attorney by the name of Robert Flournoy, who at that time was also the attorney for the City of Lufkin. He had a client in his office who wanted to talk to them.

The client's name raised some eyebrows with the detectives. It was Mark Kevin Saenz, Kimberly Clark Saenz's husband.

Corporal Shurley left the police department and went to the attorney's office, where he met Kevin, who told Corporal Shurley that he was in the process of filing for a divorce. The reason he'd called the meeting was to inform the police that he'd seen some Internet searches on Kim's computer that had disturbed him. Kevin told the detectives that he had found records of searches done on bleach poisoning. He also told Corporal Shurley that he didn't want to see Kim get into trouble for something that she didn't do, and Shurley assured him if his wife hadn't done anything wrong, she wouldn't get into trouble. The detectives said that Saenz continued to completely cooperate with police after the initial interview, until he began to see all the evidence piling up against her, and then he refused to cooperate anymore.

After Corporal Shurley returned to the station, the two detectives made arrangements to speak with the two eyewitnesses. The first one was Ms. Hall, the sixty-four-year-old mother of three who had worked at Memorial Hospital as a nurse's assistant for seven and a half years prior to becoming ill. She told them that she always took a book to read and sat in the same place, a corner seat in Bay B with a machine between her and Ms. Hamilton. On April 28, LVN Kim Saenz was the nurse for both Ms. Hall and Ms. Hamilton. Ms. Hall told the detectives that Saenz was always a nice person. They laughed and talked together, and they'd even discussed the Lord that day.

What caught her attention and made her stop reading was the way Saenz was acting. "She was fidgety—not acting like herself," Ms. Hall recalled. She watched as Saenz went to the drawer of the desk at the nurses' station and took out some syringes and dropped some paper in the trash. Saenz glanced all around as if she was checking to see if anyone was observing her, then set the bleach pail on the floor. Before squatting next to it, Kim again looked around as if making sure that no one was watching her.

Ms. Hall told them that Kim then stuck the syringe in the bleach water and drew some of it up. She stood at the station a minute looking around and then walked to Ms. Marva Rhone's station and injected the bleach into her saline port. Just as Ms. Hall was wondering if she was really seeing what she thought she saw, Ms. Hamilton became very upset. She heard Ms. Hamilton say she saw something, and Ms. Hall responded, "Lord, I did, too."

Ms. Hall told the detectives that she begged the nurses not to let Kim touch her.

Ms. Hamilton's statement was similar to Ms. Hall's. There were some minor variations because they were sitting in different places, at different distances, and had different angles. Ms. Hamilton echoed Ms. Hall's description of Kim's unusual behavior. This was what had originally captured the attention of both of them.

When Kim put the pail on the floor, Ms. Hamilton said to herself, "What is she doing?" Ms. Hall had been a dialysis patient for a year, but Ms. Hamilton had been one for eight years. She was by far more experienced than Ms. Hall, and she knew they never put anything on the floor.

In a deposition later, Ms. Hamilton related how she saw Kim pour the bleach from a Clorox bottle and she'd smelled the bleach. Both witnesses had seen her inject the bleach not only into Ms. Rhone's lines, but also into Ms. Carolyn Risinger's.

Every detective has that aha moment. For Corporal Mike Shurley, that moment came when they interviewed those two women. He said that he had an open mind going into an investigation and, as always, would let the evidence and not his preconceptions lead to guilt or innocence. He'd interviewed thousands of people by the time they talked to Ms. Hall and Ms. Hamilton, and he was leery of eyewitnesses, but what the witnesses said matched up to everything the detectives had seen and found.

Besides that, the detectives had spent an inordinate amount of time investigating the witnesses themselves— they looked to see if either Ms. Hall or Ms. Hamilton might've had an ax to grind with Saenz, if either had ever complained about her before, or said or did anything that would make them report false allegations about her. But investigators found that not only did neither of the women have any reason to lie, until this incident, they had both really liked Saenz. Far from being vindictive, Ms. Hall and Ms. Hamilton were simply stunned and scared to death to think that Saenz could've done something like that.

Another thing that helped seal the deal for Shurley: both witnesses had similar but not identical stories, which spoke volumes for their validity. Most of the time, if people collude on a story, there aren't any differences. Also, the women were absolutely positive of what they'd seen and there wasn't anything or anyone that would ever sway them from it.

Next up for the investigators was their most illuminating interview yet—Kimberly Clark Saenz.

—⋀—

CHAPTER 9

TELL NO LIES

In any investigation, it is imperative that investigators speak with potential suspects as soon as possible, especially when the crimes are of a serious nature. The sooner suspects are interviewed, the more likely they will speak, even with their rights read to them. In many cases, suspects—whether innocent or guilty—*want* to tell their side of the story. Often, guilty suspects believe they can spin a story in their favor, explain away things that might be incriminating, actually learn what the police have, and in some cases mislead or divert the investigators.

And in this case, the two witnesses' poor health made it even more imperative to get the suspect talking. Young, healthy witnesses don't always do well on a stand in the courtroom, but it would be a lot easier to confuse or discredit the accuracy of elderly, ill witnesses.

In any investigation there are two kinds of evidence: direct and circumstantial. TV has spent years creating misunderstandings about this. Far from being untrust-worthy, "circumstantial evidence" can and usually is the most important evidence in a case. DNA, fingerprints, and other scientific evidence are all considered circum-stantial evidence, and lead to the circumstances of the crime.

Say a suspect tells police he's never been in a house where someone committed a murder, but his fingerprints are inside that house and on the murder weapon. This is powerful circumstantial evidence that would lead some-one to draw an inference that the suspect was actually in that house and had held the murder weapon.

Direct evidence is eyewitness testimony, and law enforcement and prosecutors actually hold less value in this type of evidence. For example, in the same scenario as above, imagine a witness saw a man enter the house where a murder occurred, and then a little later leave it. However, this time there are no fingerprints from him in the house or on the murder weapon.

In the first scenario, if the case goes to trial, it will be almost impossible for the defense to explain how the sus-pect's fingerprints got into a house he claims he's never been in and equally difficult to offer any legitimate reason the suspect's fingerprints are on that murder weapon.

In the second scenario, the witness saw the suspect enter and leave the house, but he never saw a crime com-mitted, and in thousands of cases witnesses have turned out to be wrong about who or what they think they saw. Eyewitnesses are extremely susceptible to defense attor-neys on cross-examinations. In many instances, witnesses can be made to look wrong or even incompetent, even when they aren't. It's a lot easier for a defense attorney to challenge a witness than it is to challenge forensic evidence.

So far in the DaVita case, Sergeant Steve Abbott and Corporal Mike Shurley had direct eyewitness testimony, but while they'd collected bloodlines and syringes that might produce some circumstantial evidence, at that point they didn't even know what to do with it, and didn't have a clue where to send it. None of the forensic labs in the United States were equipped to handle the tubing and needles and tell the investigators if what they had contained bleach.

All the two detectives really had at that point was the testimony of two elderly dialysis patients. Corporal Shurley believed the witnesses and was starting to become convinced of Saenz's guilt of the two aggravated assaults. However, Sergeant Abbott hadn't reached his aha point yet.

The detectives needed to talk to Kimberly Clark Saenz, and the sooner the better. They got her address from DaVita and found out that she lived way out deep in the piney woods of Angelina County at 2203 Green Sanders Road in a double-wide trailer that sat close to her parents' house.

On this trip to Saenz's house, the two detective supervisors began playing what Corporal Shurley termed "Devil's Advocate." He was usually the Devil. Although he now believed in Saenz's guilt, he played the other hand. Whatever excuses Sergeant Abbott came up with, Corporal Shurley made him prove them with facts. This would go on for months and would be a key factor in revealing the investigation's strong and weak points.

On the afternoon of April 29, the detectives, aware that DaVita had fired Saenz that day, found her at home. They told her that they needed to talk with her at the police station. Whenever possible, detectives always conduct interviews with suspects at the police station, which not only gives them the benefit of videotaping what happens inside that interrogation room but keeps the suspect from getting too comfortable. People's words and actions sometimes come back to haunt them in those little interrogation rooms, and it helps to have it all on tape. The investigators didn't know it at the time but they had a perfect suspect in Saenz—one who thought she could talk her way out of things.

Sergeant Abbott and Corporal Shurley emphasized that Saenz wasn't under arrest, and even gave her the opportunity to drive her own vehicle to the station, but she decided to ride with them. She was very agreeable, and all she asked for was a couple of minutes to get her purse and arrange for someone to pick her daughter up from school.

Sergeant Abbott and Corporal Shurley went outside to wait for her in their car. No matter what the outcome of a case, there is never a perfect investigation. Every detective can look back and see things that they could have done better, or should have done differently. But if they are good, they don't make the same mistakes again.

Sergeant Abbott on hindsight said he wished he'd handled this part differently. It was taking Saenz too long to make a phone call and get her purse. Corporal Shurley even commented, "What's taking her so long?"

Sergeant Abbott and Corporal Shurley came to believe

that Saenz took drugs while they were waiting in the car for her. They said that when they first approached her in Pollok, she was fine—coherent, alert, not a thing wrong with her demeanor. On the way to the station, they chatted and she even showed them a shortcut to get back to the main road that took them to Lufkin.

Corporal Shurley, the one who conducted the interview, said, "Everything was fine and then she took a nosedive." They believe it took a while for whatever substance she'd ingested to take effect. These two veteran police supervisors had come into contact with hundreds of people who were intoxicated by alcohol and/or on drugs. They knew what they were seeing. Sergeant Abbott said, "The longer the interview went, the more rambling she became and she couldn't maintain a coherent thought." Because of Saenz's obvious impairment, they were left with no choice but to terminate the interview. Corporal Shurley said the fact that she'd taken something to try to relax herself was a huge red flag for him—an indicator to him of her guilt. Innocent people seldom have to take drugs to relax themselves.

The interview lasted fifty minutes, and by the time they walked her out to her waiting ride, Saenz didn't know who or where she was. Unfortunately, it was the last chance they got to talk to her.

However, this is exactly the reason detectives want to record what goes on in the interview rooms. Saenz's deterioration was obvious for all to see. She was lucid at the beginning of the interview, although very talkative. Then later her words began to slur and sentences began to run-on to each other. While the interrogation went on, her cell phone began to ring, and it continued to ring throughout. She received at least twenty calls during the fifty-minute interview. At the end, she didn't seem to know what to do with the phone—turn it off, answer it, or just take it out and see who was calling.

Despite having to end the interview after fifty minutes, it was hardly a total loss. The first rule of interviewing a suspect is that if the person is talking, shut up and let her talk. A talkative guilty suspect will usually say things she shouldn't if she's just given the uninterrupted opportunity to talk, and Kim Saenz talked quite a bit.

Many young detectives are too eager and not patient enough to sit and listen, but Corporal Shurley and Sergeant Abbott sat back like the veteran police officers they were and simply let Saenz stick her foot in her mouth. One of the things she said in the interview was that she'd used a 10cc syringe to measure the bleach for the bleach pail. She said when she used a syringe, she'd pour the bleach into a cup then fill the syringe. She told them that the reason she'd done that was because with all the monitors watching at the clinic, she wanted to make sure that she measured it perfectly.

This surprised the investigators, who'd already been told by DaVita that this was something that was never done. So why, if Saenz wanted to make sure she was doing everything correctly, would she use a method to measure bleach that was not taught by DaVita and was, in fact, taboo?

Even more alarming was that, since the weapon used to injure the two patients was bleach, Saenz had just put a smoking syringe in her own hand.

She rambled on about things like loving her job, which they later heard from other sources was just the opposite, and without provocation, she even volunteered the fact that she had not used a computer to research bleach in dialysis lines or anything like that. That got the detectives' attention quickly, because it was that very morning that Kevin Saenz had told them about the Internet searches on bleach poisoning he had found on Kim's computer.

There were still other things in that interview that caught their attention. Saenz stated positively that two employees had to verify the testing of the dialysis machines when they were tested for bleach, and they always did. She had her opportunity to say right then that they didn't always do this, a position her defense attorney later tried to take, but of course, she didn't think that far ahead at the time. Another thing she told them that came back to bite her was that there weren't any measuring cups at the clinic that day—that the clinic was often out of supplies. Sergeant Abbott and Corporal Shurley knew this last statement was just plain false; everyone else they'd spoken to had said there was always an abundance of measuring cups on hand, and besides that, they'd been at the clinic the day before and knew DaVita had them on hand.

Saenz also informed them that she was taking a prescription drug for depression and had been on it for six weeks.

As she rambled on, she said other odd things—for example, that she thought the problems the patients at DaVita were having had to do with blood pressure.

It really left them scratching their heads when she

couldn't remember the last day she worked, or the patients she'd treated, even though it had been the day before.

After Saenz left the station, both detectives now strongly suspected that she was guilty of two aggravated assaults. But both detectives were determined, despite their suspicions, to keep an open mind. They also realized they would have to dot their *i*'s and cross their *t*'s on this one, sensing that it was going to turn into a high-profile case.

Not that they had any idea, at that moment, just how big it would become.

For now, they focused on the great deal of work ahead of them. Besides the two witnesses they interviewed, they also interviewed all 130 DaVita patients to see if anyone else had seen Saenz, or anyone else for that matter, doing anything they shouldn't. But the hardest part of what they had to do was take care of the evidence they'd collected at DaVita. Besides the bloodlines that DaVita had stored in their evidence freezer, the detectives also took every vial of the clinic's heparin, a drug that helps prevent blood from clotting. Sergeant Abbott wanted to leave no stone unturned, as the old cliché goes. He didn't want a defense attorney to come back later and blame him for not collecting it, or to blame the heparin itself for the problems. That left those thirty sharps containers they had collected. The biohazard people only came around to DaVita every so often to empty the containers, and when Sergeant Abbott collected all of them on the night of April 28, they hadn't been emptied in a while. Most of the approximately thirty containers were at least half full, and Sergeant Abbott believed that they would need to test all the syringes.

Because of the sheer volume of needles the crime scene techs had to test and the equipment they had to wear to protect themselves from the jumble of uncapped dirty needles—they knew that some patients at DaVita had the AIDS virus—the process took days. The techs used small test strips, the kind most people use to test pools or spas. Sergeant Abbott's decision to test all those syringes no matter how long it took became the single most important part of the investigation.

One person Sergeant Abbott rightfully deflected credit to was Christy Pate, a crime scene tech who took part in testing the syringes. Pate was an attractive woman with blond hair and blue eyes, and born and raised in Lufkin. She'd graduated from Lufkin High School in 1990 and started work at LPD when she was nineteen years old. As a crime scene tech, her main jobs were to collect and maintain evidence, and maintain the custody of evidence—a vital role in an investigation. In April 2008, she'd worked for the police department for almost nine years.

Pate was also one of the crime scene techs who had responded to the call to collect evidence at DaVita on the evening of April 28. Later, after she was told what was going on, her initial impression was what they were saying wasn't right—somehow they were missing something. It was just too outlandish to believe that a health care provider would inject her patients with bleach.

They'd collected all the sharps containers the night of April 28, a Monday. That night they stored them in the evidence room and Pate got a glimpse at the list of patients who'd died at DaVita, but they didn't begin to test the syringes until the next day. Because Saenz had told them she used a 10cc syringe to measure bleach, they were only checking the 10cc syringes. By Friday night, they had made their way through all of these syringes in the sharps containers, and had found a couple that tested positive for bleach.

That Friday, May 2, exactly one week after Ms. Opal Few died, and almost the same hour, Christy Pate returned to the evidence room by herself to recheck the sharps containers. For some reason she wasn't satisfied with what they'd done and wanted to go over it again. Pate said later that it must have been a sign.

On this morning, Pate picked up one of the containers and opened it. She could only stare. Right on top was a syringe with a patient's name on it—a name that flashed in Pate's memory. The detectives had been given a list of all the patients who had died of cardiac arrest while hooked up to the machines, and she recognized this name. Pate knew this syringe hadn't been tested, because it wasn't a 10cc syringe but a 3ml one. The 3ml syringes were way too small to use to measure bleach, and were only used at DaVita for small doses of a certain drug.

The patient's name on that syringe was Ms. Opal Few. With trembling hands Pate picked it up and tested it. What she discovered literally took her breath away. The test strip was positive for bleach. She grabbed the phone to call her boss, Sergeant Abbott. They now had a murder investigation on their hands.

---/\\/---

CHAPTER 10

SIGNS OF VIOLENCE

The evening of April 28, 2008, the same day the two witnesses had accused her of injecting bleach into patients, a DaVita employee called Kimberly Saenz at home to tell her about the meeting that was to take place with all DaVita employees the next morning. Later, Saenz's friend and coworker Werlan Guillory called as well. He specifically asked her if she was coming to the meeting. She told him no. She was going to the Expo Center for her daughter's school field day. Guillory told her that they would fire her if she didn't show up.

The next morning, after the meeting at DaVita, which Saenz didn't show up for, and before she met with the police later that day, Guillory drove to the Expo Center to talk to Saenz and got a huge surprise. She was crying, her eyes were swollen, and her hair was disheveled. Besides that, she acted like she didn't recognize him even though he'd worked with her for almost eight months. When he asked her what was wrong, she told him she was having trouble with her husband and he'd accused her of hurting the patients.

When Saenz left the Expo Center, she returned home and received another call from DaVita, but this one was to tell her that she was fired. Saenz had accomplished one thing at DaVita—she'd worked there for eight months, longer than any of her other nursing jobs. However, her problems were far from over. That very afternoon, she'd had an interview with the Lufkin detectives that hadn't gone well at all.

Then around eight thirty that night, Bradley Baker, a Lufkin police officer, was called to a Tulane Drive address in Lufkin because of a dispute. When he arrived, he found Kim Saenz banging on the door of the house. The officer issued a criminal trespass warning, but since she appeared to be under the influence of something—her eyes were glassy and she was having trouble answering questions— he arrested her for public intoxication. Saenz spent the night in jail and was released on a $500 bond on April 30, 2008.

Kim Saenz had had trouble with depression for a long time, and according to her husband, when she went to work at DaVita, she not only was under a psychiatrist's care, she was also addicted to prescription drugs. He said that by that point in time, she was buying prescription drugs over the Internet, doctor hopping to get medications, and even stealing his medication.

During the time she worked for DaVita, Saenz's depression had worsened. She and her husband were having problems, and as before, it was highly likely that

financial troubles were contributing to their marital strife.
Prescription drugs on the Internet and at pharmacies
aren't cheap, and neither are doctors who prescribe them.
Besides that, she also had two children, who weren't cheap
either.

When she got out of jail on April 30, Saenz came home
to find that the problems with her husband had magnified.
A week after Kevin Saenz had met with Corporal Shurley,
he repeated his statements under oath. On May 6, in front
of a county court at law judge, Kevin swore in an affidavit,
"My wife is addicted to drugs and unable to function.
She is violent at times and unable to drive a vehicle safely."
He went on to say, "My wife has been charged with public
intoxication. I believe she is a danger to our daughter and
to herself and should not be permitted to have possession
or custody of our child at this time."

The judge issued a temporary restraining order against
Kimberly Saenz—the second one her husband had taken
out against her. In that order, the judge listed thirty-two
separate restraints. In many cases the wording of restraints
in a protective order are standard, but one protective order
does not fit all. The judge compiles the specific restraints to the cause of action that brought it before his
court. In this case, the judge personalized the restraints
by using Kevin's name. According to the order, Kimberly
Saenz was:

  – Restrained from communicating with Kevin in per-
    son, by telephone, or in writing in a vulgar, profane,
    obscene, or indecent language or in a coarse or profane
    manner.

  – Restrained from threatening Kevin in person, by tele-
    phone, or in writing to take unlawful action against
    any person.

  – Restrained from placing one or more telephone calls,
    anonymously, at any unreasonable hour, in an offen-
    sive and repetitious manner, or without a legitimate
    purpose of communication.

  – Restrained from causing bodily injury to Kevin or to
    a child of either party.

  – Restrained from threatening Kevin or a child of either
    party with imminent bodily injury.

  – Restrained from visiting with a child in an unsuper-
    vised manner.

From the affidavit and the restraining order, it was clear
to see that Kevin Saenz feared his wife. However, at the
time the detectives didn't know that Kim had also told
her former DaVita coworker Werlan Guillory that her
husband had accused her of harming the patients at
DaVita.

Kimberly Saenz was about to receive yet another blow.
For almost three years, she had skirted the suspension of
her nursing license in spite of her poor track record. From
August 2005, when Woodland Heights filed the charges
against Saenz's nursing license for stealing Demerol, she
had worked as a nurse at Wright Choice Home Health,
The Lufkin State School, The Children's Clinic of Lufkin,
and the DaVita Lufkin Dialysis Center without those
charges ever appearing on her nursing license.

Finally, on May 14, 2008, the Texas State Board of Nursing suspended Saenz's license.

———————

Sergeant Steve Abbott realized that he needed help with this investigation, so he sought out Clyde Herrington, the Angelina County district attorney.

The DA's office worked well with the Lufkin Police Department and its detectives. Herrington knew Sergeant Abbott, and the fact that the detective supervisor who didn't usually handle a caseload was now investigating a case surprised him—but not nearly as much as the tale Sergeant Abbott told him. Herrington had been in the DA's office at the time for twenty-eight years, eighteen as district attorney, and though he thought he had seen and heard just about everything, never before had he encountered a crime like this one. After Sergeant Abbott finished telling him everything they'd found out so far, Herrington's first coherent utterance was, "Holy cow, that can't be true."

It was the same reaction from everyone who heard the story. It was almost unbelievable anywhere, but especially in Lufkin. Things like this just didn't happen here.

What neither Sergeant Abbott nor Herrington knew at that moment was that things like this had never happened *anywhere*.

Herrington knew he would need every ounce of his experience for this case. He and Abbott were facing some serious problems with the investigation. As soon as Herrington began to look into instances of doctors, nurses, EMTs, or other medical people being accused or indicted and put on trial for killing or causing harm to patients, he found there were far more cases than he'd anticipated. Even so, however, these individuals were hardly ever convicted, owing to a lack of evidence.

As Herrington pondered what evidence they had and what to do with it, he began calling people to ask their opinions—medical and legal professionals, anyone who might help him. His apprehension about the case grew as he discovered that no one—or at least no one anyone had ever heard of—had used bleach as a weapon before. And there was still worse news for the prosecution. Herrington discovered that bleach doesn't act like other solubles in the blood: it rapidly mixes in and attaches itself to all the different components of blood and becomes undetectable.

At this point in the investigation, Herrington and Abbott were looking at two cases of aggravated assault on Ms. Risinger and Ms. Rhone, but Herrington also recognized another looming problem. Both his witnesses were getting on in age and were obviously not in the best of health to begin with. After talking to Dr. Nazeer, the medical director of DaVita, Herrington found out that the average dialysis patient lived only three or four years after starting treatment. From a legal standpoint, this was a problem because if the case was as extensive as it appeared to be, it could take several years before it came to trial. Without the witnesses, Herrington knew he might not have a case. He took advantage of a new law that allowed prosecutors to video a witness's deposition if there was reason to believe that health reasons might prevent that witness from testifying at a later date. He had Dr. Nazeer put the patients' medical conditions and the average life expectancy of dialysis patients in a document to him, and then used that as a basis to get video depositions of the two witnesses. This decision proved crucial in the long run—the case ultimately took four years to come to trial, by which time one of his witnesses had indeed passed away.

By this time, Christy Pate from the Lufkin crime scene unit had discovered Ms. Few's bleach-laden 3ml syringe, and the investigation tilted from aggravated assault to murder. However, the main question was if someone had murdered Ms. Few using bleach, what about the others on the list? Abbott had syringes and biohazard bags with other patients' names on them.

Herrington joined Abbott in searching for a lab that could handle their specialized kind of evidence. They needed to find a crime lab that could accept the bloodlines and syringes the police had confiscated from DaVita, test them, and tell investigators definitively that bleach was present in them.

At first blush, if Kimberly Saenz had indeed killed the DaVita patients, it appeared that she might have found the perfect weapon.

This lack of crime lab left Herrington with a dilemma. He might be able to convict Saenz on the first two aggravated assaults. They had two very good and credible eyewitnesses who would not be swayed from their testimony. They also had the CSU testing with the positive bleach results of the syringes found in the sharps containers, but since that testing hadn't been done in a laboratory setting with scientific equipment, and with trained personnel, it could be challenged in court.

They couldn't convict Saenz of Ms. Few's murder or any of them on the list—if she was guilty of them—without valid, scientific evidence. Herrington continued looking for someone to handle the testing. Finally, in the middle of May, just about the time Saenz's nursing license was suspended, Herrington uncovered a possibility that he'd never previously considered: the FDA, the Food and Drug Administration. The FDA had the only lab that thought they might be able to test the bloodlines and syringes to determine if a chlorinating agent were present. However, they weren't *certain* they could do it, and even if their labs did reveal a "chlorinating agent," that would not be good enough in trial. They needed to be able to say that the lines and syringes held *bleach*. Herrington followed up with the CDC, the Centers for Disease Control, who said they thought they could handle the delicate medical analysis to determine whether the patients had been injected with bleach, and if so, what effect the bleach had on the ones injected.

Still, Sergeant Abbott exercised caution. Because of the unknowns in whether the FDA and the CDC could handle the tests on the possible evidence, Sergeant Abbott only sent the FDA Ms. Rhone's bloodlines and syringe. When the FDA was through with the evidence, they would in turn ship the evidence to the CDC to see if they could handle their part.

Abbott and Herrington had witness testimony of Ms. Rhone's aggravated assault, as she was one of the two patients whom witnesses claimed to have seen Saenz inject. (For some reason, DaVita had not kept the bloodlines of Ms. Risinger, the other patient.)

The report he got back from the CDC and the FDA on Ms. Rhone's bloodlines and syringe took some pressure off Sergeant Abbott and Herrington. These agencies found traces of bleach not only in the bloodlines, but also in a syringe that had Ms. Rhone's name on it. After these results came back, Abbott sent them the rest of the evidence to test, but he did it in a way that would be crucial. He sent the evidence as a part of a "blind study." He sent fifty-one samples with no identifying marks except numbers marked from 1 to 51. Among the fifty-one was the evidence, and the lab technicians had no idea which samples belonged to the victims.

However, before they received the test results, Herrington discovered some other problems. After studying what other agencies had done with incidents of medical professionals accused of hurting their patients, one thing was clear: most of the convictions came not from a jury, but with a confession. Their best chance in this case would be to get Saenz to confess. By that point, there was little doubt in any of the investigators' minds that she was at least guilty of the first two aggravated assaults.

Fortunately they also had Sergeant Abbott's quick wits to rely on. Early in the investigation, using information obtained from Kevin Saenz, Abbott had obtained search warrants for Kimberly Saenz's home computer as well as her parents' computer. Her husband was the one who'd told investigators that his wife sometimes used her parents' computer—a habit that came back to haunt her.

After retrieving the computers, investigators stored them until they could be examined by computer forensic experts. The results of the computer analysis chilled them. At 4:14 in the morning on April 2, 2008, the morning after the deaths of Ms. Strange and Ms. Metcalf, someone had done a Yahoo! search on bleach poisoning. This search was followed up on May 5, by "Can bleach be detected in dialysis lines," and "Dialysis patient's symptoms of bleach poisoning."

The evidence began to pile up, but the investigators still didn't have enough to convict Saenz of murder. In most cases, an autopsy of the victim helped in determining the cause of death. DaVita had given Abbott a list of patients who'd died at DaVita, but none of the patients who'd died had received autopsies. Also, he only had bloodlines and syringes for Ms. Strange, Ms. Metcalf, and Ms. Few, and he believed that all three of them had been murdered. At the time, Mr. Kelley and Ms. Bryant were still alive. But the three deaths that he had evidence on had problems with their death certificates. All three certificates listed their deaths as natural causes. At the time of their deaths, there had been no reason to think otherwise, so there was no reason to do autopsies. All the patients had been of advanced age, with health problems in addition to the renal failure that required them to take dialysis treatments.

Herrington, in an interview later, shook his head and sighed as he said, "It took us a long time—months—to understand what we were dealing with. We continued to learn for four years."

Indeed, nothing in the Saenz case proved easy. In the

meantime, they had two patients in the hospital, Mr. Kelley and Ms. Bryant, and they needed evidence from them. At minimum they thought these two would turn out to be aggravated assaults, and if they died—and the doctors weren't giving them any chance—they'd have two more murders on their hands.

CSU Christy Pate went with Sergeant Abbott to the hospital to talk to the doctors about the patients' conditions, to have blood collected, and to discuss where and how the blood needed to be preserved and shipped for testing. She was amazed when Abbott, her sergeant, who had no prior medical knowledge or experience, began talking with the doctors in a medical language she didn't understand. It was obvious to her, and to the doctors, that Sergeant Abbott knew as much about this as they did.

Once they left the hospital, Pate couldn't hold back any longer. She asked Abbott where and when he'd learned all the medical stuff. His simple answer was one that epitomized Sergeant Abbott. "I've been studying."

After the trial ended, other LPD officers said that medical experts on the subject of bleach and its effects on people and blood called to consult Sergeant Abbott about it—not each other.

Sergeant Abbott endeavored to keep an open mind as the case began. However, the longer he investigated, the more the evidence began to pile up, and the evidence kept bringing him back to Saenz.

With enough evidence in place, the investigators were finally able to make an arrest. Sergeant Abbott arrested Kim Saenz on May 30, 2008, for two counts of aggravated assault with a deadly weapon, for allegedly injecting

Ms. Risinger and Ms. Rhone with bleach. These were the two patients that both witnesses had claimed Saenz injected.

Instead of having a lawyer appointed, Saenz and her family decided to hire an attorney, Scott Tatum of Lufkin's Tatum & Tatum law office. Quite a few people in and around the courthouse said that Scott Tatum was a darn good attorney. He was intelligent, knowledgeable, direct, and a veteran of many court battles.

Tatum handled the depositions from Ms. Hall and Ms. Hamilton, the two witnesses who claimed to have seen Saenz inject bleach into the patients, and he posted her bond—a $50,000 attorney bond on each count, for a total of $100,000. Saenz was released from jail on June 2. One of the stipulations of the bond was that she would not work in any way in or around a medical facility.

As the news of Saenz's arrest and the allegations began sweeping the country and parts of the world, the mood inside Herrington's office wasn't one of celebration. He and Sergeant Abbott thought they had a serial killer on their hands, and they were earnestly hoping for a confession. That was the real reason they had carried out the arrest when they did. Unfortunately, none was forthcoming. Kim Saenz had an attorney, and they couldn't even talk to her.

CHAPTER 11

A CALL FOR HELP

Clyde Herrington's unthreatening appearance, along with his soft-spoken, slow speech pattern and the friendliness of his bearing and gestures, gave him the look of an old country attorney from Central Casting. But while his even temperament and affable nature might conjure up the image of a bumbling bumpkin, the truth was far different. In fact, Clyde Herrington was an intelligent, shrewd, and wily veteran of the courtroom.

Herrington had a deep dedication to community welfare—especially when it came to the victims of crime. Most people who came into contact with him knew instantly that Herrington actually cared. And he was ethical—he never wanted to stand in front of a jury and ask them to do something he wouldn't do if he were in their place. One of his biggest fears was to discover he'd put an innocent person in prison.

In his own words: "People sometimes think a trial is

not about the evidence but who is the best attorney. When that happens, guilty people either go free or innocent ones go to prison." According to Herrington, "A prosecutor's job is not to convict but to see justice is done." As he says, "The purpose of a trial is to find the truth."

Herrington grew up blue-collar in Angelina County. His grandfather worked at Lufkin Industries and his father followed suit for forty-two years. His mother worked at JC Penney. There were no silver spoons awaiting him at birth; like many East Texas boys, he was expected to work and do the chores.

As he grew up, tending farm animals had an effect on him that lasted all his life. Unlike his grandfather and father, he didn't want to work at Lufkin Industries—he wanted to be a veterinarian. In high school he participated in the Key Club and the Kiwanis Community Service Club, and spent four years in FFA, Future Farmers of America.

After high school, Herrington attended two years at Angelina Community College in Lufkin, and then traveled twenty miles north of Lufkin to attend Stephen F. Austin State University in Nacogdoches. There he took a slight turn from his veterinary dream. Although he majored in agricultural science, he minored in education with a plan to obtain a teacher's certificate to teach agriculture in school.

Although he did, in fact, obtain a Texas teacher's certificate, his path diverged even further. An uncle of his, who was a professor at Baylor University in Waco, Texas, convinced him to apply to law school. In an interview after the trial, Herrington said that, growing up, he'd never thought about becoming an attorney. With his uncle's encouragement, he said why not, and applied to the Baylor Law School. He was actually doing his student teaching in agriculture at Hudson High School, just west of Lufkin, when he was accepted.

After earning his law degree from Baylor in 1981, Herrington returned to Lufkin to settle down. He went to work for a local defense attorney and remained at the firm for three years. Defense wasn't for him, though—he didn't like it when the court appointed him to represent bad people. In 1983, then–district attorney Gerald Goodwin, who'd had his eye on Herrington since he'd graduated from law school, hired him to work for Angelina County as an assistant.

In 1990, Goodwin stepped down as district attorney in order to run for election as a district judge in the county. In doing so, he left an unexpired term, and Texas Governor Bill Clements appointed Clyde Herrington to serve out the remaining time as the district attorney of Angelina County until the next elections were held.

When the time came for the DA elections, however, Herrington ran unopposed. As it turned out, this wouldn't be an unusual occurrence. Herrington ran for DA five times and never once had an opponent in the general election. When he finally left the DA's office on December 31, 2012, it was because he retired, not because he'd ever lost.

Never in his law career had Herrington ever been involved in a case remotely like that of Kimberly Clark Saenz. In an interview after the trial, he said, "I really don't think prosecutors should avoid cases because it's tough, and I knew from the moment Abbott had first walked into my office that this one would be the hardest of my career."

Unfortunately for Herrington, Saenz's arrest and charge didn't lead to the confession he'd hoped for. He felt secure that he could convict Saenz on the two assaults, but he also believed she'd murdered patients, and he wasn't going to stop until he could find the truth.

Although he'd finally found the two government agencies that were testing the evidence, the FDA and the CDC, Herrington was dismayed to realize that both agencies were exempt from processes—meaning they couldn't be subpoenaed to testify in court. And if he couldn't get them to testify to the results of the tests, no matter what those results might be, that would put the investigation back to day one.

So Herrington called on an old friend—Malcolm Bales, the U.S. Attorney for the Eastern District of Texas—reasoning that if the U.S. Attorney's office, also a federal agency, was involved, it might help smooth the way to get the other agencies to testify. Herrington even knew of an assistant U.S. Attorney who worked in the East Texas area who wanted to be a part of the case. He just didn't know if he could get him. As it turned out, he'd get lucky on several fronts with that phone call to his old friend. That phone call produced help in the form of a young attorney by the name of Chris Tortorice (pronounced "ta-TORres").

Chris Tortorice was thirty years old when he became involved in the prosecution of Saenz. At a slender six feet, with glasses and short brown hair parted in the middle, Tortorice looked like a mild-mannered if well-dressed geek. In truth, he *was* mild-mannered and likable with no hint of cockiness.

Born and raised in Beaumont, Texas, Tortorice attended Catholic schools through high school, and upon graduation took off for Texas A&M, and then law school at South Texas College of Law in Houston—one of the largest private law schools in the country. In 2010, *U.S. News & World Report* ranked the South Texas School of Law third in the country in trial advocacy.

After passing the bar and being licensed as an attorney in Texas in May 2005, Tortorice first spent a couple of years in the Navarro County DA's office before becoming the Special Assistant to the Texas Attorney General. After a short stint there, he went to the U.S. Attorney's Eastern Division of Texas headquartered in Beaumont. He'd just begun there when he became involved in the Saenz prosecution—an assignment that would consume four years of his life. Tortorice was a newlywed when the assignment began, and he and his wife had settled down in Beaumont. They both wanted children, but couldn't have guessed that they would have two sons before Saenz even came to trial. To emphasize the type of person he is, Tortorice's wife tells the story of how they'd planned home births for both of their boys, but each came so fast that their midwife didn't make it in time. Chris had to deliver them both himself.

In 2008, Tortorice had prosecuted quite a few cases, ranging from child sexual assault to one where a man threatened to kill and eat the President and First Lady, but he'd never been involved in a capital murder case before. However, what Herrington got in young Chris Tortorice was an attorney who was intelligent and willing to work and put his all into the prosecution. Even more important, he got someone willing to learn what turned out to be the hardest part of the trial: the sciences involved in the case.

The third member of Clyde Herrington and Chris Tortorice's prosecution team—later referred to as "Team Justice"—was Layne Thompson. Thompson, a short, slim man with a craggy face under steel gray hair, was the type of person who looked like he was going ten miles an hour while sitting still.

Born and raised in Lufkin and East Texas, Layne Thompson had attended high school with Herrington, then lit out for the University of Texas and its law school. Graduating in 1982, he took his degree to Houston and Harris County, where he said he worked in a large law firm for twenty-two years, defending doctors, hospitals, and medical offices against malpractice charges. Thompson, like Herrington and Tortorice, was a humble, intelligent man who got along well with everyone. In fact, in his humbleness, he neglected to mention that he not only had worked for that huge law firm in Houston, but had been a partner.

However, Thompson eventually tired of civil litigation. He said he'd had the idealistic belief that he would be a part of changing the world when he went to law school. But he wasn't changing anything in civil litigation. His thoughts turned to prosecution and to the Harris County DA's office. One thing Houston has is crime, after all, and it needs a lot of people to help change its world.

Thompson thought he could do this in a small way, one case at a time, one defendant at a time, and thus began a new stage in his career—criminal prosecution. It was a step down in salary, for sure, but people around Layne Thompson said that money had little bearing on what he did.

When he made the switch to the prosecution side of law, Thompson rediscovered his passion—the passion that had sent him to Austin and law school. He said, "As an assistant DA I had to make some tough decisions. Plea bargaining is difficult—figuring out what to offer someone. Can we save that person, or is he or she incorrigible with no way of saving or helping them? However, the first choice always had to be to protect society from that person."

The pull of East Texas made Thompson want to return home, but in order to do that, many things—some of them out of his control—had to come together just right. First of all, he didn't want to uproot his family until his son graduated from high school. Second, the Angelina DA's office would have to have an opening, and Herrington would have to want to hire him. Thompson had laid the groundwork for that when he'd run into Herrington several years before. "They're working me to death here and I want to come back home. Let me know if anything ever comes open."

May came and his son graduated from high school, then out of the blue, the stars aligned. Clyde Herrington called to tell him that he had an opening. With his new-found passion for the law, his desire to change worlds, Layne Thompson returned to his roots. However, he soon discovered the roots he returned to would also want him to take part in a trial that would put his skills and abilities on display for the entire world to see.

Herrington said, "Layne coming to the Angelina County DA's office was a Godsend. No way could Angelina County get an attorney of Layne's caliber and experience under normal circumstances, but Layne was from Angelina County and that is the only reason I could get him."

An Angelina grand jury had just indicted Kimberly Clark Saenz on several charges including five capital murders by injecting bleach into dialysis patients. In other words, this would turn out to be a medical malpractice case with the death penalty on the line.

As they prepared for the trial, Thompson and the defense team referred to as Team Justice had a couple of fears. First, they worried that the inordinate amount of science and medical expertise involved in the case would overwhelm the jurors and take their focus off the real facts in the case. Second, while by law they didn't have to prove motive to convict, they worried that the jury wouldn't be able to get past the why. It's human nature to wonder, but could the jury get past it?

And last, Thompson worried about the youngest member of Team Justice—Chris Tortorice. He was worried because Chris would handle the brunt of the sciences in the case and he didn't have a lot of experience in that area. He had a lot to learn and a short time to get there.

_____

As the attorneys came together, the investigative side was also transitioning. Sergeant Abbott got help in the form of Jim Hersley and Bill Horton, investigators for the Texas Attorney General's Office. Joe Reiker, a special agent with the U.S. Office of Inspector General, also provided a lot of help in the investigation. In fact, Reiker was instrumental in getting Tortorice in the case. Even before Herrington called the Attorney General, he'd heard of Tortorice and that he wanted to be involved in the Saenz case. Reiker had worked with Tortorice before and recommended him to Sergeant Abbott and Herrington.

They needed all the help they could get. One fact was becoming increasingly clear. DaVita Lufkin wasn't the poster child for well-run medical clinics.

On April 28, 2008, once all the patients had left the clinic, DaVita "voluntarily" closed their doors in what was likely a preemptive public relations move. Would state and federal agencies have forced them to shut down anyway? Odds are good that they would have.

In a statement to the *The Lufkin News* in mid-May, DaVita officials said that they believed, "the events that led to our voluntarily closing the DaVita Lufkin dialysis center are the result of a criminal act by an individual who has been terminated and is no longer working at the center." DaVita was playing the only PR card it had at that time, doubtlessly attempting to repair some of the damage done to their image, but the statement put the police investigators in a bind. The police department's job was to investigate and convict *whoever* was responsible, and they weren't about to make the same declaration DaVita did.

One of defense attorneys' favorite ploys in trials is to blame investigators for having tunnel vision—for locking in on one suspect too soon, to the exclusion of others. Obviously DaVita's statement was fuel for a defense attorney, and LPD was quick to counter it.

Lieutenant David Young, LPD spokesman, put a different slant on it in reaction to DaVita's statement. He said, "The investigation is focused on a lot of things, including an investigation into one person."

There were those who also said that the DaVita statement was more than a mere PR move—that it was an attempt to take the focus off some other things that were going on at the time. For example, DaVita issued the statement on Thursday, May 15. The very next day, they received a letter from the Texas Department of State Health Services and the Centers for Disease Control, which had conducted an in-depth inspection of every aspect of DaVita Lufkin's operation, stating the inspection found "potentially serious or life-threatening risks to patients requiring the highest level of corrective action to be carried out before reopening."

Among the problems DHSH found were staffing and operational problems that didn't meet state-required standards. However, those were far from the only issues that existed at the DaVita facility. The investigation revealed that DaVita Lufkin failed to monitor care provided to patients and did not immediately detect an increase in adverse events related to health and safety. It also found that the facility did not keep complete and accurate patient medical records, including patient deaths, which had not been properly documented. Included in these lapses was that cause of death or possible death trends among DaVita patients from September 2007 through April 2008 had not been documented. Along the same lines, the inspection found that the staff hadn't properly documented an Adverse Occurrence Report Policy, which staff are instructed to fill out for "any unexpected event that is inconsistent with routine operation of a dialysis facility." A review showed that although thirty-four patients were transported to a local emergency room in April, only nineteen of those patients had been documented by the facility.

DaVita Lufkin had some serious hoops to jump through before they could reopen, and the DSHS gave them ten days to submit a plan that corrected the problems.

One of the state's requirements was that DaVita appoint four monitors—a physician, two nurses, and a dialysis technician—independent of the DaVita company. The doctor would oversee all operations and training, including verification of competency. The two nurses had to be on-site for five days a week for the first month the facility would be open. Their job was to ensure patient safety. The technician would monitor the facility's existing water treatment system, machine maintenance practices, and all other related policies. DaVita would also have to pay these monitors' salaries.

Furthermore, DaVita would also need to undergo what the state called a "Safety Net" program. This involved checks by nursing staff to ensure that correct dialysate, medications, blood flow rates, and safety checks were utilized.

To DaVita's credit, they quickly did everything that the DSHS ordered. While they were closed, they'd been busing patients at DaVita's expense to other area dialysis centers for treatment. They hired the monitors recommended by the state, fixed the problems, brought in a new facility director, and retrained their staff.

As the date for their July reopening neared, DaVita also renewed their PR machine. A Wednesday, June 18, newspaper headline read, DAVITA: CHARGES AGAINST NURSE UNPRECEDENTED. A gentle reminder to the public that someone was being charged and it wasn't DaVita. The article even said, "Criminal allegations against a former DaVita nurse are unprecedented in the dialysis industry," and went on to relate how DaVita itself had first spotted the problem and brought in their own investigators and monitors to try to find what the problems were. Michael Chee, the DaVita spokesperson, told the *The Lufkin News* about Saenz's suspended nursing license for allegations of stealing Demerol from another employer, and called her "a very deceitful person. This was a person trying to hide their actions, we believe."

He wouldn't be the last person to call Saenz deceitful.

On Monday, June 30, the state gave DaVita permission to reopen in phases and gradually build up to operating at full strength. However, the independent monitors remained at the facility for six months to ensure that DaVita remained in compliance with state and federal guidelines.

The doors reopened for nine patients on July 2, 2008. Not everyone was happy about the reopening. That morning, Wanda Hollingsworth, daughter of Ms. Thelma Metcalf, one of the patients who died on April 1, led a group that included her daughter, nephew, and sister-in-law to picket the clinic's opening. Passing cars honked as they waved signs. One sign said, BEWARE. THEY DON'T CARE. MY GRANNY WAS MURDERED THERE.

Hollingsworth left before the official opening. She later

told *The Lufkin News* that DaVita had told them to get off the property. "I wanted to ask a few questions or at least listen to what [DaVita spokesperson Chee] had to say. [. . .] If he was so sure of himself and his statement, then he shouldn't have had a problem with one of the victims' family members being here. But with how they have handled things, it doesn't surprise me. I want the facility to shut down, DaVita to take responsibility and the nurse who has been charged to serve jail time. You can't tell me that someone else did not know what was going on."

Before the clinic reopened, DaVita told the newspaper that the patients were anxious to come back home, as Chee put it. "All but two patients were anxious to return. That's two out of 130."

He didn't say which two weren't anxious to come back, but Ms. Marie Bradley was quick to put her name on that list. She told *The Lufkin News*, "I'm not going back. I'd be petrified. They tried to kill me." Ms. Bradley had been rushed to the hospital from DaVita in cardiac arrest. She woke up at the hospital two and a half days later with no memory of what had happened.

July and August 2008 brought more deaths to East Texas. On July 15, Ms. Cora Bryant died in the hospital, and then on August 15, Mr. Garlin Kelley Jr. added his name to the list of possible murder victims.

As the investigation continued, *The Lufkin News* was finally able to get a comment from Sergeant Steve Abbott. In October he said, "This is a very complicated investigation with a huge amount of medical information involved and requires us to go outside our normal investigative resources to seek medical expertise for review of the facts."

Lieutenant David Young added, "Once the police investigation is completed it will be presented before an Angelina County grand jury, which will decide whether or not to issue an indictment for Saenz."

Obviously, with or without Saenz, DaVita had some problems at the clinic. However, the question paramount to the Lufkin Police Department and to the citizens of East Texas was this: Was DaVita responsible for the injury to the two patients, and the deaths of the others, or were those acts by one individual?

CHAPTER 12

BIRTH OF THE SCAPEGOAT

When someone dies of old age or natural causes, the family grieves, but they are eventually able to get on with their lives the way most of their loved ones would want them to. After all, painful as it may be for the ones left behind, dying in such a manner is a natural process—something we all expect.

But no one expects their loved ones to be murdered—especially not by the medical professional trusted to care for them.

Murder is a crime against nature, willfully robbing an individual of his or her remaining natural life, and taking that person away from his or her loved ones. Murder isn't just a crime against a single person, but against that person's loved ones, too.

This is the reason motive plays so big a role on TV crime shows. People really do yearn to know who committed the crime and, more important, why. It is almost impossible to go from grief to closure without answers to these questions.

At issue in the DaVita case was that the loved ones of the dead not only didn't have the who or why answered, but didn't even know if their loved one died from natural causes or if they were robbed of that person's love by murder. They were in suspended animation. Their grief couldn't end, and they couldn't get on with their lives. Did the Good Lord call one of His own to heaven? Or did someone interrupt the natural process and kill their loved one? If so, why?

Although the families weren't getting any answers, as 2008 came to a close, Sergeant Steve Abbott and the investigation were starting to see some results. Even though they'd expected it, the results of the blind study conducted by the FDA still surprised them. They'd sent fifty-one numbered samples with the victims' samples intermixed. The FDA had no idea which sample belonged to the victims. However, the report they sent back indicated that every single sample from a victim showed traces of bleach, while not one of the other random samples showed any.

Although the large biohazard bags containing the patients' bloodlines were all labeled with the patient's name on the outside, Sergeant Abbott had gone the extra mile and had each of the bloodlines tested using DNA.

The DNA lab compared blood samples from the lines themselves to each individual patient's blood. (In the case of Ms. Few and Ms. Metcalf, for whom blood samples weren't available, DNA was compared to blood from daughters of the victims.) DNA results indeed confirmed that the bloodlines inside each bag actually belonged to the person whose name was marked on the outside.

Along with this, Abbott had hundreds of people to interview, including all of the DaVita employees. He even went to the trouble to interview ex-employees who'd been fired by DaVita. This also turned out to be a smart move in the investigation.

By the end of the investigation, he had sorted through 16,000 documents. Some of those documents that Sergeant Abbott examined were DaVita employment time records, which were very revealing. By this time, he was investigating what he believed to be five murders and five aggravated assaults. As he studied the time sheets, he discovered that the ten occurrences had occurred on six days, and there was only one DaVita employee present and working on the days that all of the occurrences happened: Kimberly Clark Saenz.

As 2008 closed and a new year began, Herrington and Abbott knew that they had a ways to go for trial, but they were almost ready for that grand jury Lieutenant Young had spoken of.

———

By the end of 2008, everyone in East Texas knew that the police were investigating not only the two aggravated assaults but possible homicides, too. Rumor after rumor swept through the small community about the possible serial killer; that it was a nurse sworn to help the sick made it even more unconscionable.

And then there was the accused method—the idea that she'd used bleach via IV was seen not only as heinous but cowardly in the gun-loving area. East Texas is a land that respects courage and the American way. It's a land where they really would need to pry the guns from an East Texan's cold, dead hands, a land where hunting and shooting are a way of life—almost a religion of its own.

By January 2009, Saenz had changed attorneys—from Scott Tatum, a veteran local attorney, to Thomas Ryan Deaton, a young attorney. Also, since it was quite obvious that she was never going to get another nursing job (and in any case, wasn't allowed to work in a medical facility as part of the terms of her bail), she voluntarily surrendered her license. This also saved her the trouble of having to testify or respond to the allegations from Woodland Heights or the State Board of Nursing, where her testimony could be subpoenaed by the district attorney.

Despite surrendering her license, however, Saenz did violate the stipulation of her bond agreement when she got a job with Dr. Matthew Rowley, a local dermatologist, and in March 2009, went to work at the Lufkin Dermatology Clinic—though as a receptionist, not a nurse.

But with her name splashed across the state and the nation under serious charges, how was she even able to get the job at the Dermatology Clinic? Although the news carried Saenz's name, few East Texans could tell you what it was. Most people simply referred to her as the DaVita nurse, and even after the trial, still did. And besides that, she also lied on her application. Naturally she couldn't put down her work history. So she didn't. She put on the application that she'd been working for a roofing company and gave her husband's cell phone number as a reference.

While Kim Saenz began what was to be yet another short-lived job, in downtown Lufkin at the courthouse, Herrington had convened a grand jury to listen to evidence of cases in Angelina County, but one in particular involved Herrington, Sergeant Steve Abbott, Corporal Mike Shurley, and several others. How she was able to get off of work to attend the grand jury session is anyone's guess, but the members of law enforcement were surprised when the doors to the grand jury room opened and Saenz marched in.

Herrington said that in Angelina County, suspects are welcome to speak to the grand jury if they want to, though people accused of crimes don't often appear to testify. Seldom will a suspect's attorney let them. For one thing, if they appear, they are by themselves—their attorney can't appear with them. Second, the testimony is a matter of record and can and will be used in a criminal trial. And third, the members of the grand jury are empowered to investigate as well as review evidence, and are allowed to ask questions of the suspect, who very well could incriminate herself—especially without an attorney by her side.

Some people later said that it was a ploy by the defense attorney to get certain things on the record to try to combat what Saenz had said in the police interview, and that she walked in with a script. Herrington called it the birth of the "scapegoat" theory, which would become an integral part of the defense strategy.

As a matter of fact, Saenz's entire testimony to the grand jury contradicted what she'd told the police in her earlier interview.

On the other hand, her stated purpose for appearing and asking to speak to the grand jury was that she'd been accused of some things and she wanted to clear her name. But if it was meant as a means for Saenz to try to talk her way out of trouble—and it was noted that she was sober, a stark contrast to what the grand jury had already seen from the police video—it didn't work.

Big bold headlines in the April 1, 2009, newspaper declared: GRAND JURY INDICTS FORMER NURSE ON CAPITAL MURDER CHARGES OF FIVE PATIENT DEATHS. The news swept through Angelina County and across the entire country. Finally, the family members of the dead patients knew without a doubt that the investigators and the district attorney believed that their loved ones had been murdered by Kimberly Clark Saenz.

In an odd twist of fate, the newspaper headlines came out on the one-year anniversary of the day that Ms. Thelma Metcalf and Ms. Clara Strange had coded on their machines at DaVita, within five minutes of each other. Near the headlines about Saenz's indictment was a picture of Walter Metcalf Sr., husband of Ms. Metcalf, flanked by their children. On his right were their two sons, Johnny and Walter Metcalf Jr., and on his left, their two daughters, Patricia Metcalf and Wanda Metcalf Hollingsworth. In the picture, Ms. Metcalf's loved ones were standing by the creek in Arkansas where she had played as a child. Nearly a year earlier, they had spread Ms. Metcalf's ashes over this area.

Johnny Metcalf's statement to *The Lufkin News* in many ways reflected the feelings of other victims' family members. "I have mixed feelings about the nurse being

accused of murdering my mother. Evidence will show if
she was intentionally hurting those patients or if she is
being blamed for others' wrongdoings. I have to have
faith that the justice system will decide if she is guilty or
innocent, only time will tell. I do feel that something
horrible was happening at DaVita and the clinic is guilty
of not properly supervising its staff and protecting the
patients from harm. We sent our loved ones up there to
be cared for and treated humanely, instead all our families
have had to live this horrible nightmare."

In other words, while a jury would decide Saenz's
guilt, DaVita still ought to shoulder some responsibility
for the actions of one of its employees. DaVita, meanwhile, was trying to distance itself from the indictments,
and released a statement saying, "Yesterday's grand jury
indictments of a lone individual for murder of patients at
DaVita Lufkin Dialysis Center in 2008 is a painful
reminder of the terrible tragedy that has impacted our
teammates, our patients, their families and our community." Obvious PR from a Fortune 500 company facing a
mounting pile of lawsuits from family members of the
victims. (To their credit, they ended up settling most of
them.)

Ms. LaFrancis Kelley, Mr. Kelley's wife, said to the
paper, "It's hard to understand what happened and how
she could've done that because [my husband] was the love
of everybody." Even so, LaFrancis said she forgave Kimberly Saenz for what she'd done. She said, "Love does not
delight in evil, but rejoices in the truth, it always protects,
always trusts, always hopes."

The grand jury indicted Saenz on the five counts of

capital murder: the murders of Ms. Metcalf, Ms. Strange, Ms. Few, Ms. Bryant, and Mr. Kelley. However, that would not be all. Seldom does law enforcement charge anyone with attempted murder in Texas—it's difficult to prove—but the grand jury also indicted Saenz on five counts of aggravated assault, against Ms. Risinger, Ms. Rhone, Ms. Castaneda, Ms. Oates, and Ms. Bradley. Aggravated assault is a serious charge that could result in a twenty-year sentence for each count. Even without the murders, Kimberly Saenz would spend most of her life in prison if convicted of the assaults. Linda Few James, Ms. Few's daughter, voiced what many East Texans were thinking when she said to the paper, "This many people? It's blowing my mind. I mean, we live in Lufkin. How can a person that sick walk around like a normal person?"

The news of the indictments told nothing about the victims. The ten victims listed were just names to most—just numbers. Angela Scott, the daughter of Ms. Cora Bryant, called up *The Lufkin News* and told them she wanted people to know who her mother was. She went on to tell them about the values Ms. Bryant had instilled in her, how her mother had passed on the will to never give up, and how Ms. Bryant had given her strength to carry on. "We knew my mother was going to die eventually of kidney failure, but not this way. Not by the hands of someone else."

The one divergent voice in all this, unexpectedly enough, was Ms. Carolyn Risinger, one of the victims whom the two witnesses saw Saenz inject with bleach on the morning of April 28.

Ms. Risinger told her story about that day to KTRE-TV on April 2, 2009. "It started out with a pressure on my chest. It felt like somebody was pushing on me and then my stomach started a severe hurt." She said, "It turned into a nightmare, and so many had died I thought it was my turn."

Her husband, Jim Risinger, also told the reporter, "You don't go in there [to the dialysis center] expecting to be up dancing or anything, but you'd like to see them still be alive."

But neither Ms. Risinger nor her husband blamed Kimberly Saenz for killing the five patients or attempting to kill or harm her. On the contrary, they told about a time when they thought Saenz tried to help her. They put the blame squarely on DaVita's shoulders. "The fault lies with more than a single person," Ms. Risinger said. "DaVita was such a rat hole that I said they're using her as a scapegoat."

Interestingly enough, Ms. Risinger would be the first person to use the word "scapegoat" in public. Saenz had said it to the grand jury, but that was sealed and no one knew it at the time. Saenz's new attorney, Ryan Deaton, would also use it in an interview with the paper, but not until later. Ms. Risinger was also the only patient to refer to DaVita as a "rat hole."

Unfortunately, Ms. Risinger did not live to see the Saenz trial. A year and a half after Saenz's indictment, she and her husband were in an early-morning one-car accident in Nacogdoches. Jim Risinger, the driver, sustained some head injuries as a result, but his wife died. Mr. Risinger, a witness for the defense, was not allowed to listen to testimony. Perhaps a small mercy, since at trial former DaVita employee after employee swore that Ms. Risinger was one of the patients Saenz disliked the most, and would get really upset if assigned to care for her.

———————

Just as it can be argued that the families of murder victims are also victims, the family of the suspect could be victims as well. Imagine being the parents of an accused serial killer.

After the indictments, only one member of Saenz's family spoke publically in her defense. Kent Fowler, Saenz's father, told KETK-TV, "My daughter is a Christian woman and the truth will eventually come out. She is the victim and that DaVita is the one to blame for the deaths. She was only using bleach because her superiors at DaVita told her it was part of her daily cleaning duties."

The public as a whole still had little idea who Kimberly Clark Saenz was. All they knew was that she was charged with some pretty horrific crimes—ones almost too unimaginable for the little town of East Texas to contemplate. Her immediate family, church members, and other people who knew her would or could not believe her guilty of these crimes.

With all the media coverage, it seemed inevitable that the Lufkin Dermatology Clinic where Saenz worked was bound to find out about her indictment and arrest. After all, the news had swept the country like wildfire. But it actually wasn't until her husband called to inform them that she couldn't come to work because she was being indicted for murder that they fired her on March 31,

2009—the same day she was indicted by the grand jury, arrested, and put in jail.

About a week later, on April 8, 2009, Saenz was released from jail on a $500,000 attorney bond from her new attorney, Ryan Deaton. On Thursday, April 16, most Angelina County residents got their first look at Kimberly Clark Saenz, when a picture was published in the newspaper of her standing next to Deaton in the Angelina County Courthouse.

Saenz, along with several other people, was awaiting arraignment before Judge Barry Bryan, one of the district judges. Saenz stood out in a vibrant, almost fluorescent, green shirt, which seemed to draw attention to her like a bug to light.

Saenz would have commanded people's attention even without her bright clothes. Not many people are charged with five counts of capital murder. "Capital murder" differs from "murder" when the murder in question happens during the commission of a felony. For example, the murder of a policeman or fireman in the course of their duties; murder for hire; murder in an attempt to escape; murder during a robbery; murder in retaliation; murder of someone under ten years of age—or multiple murders (defined as two or more murders during the same "criminal act," which can involve a series of events not taking place at the same time), which was what applied to Saenz.

Perhaps the largest difference between murder and capital murder in Texas is this: those convicted of murder go to prison; those convicted of capital murder can be put to death. And the world knows how Texans feel about the death penalty.

Deaton gave a statement to the press defending his client against the allegations. "Police have not offered a motive in the case. Saenz is a married mother of two and has no motive for the crimes she is accused of committing. She has no motive to kill anyone." He then plugged the theory that DaVita was using her as a scapegoat, and said, "The investigation is very narrow. I think when the dust settles the truth will come out."

What he said was in part true. Saenz was a married mother of two, and the Lufkin Police Department had not offered a motive. Of course, what Deaton failed to say was that police departments seldom if ever speak to the media before a trial, and the Lufkin Police Department was no exception—especially Sergeant Stephen Abbott.

Nor was motive part of the proof that the prosecution needed to convict.

PART III

THE ARMIES PREPARE

When men are most sure and arrogant
they are commonly most mistaken,
giving views to passion without
that proper deliberation which alone
can secure them from the grossest
absurdities.

—DAVID HUME

CHAPTER 13

THE DEFENSE GROUP

The definition of arrogance: having or showing an exaggerated opinion of one's own importance; being conceited; or overbearingly proud. When people survey the American public about which profession exemplifies this persona, most say attorneys—especially defense attorneys. In a recent survey done by the American Bar Association, the results concluded that the public considers the legal profession among the least reputable institutions in America. The only group that ranked lower was the media, but even then, it was close.

And although the media itself, mainly TV, can be blamed in part of this perception, some of that blame has to fall on the attorneys themselves.

Some seem to be drawn to the spotlight. In many cases, these are the ones perceived to have overinflated opinions of themselves—the self-centered egomaniacs. Others choose to keep themselves as far away from the public spotlight as they can, recognizing that, like cops and the clergy, they are always in the public eye. They are judged by their behavior not only in the courtroom, but also in the hallways, grocery stores, and even church.

At the moment of the arraignment, Kimberly Clark Saenz and her family had retained Ryan Deaton to represent her against the charges. However, in July 2009, prosecutor Clyde Herrington notified Deaton and the court that he planned to seek the death penalty against Saenz. This meant the structure of the defense would have to change—Deaton was not a certified death penalty specialist, and the defense was required to have one appointed by the court.

Like most states, in order for an attorney to defend someone facing the death penalty, that attorney either needed to be certified by the State of Texas as a death penalty specialist or had to have someone at the defense table who was certified. Most counties like Angelina in Texas have an abundance of attorneys, but few are certified to handle death penalty cases.

Stephen Christopher Taylor, an attorney from Conroe, Texas—approximately a hundred miles south of Lufkin— was a certified death penalty specialist. He was an extremely experienced attorney—twenty-three years— and a board certified criminal defense attorney whose practice included North, South, and East Texas. He was also one of the first attorneys in Texas to receive certification in criminal appellate law. With this certification, he could appeal on a client's behalf in state and federal courts, and other aspects of the appeal process. Like certification to defend clients facing death, to become a certified criminal appellate attorney, there are many processes to undergo, and Taylor had successfully completed them.

In truth, Taylor could have been that defense attorney that everyone talked about—the one who strutted around, the one the public had a low opinion of. But he wasn't. He'd taken a circuitous route to becoming a lawyer— born, raised, and educated in Houston, he began working in the computer industry after graduation from high school, and several years later started taking college-level night classes. Eight years after he began those college classes, he graduated with a bachelor's degree. Three more years of night school followed as Taylor obtained a master's degree in business administration.

At the age of thirty-six, Taylor began what he calls a midlife change. He entered law school at the Thurgood Marshall School of Law at Texas Southern University in Houston. In true Taylor fashion, he chose this school because it was only a couple of miles from where he worked.

After graduating from law school at the age of thirty-nine, Taylor had to decide what he wanted to do, but in many ways, his decision was taken out of his hands. In his own words, unless he wanted to chase divorces, he didn't have enough money for civil litigation unless he was lucky enough to get into one of the big civil litigation firms. Also, Taylor said, he didn't go into the prosecution side of criminal law because no one wanted to hire a thirty-nine-year-old baby fresh out of law school. That left criminal defense, an area he immersed himself in.

However, the baby would grow into a sixty-three-year-old intense, tenacious attorney. The short, solid attorney had thinning, short gray hair, full cheeks, and high blood pressure, which revealed itself in his face when he was angry or upset. His attitude at times seemed like that of a tenacious little bulldog who would sink his teeth into something and not let go until he was ready.

Although intense and focused both in and out of the courtroom, Taylor had an unpretentious, engaging personality. He talked to people and made friends. At times he could be seen talking to an attorney or judge, and the next time a bailiff. He engaged just about everyone in conversations, including long discussions with the janitor.

In order for someone to earn respect, they first must respect others, and this seemed to be a Taylor calling card. He appeared to truly respect other people's feelings, opinions, and jobs—no matter what they did. Even the prosecution team thought he was genuine. When they spoke about Steve Taylor, it was always with respect. Not a single attorney from the prosecution team ever doubted that a client of Taylor's would get anything but the absolute best defense from him that was humanly possible. At the same time, they didn't need to worry about his conduct in a courtroom. They also never doubted that he'd be honest and respectful in his dealings with everyone.

Kim Saenz's other lawyer, Thomas Ryan Deaton, was another story.

Deaton had been raised in Lufkin and looked East Texas country all the way from the cowboy boots he wore with his suits to the smokeless tobacco he dipped and spit during court sessions. He was one of Lufkin's all-American boys—all about hunting, fishing, dipping, and football—an image he seemed to promote.

In many ways, Deaton was like that person who was born on third and thought he hit a triple. Without a doubt he had to work in high school, college, and law school to get where he was—college degrees aren't given away and neither are doctor of jurisprudence degrees or admittance to the state bar. But he didn't have to scrape or pinch pennies getting there, and the probability of eleven years of night school to obtain his goal likely would've never entered his mind.

Deaton's list of high school activities can make even an active person tired. Besides starting on the football team's offensive line, he also played basketball, ran track, and was a member of the LHS student council; the Key Club; and Kyssed, the high school's drug-free club. He was also a member of Young Life, a national program that benefits all high school students, but is a multicultural ministry focused on kids in diverse cultural communities and those in economically depressed areas. His activity on the football field came to the attention of several colleges, and even with all his extracurricular activities, Deaton graduated with honors. This didn't hurt when Tulane, a very prestigious private research university in New Orleans, came calling to offer him a football scholarship—a fact that he was rightfully proud of.

After graduating from Tulane, Deaton married his high school sweetheart, then followed in his father's footsteps to law school. Like prosecutor Chris Tortorice, Deaton attended the prestigious South Texas College of Law in Houston. When he graduated from law school in 1998, he returned to his East Texas roots and the newly created Deaton & Deaton law firm.

Quite a few people seemed to think Deaton was conceited and full of himself. The polite word most used for him was "cocky." It certainly appeared that Deaton had never read Dale Carnegie's *How to Win Friends and Influence People*—especially when it came to law enforcement. He wasn't bashful about making comments and accusations against law enforcement in the newspapers.

Taylor, the most experienced attorney and a death penalty specialist, had been assigned by the court to defend Saenz. But Deaton was Saenz's attorney of choice, the one she paid and listened to, and whose directions she followed.

Few people in the Angelina Courthouse had doubted that Deaton would be first chair in Saenz's defense. They said that his ego wouldn't let him take a backseat to Taylor. If he lost the case, no one would blame him—the state had the evidence against her. However, he'd be a big hero if he won, and everyone recognized the size and scope of the trial.

Some people said that, for Deaton, the trial was less about Saenz's innocence than it was about what he would get out of it. At one point, Deaton had attempted to back out of the defense because he wasn't getting paid enough, but Judge Bryan had already given one continuance because of a change of attorneys and wasn't going to give another.

People on the defense team said that Deaton was so confident that he was going to get Saenz off that he had plans to hire her to work at his law firm when the trial was over—once she returned from the cruise that, rumor had it, she'd already booked. This would be the prelude to a $10 million lawsuit against DaVita, which, of course, her attorney would get a hefty chunk out of.

Personality issues aside, some professionals in the Angelina County Courthouse doubted whether Deaton had the ability to win the trial.

According to his adversaries, he also had a problem with leading questions. A leading question is one that lets the witness know what answer is expected of them. "Did you have a hamburger for lunch?" is an example of a leading question. It's obvious from the question what the expected answer is. In contrast, an open question would be: "What did you have for lunch?"

Leading questions are allowed when attorneys cross-examine a witness but not during direct examination, and Deaton had a reputation for either being unable or unwilling to conform to this legal requirement in the courtroom. Attorneys in the DA's office knew this.

But leading questions weren't all Deaton had a poor reputation for in the DA's office. When the office attorneys opposed him in court, they had to be ready for what they called Deaton's propensity for "misrepresentation of facts." And then there was the issue that one prosecutor predicted. He said, "In the Saenz trial, we will mostly present circumstantial evidence with forensic experts to testify to the veracity of that evidence. Deaton has to counter that testimony with his own experts, and Deaton's understanding of the rules of evidence is as bad as any attorney I've ever seen."

CHAPTER 14

---∧---

INEFFECTIVE COUNSEL

After Kimberly Clark Saenz's indictment, Clyde Herrington could easily have asked for no bail to be granted. The posting of bail is not required in capital murder cases. However, if Herrington asked for no bail, the defense attorney could have filed a writ of habeas corpus, a legal action that requires the arrested person to be brought before the court. The writ ensures that people aren't detained unlawfully or without evidence.

If the writ was filed, Herrington would then have been forced to put on his case before the court. With all of his expert witnesses out of state, it would have cost thousands of dollars to get them to Lufkin for the writ hearing, then he'd have to do the same thing again when the trial actually began—all at the cost of the taxpayer. Plus, he wasn't ready to put the evidence on yet. For all those reasons, he didn't make a recommendation for no bail.

Judge Bryan had set her bail at $500,000, which

required her to post 10 percent, i.e. $50,000 if they used a bail company.

However, Texas is actually one of the few states that allow attorneys to act as bail bond agents. A bond is simply a guarantee that the accused will show up in court if let out of jail. In most cases, a bail bond company handles the bonds. The accused or family of the accused puts 10 percent of the bond down, and then the bail bond company guarantees the rest to the court. The 10 percent paid to the bond company is their fee for getting the accused out of jail. This is money the person will never get back. In Saenz's case, she or the family needed to post 50,000 nonrefundable dollars. If the person skips and doesn't appear for the court hearing, the bond company would be required to pay the entire bond.

Attorney bonds in Texas work almost the same but with an exception: the money paid for the bond is supposed to be used in the person's defense. However, the American Bar Association is not an advocate of the Texas law that allows the practice. The Association believes that the practice can lead to conflicts of interest, and pit the attorney's own financial interests against his or her duty to fight for clients in court.

Because Herrington didn't oppose bail, and Deaton posted it for Saenz, the country got to see a rarity—an accused serial killer walking the street for almost four years waiting for trial. The fact that Saenz, accused of five murders and of severely harming five others, had the run of the courthouse was a topic much discussed by courthouse people as well as citizens.

Defense attorney Steve Taylor said after the trial,

"Jacob Hopper's college fund was raided to pay Deaton, and he was devastated." Jacob was Saenz's son from her first marriage. Cheryl Pettry, a mitigation specialist, said, "Saenz's parents apparently had control of Jacob's college fund and used it for the bond." She echoed what Taylor said about the young man being devastated.

Saenz also had some stipulations beyond money set on her bail. She would have to wear a GPS tracking device on her ankle, and she was limited to movement inside the county line. She was not allowed to contact any of the victims, and like before, she was not to seek jobs in the medical profession.

After Judge Bryan set bail, the date of April 5, 2010—almost exactly a year later—was set for the beginning of jury selection for the Saenz trial, later moved to August 9, 2011, for *voir dire*, and September 2011 for the trial.

However, in early August 2011, the defense team again asked for a continuance—Ryan Deaton said that he hadn't had time to properly prepare for the expert witnesses—and it surprised a lot of people when the judge granted it. Very few people knew that this was the right thing to say to Judge Bryan at that moment.

The Saenz investigation and case involved many interesting and unique people, but none like Judge Barry Bryan.

Physically, he tended not to conform too slavishly to any one look. His silver hair was sometimes on the short side, and sometimes longish. Sometimes he had a silvery half-beard, and sometimes he was clean-shaven. He seldom wore a robe in the courtroom and his bailiff didn't announce his arrival. He just opened the door and walked in as he waved everyone to remain seated. Pretentious, he was not.

When asked about his childhood activities growing up, Bryan's response was, "Any club worth being in wouldn't have me," a twist on the classic Groucho Marx line. Judge Bryan may never have been in the Boy Scouts, but he did serve as the district chairman of the Boy Scouts as an adult.

In many ways, Bryan's career path mirrored Steve Taylor's. After high school, he built houses for several years. Then he graduated from Stephen F. Austin in Nacogdoches in 1986 and then law school at SMU.

He was a criminal defense attorney from 1990 until 2003, and like Taylor, was certified in death penalty cases. He'd defended several clients charged with capital murder in Angelina and Jasper Counties, but never went to trial.

Prior to 2003, he was a member of the Angelina County Bar Association, State Bar of Texas, National Association of Criminal Defense Lawyers, and the National Homebuilders Association. In 2003, he became the Angelina County Court at Law 2 judge. He was the County Court judge until 2006, when Texas Governor Rick Perry appointed him to serve the unexpired term as judge for the 217th district court in Angelina County.

As the presiding judge of the 217th district court, Bryan now had the responsibility of overseeing the most high-profile case in the county's history. However, an unrelated case in Angelina County that occurred in June 2005 before he became district judge seemed to have an influence on Judge Bryan's decision to grant Deaton's request for a continuance.

In late May 2011, three months before the Saenz trial was scheduled to begin, Gerardo Flores, serving two life sentences for stomping his pregnant sixteen-year-old girl-friend's stomach, causing the deaths of their unborn twin boys, was brought back to Angelina County.

Flores was scheduled to appear before Judge Bryan, who heard an argument for ineffective council against the original trial attorney. The appeal's attorney believed the original attorney—Ryan Deaton—was ineffective because of the way he handled the expert witnesses in the Flores case.

Deaton told Jessica Cooley of *The Lufkin News*, "That is pretty common in a case like this where a life sentence is issued," but when Deaton asked the judge for the extra time to properly prepare for the expert witnesses, the judge allowed it. Judge Bryan's worst enemies would say that he was fair, and if Deaton was ineffective in the Saenz trial, it wouldn't be because Bryan hadn't allowed him the time to prepare. The judge set a new date of March 5, 2012, for the trial.

Trial preparations were a different process for both sides. Clyde Herrington, though he was the clear leader of the prosecution team, delegated areas of responsibility. Layne Thompson would handle all the questions about the water in DaVita, the expert witnesses, and everything to do with the water purification process. Chris Tortorice would handle the sciences and the medical experts in the case, and Herrington would handle all the rest of the witnesses.

It was an equitable partnership of the humongous caseload.

While Herrington was taking care of the legal end, he gave a lot of credit to Sergeant Steve Abbott. "Abbott's the most modest person I've ever seen," Herrington said. "He's quiet but very bright. Not only that, but he has the ability to get people to cooperate with him." Herrington went on to say, "Abbott was able to work well with the different law enforcement agencies that were helping in the investigation. In a lot of cases, there are jealousies and rivalries with law enforcement groups, but not in this case, and Abbott was the reason."

He also pointed to Abbott's tireless work ethic. In January 2011, Abbott moved his office from the police department to the courthouse. Herrington said, "It was nothing for Abbott to work from seven in the morning to ten at night."

By now, the DA wholeheartedly believed that Kimberly Saenz was a serial killer. The important thing to him was getting this person out of society so no one else died.

In Texas, the prosecutor is responsible for proving every one of the "elements of a crime" in order to convict the person charged. One of the hardest elements to prove in the Saenz case was that the victims had actually been murdered. In most homicides, that's the easy part—a homicide victim's cause of death is usually pretty obvious, like a gunshot wound. However, the death certificates listed Ms. Clara Strange's, Ms. Thelma Metcalf's, and Ms. Opal Few's causes of death as natural. Two of the women had been dead almost a month before the witnesses saw

Saenz inject the two other patients with bleach, and before anyone would even consider something like this was possible. Second, Herrington had to prove that these crimes took place on a certain date and time, and third, that Saenz had intentionally or knowingly caused the deaths, and finally, that these crimes happened in Angelina County, Texas, where he had jurisdiction.

Complicating matters further, Saenz wasn't merely charged with murder—she was charged with *capital murder*. In other words, the prosecution had to prove all the elements of murder plus the fact that Saenz had killed more than one person in the same way. Usually only one of the elements would be in dispute, but in the Saenz case, they had to fight for each one of them.

Still, while the prosecution team's preparations went like a greased pig sliding down a chute, the defense team at times seemed to be stuck in the slop.

Cheryl Pettry was a mitigation specialist brought in by Steve Taylor. The American Bar Association stipulates that a mitigation specialist is a mandatory part of the defense team. The Association goes on to say that the mitigation specialist ensures that the presentation to be made at the penalty phase is integrated into the overall preparation of the case rather than being hurriedly thrown together by defense counsel still in shock at the guilty verdict.

Every trial has a second phase called the punishment phase if the defendant is found guilty in the first. The defense attorney may believe that he or she will get the client off, but has to prepare for that guilty verdict just as he or she does for the first phase. In capital cases, that's where the mitigation specialist comes in.

At the time of the Saenz trial, Cheryl Pettry had worked close to eighty capital cases—more than all the attorneys on the prosecution team and defense team put together—but she said the Saenz trial was one of the most unpleasant cases she'd ever worked on. While Pettry had good things to say about Kent and Bennie Fowler, and she was especially complimentary about Saenz's son, Jacob Hopper, she said that Kimberly Saenz, Ryan Deaton, and Vann Kelley, Deaton's investigator, made her job extremely difficult. For example, neither Saenz nor Deaton agreed to meet with Pettry or the psychologist about the case. Deaton insisted that Saenz was going to be found innocent, and Saenz believed him.

Pettry even had trouble just getting Saenz to confirm basic facts. For example, Saenz told the mitigation specialist that she'd graduated from Central School in Pollok, but when Pettry sent Central a subpoena for the school records, she only got the records up to the eleventh grade. It wasn't until much later that Pettry found out that the school hadn't sent the twelfth grade records because there weren't any—Saenz didn't graduate from high school. She quit after the eleventh grade.

"She's awful; she doesn't know how to tell the truth," Pettry said. "I found out that she didn't even tell me the truth about most of her jobs. For example, she never told me she worked for the State School. I found that out on my own."

Saenz also insisted that all of her family sit in the courtroom as the trial was in progress. That included her cousin, Jennifer Kujala, whom Saenz referred to as her best friend. However, if the family is in the courtroom, they can't be witnesses, and if it went to the second phase, Pettry would not have the people who knew Saenz best to attest to her character. Pettry said Kelley sent her e-mails saying they wouldn't need character witnesses because Saenz was going to be found innocent and there wouldn't be a penalty phase. Steve Taylor reiterated what Pettry said. "Kim insisted in writing that her family be allowed in the trial, and that made them ineligible to testify in the punishment phase."

The one close family member who did not attend Saenz's trial was her brother, Cody Fowler. However, Pettry said she met him once briefly and knew instantly that they didn't want him on the stand.

Pettry said she would never work with that group again.

Taylor echoed her sentiments. "The defense of Saenz, preparations, and the trial was not a good experience for me. It was not a good experience working with Deaton— not a good experience at all. I wouldn't do it again."

Taylor used the analogy of Deaton wanting to go to the big dance but not being able to go there by himself. He needed a partner to get there, but once he got in the door, he dumped his "date." From that time on, Taylor was excluded from everything. He didn't know who the experts were or what they were going to say. He had the documents that listed who would testify, but he had no idea what they would say.

Taylor, the death penalty specialist, who also had a number of murder and death penalty cases under his belt, said his philosophy of criminal defense is to do the best he could for the client. Part of his job was to make sure that they are aware of all options and consequences so they could make the best decision. Because in the end, the client makes the decision.

Taylor said, "Capital litigation isn't pretty—someone is dead and someone caused that death. The best way to keep the client away from death when facing solid evidence in a capital case is to stop it before trial. You don't put your life in the hands of twelve strangers unless it is absolutely necessary."

In cases of multiple deaths, Taylor said he didn't think there was ever a not-guilty verdict.

He said that there was a deal on the table from the prosecution leading up to trial, but it was never going to happen. According to Taylor, for some reason, Deaton and Saenz's husband were there to ensure she didn't take a deal.

In the time leading up to trial, meetings with the DA and hearings before the court on all matters of the judiciary process took place—normal proceedings in any criminal trial, but especially so in a death penalty case. Like most defendants, Saenz was present for all of them, but unlike most defendants, Saenz seemed to enjoy them, revel in them. As preparations for the trial intensified, it was Saenz who spent time going through all the documents that were in the case. She went with the defense group when they toured DaVita—showed them where everything was, did measurements, and demonstrated the lines of sight. Her attitude and actions caused quite a few raised eyebrows with the prosecution team and others who observed her in these situations. One psychologist concluded that Saenz might be a sociopath.

Saenz's mental state aside, the trial preparations for the two sides were vastly different. While the prosecution was preparing for battle, the defense proceeded as if they believed conviction was impossible. Following Deaton's lead, Saenz never seemed to consider any other outcome.

In early 2012, right before *voir dire*, Saenz in all her effervescent glory appeared before Judge Bryan with Ryan Deaton and his father, Thomas W. Deaton, to argue against allowing a prosecution expert witness to testify about the effects of bleach on living tissues. The expert witness in question was Dr. Mark Sochaski, director of analytical chemistry at the Hammer Institute for Health Research. Dr. Sochaski's knowledge came about because of his study of chlorine gas and its effects on rats.

One of the reasons the case was so hard to prove was because bleach in blood was undetectable. Bleach almost instantly attaches itself to the substances in blood like amino acids. But the *effects* of the bleach can be seen by the presence of 3-chlorotyrosine, a specific marker of protein damage in the body caused by bleach. The presence of elevated 3-chlorotyrosine levels is an indicator of the effects of bleach on a person's blood. The prosecution badly needed Dr. Sochaski to testify—and the defense just as badly wanted him not to.

In defending the witness testimony, Herrington told the judge about Mr. Garlin Kelley, who had entered the clinic on the morning of April 16, 2008, in good spirits. He was doing fine, and then five minutes later, he was unconscious. He died a few months later without regaining consciousness. Herrington went on to say that Mr.

The DaVita Lufkin Dialysis Center in Lufkin, Texas. In April of 2008, thirty-four patients were rushed to the emergency room. *(John Foxjohn)*

Downtown Lufkin, Texas—no one believed that such a heinous series of crimes could have occurred in this nice East Texas town. *(Beth Folsom)*

Opal Few.
At ninety-one,
she was the oldest alleged
murder victim, but had been
in excellent spirits right up
until her death.
(Linda Few James)

Clara Strange.
Marisa Fernandez,
her granddaughter,
kept her grandmother's
number in her cell phone,
wishing she could
still call her.
*(Texas Department
of Motor Vehicles)*

Cora Bryant.
She left her family with
the will to never give up.
*(Texas Department
of Motor Vehicles)*

Garlin Kelley Jr.
Mr. Kelley, here with his wife, LaFrancis, at a Lufkin Dunbar High School reunion, was an inspiration to all who knew him.
(LaFrancis Kelley)

Thelma Metcalf.
Ms. Metcalf's death on April 1, 2008 was one of two that sparked the initial DaVita investigation.
(Texas Department of Motor Vehicles)

Marva Rhone.
Ms. Rhone was one of the patients whom witnesses saw Saenz inject with bleach on April 28, 2008.
(Texas Department of Motor Vehicles)

Carolyn Risinger.
Ms. Risinger was the second patient whom witnesses saw Saenz inject with bleach on April 28, 2008.
(Texas Department of Motor Vehicles)

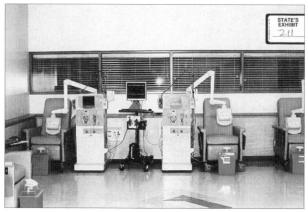

Inside the DaVita Lufkin Dialysis Center.
(Lufkin Police Department)

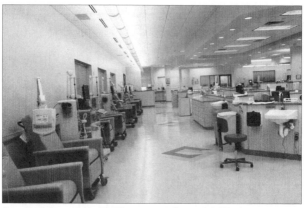

A typical four-chair DaVita care station, with TV hanging over chair, dialysis machine, sharps container in front of chair, and caregiver's computer. *(Lufkin Police Department)*

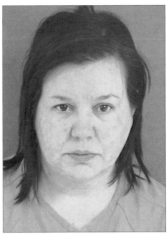

Kimberly Clark Saenz had only gotten her nursing license two and a half years earlier, but had already gone through five jobs by the time she landed the position at DaVita Lufkin. *(Angelina County Sheriff's Department)*

Kimberly Saenz's husband, Kevin Saenz, had a police record in Houston dating back to 1994, but had recently settled into a well-paying job as an appraiser at the Angelina County Appraisal District. *(Houston Police Department)*

Kimberly Clark Saenz and her defense attorney, Ryan Deaton, leaving Angelina County Courthouse. Both seemed convinced throughout the trial that Kim would never be convicted.
*(AP Photo/*The Lufkin News, *Joel Andrews)*

Prosecutor Clyde Herrington conferring with defense attorney
Steve Taylor, the only member of the defense who had experience
with death penalty cases. *(John Foxjohn)*

District attorney Clyde Herrington at his desk.
(John Foxjohn)

"Team Justice," aka Chris Tortorice, Layne Thompson, and Clyde Herrington (left to right). *(John Foxjohn)*

The twelve jurors and two alternates for the Saenz trial. *(John Foxjohn)*

Kelley had very elevated levels of 3-chlorotyrosine, a marker for bleach poisoning in his blood.

Thomas Deaton argued to the court that Mr. Kelley's 3-chlorotyrosine level was due to a "massive infection."

Judge Bryan, an intensely intelligent man, looked at Deaton Sr. for a long moment, then read the toxicology report out loud. It stated that 3-chlorotyrosine does not occur naturally from infection. The judge asked, "Did he have a raging infection when he was transported?"

The elder Deaton's next comment drew expressions of skepticism. "I think it's pretty clear he did."

Ryan Deaton only made matters worse when he called the study with rats bad science, and emphasized his point by saying it had never been replicated in humans.

How Judge Bryan responded to this statement with a straight face is anyone's guess, but it did take him a few moments to formulate his words. He said, "I understand that there is a lack of research with humans being injected with bleach. Wouldn't that kind of study raise some ethical questions?"

With this statement, it took everything the people in the audience had not to burst out laughing.

Needless to say, the state's expert witness was allowed to testify at the trial.

CHAPTER 15

VOIR DIRE

Monday, January 23, 2012, was a beautiful spring-like day in Lufkin. With temperatures in the sixties, a light wind, and no rain, Angelina County citizens flocked to the courthouse. Some were called to jury duty, but most of the others were there to observe the potential jurors.

Voir dire is a French term that means "to speak truth," although "jury selection" is a more common term. In a legal setting, the term has several meanings, and of course, jury selection is only one of those. It can also mean to examine a potential witness before testimony, or even examine evidence to determine whether or not it can be admitted to trial.

Attorneys examine prospective jurors during *voir dire* to see if they have bias against the attorney's case and can follow the law, or just to see what kind of people they are. Potential jurors who are biased or don't believe they can follow the law can be released for cause.

Each attorney can use a limited number of challenges without giving a reason. The potential jurors accepted by both sides are the ones that will hear the case.

It's a simple-sounding process, but a complex issue and vitally important to both sides. In the Saenz trial, the jury selection was even more important than usual—a person's life was on the line. The official date of the Saenz *voir dire* began on January 23, 2012, but in all actuality, it began the day she was first arrested. From that day on, nothing other than normal public information from open records came from the DA or the police department. The reason: Herrington didn't want to give out information that would compromise a jury pool. Most information reported about the case came from the defense side.

Voir dire was one of the reasons Herrington chose to pursue the death penalty. He said, "I have a legal right and obligation to ask for the death penalty but a death penalty *voir dire* gives me a better way of choosing a jury."

He went on to explain his decision: "In a normal situation, all the potential jurors file into the courtroom and have a seat. The two attorneys get to talk to them as a group. The attorney will pick one out of the group and ask that person a question. Then pick another and ask another question. However, they never get to ask all of them a question or even talk to everyone. Both sides know little if anything about the potential jurors."

With a desire to impanel an impartial jury, both attorneys and the judge could ask questions and dismiss jurors. However, the normal process is basically a crapshoot. Herrington said, "This case was too important to select jurors the normal way."

In most cases the defense and the prosecution desire different types of jurors and the selection process is as much about getting the type of person that each side needs as anything else. In the Saenz *voir dire*, both sides wanted smart jurors, with the ability to stay focused for a long time period. The trial was expected to take four to six weeks. The case was complicated, both sides would be putting on expert witnesses in all fields of forensic science as well as dialysis experts, and the jurors had to have the ability to understand and not get lost or caught up in the medical and scientific testimony.

In the capital murder *voir dire*, a potential juror filed alone into the 217th district courtroom and was directed to the witness box next to Judge Bryan. For most of them this was the first time they'd ever been in a courtroom, and definitely the first time in the witness stand. The judge swore them in as not only the prosecution attorney and the two defense attorneys but even the defendant sat watching. In the audience were also several with pens, papers, or in some cases, computers open and ready to write down everything they said.

The citizens had first reported for jury duty up at the courthouse on a Monday morning with no clue as to what kind of jury they might get on or who the defendant was. By the time both attorneys had spoken with the group as a whole for a while, the judge had dealt with the ones claiming exemptions from service for a mélange of legal reasons, and the citizens had spent a few hours filling out that autobiography that the court called a survey, they all knew they were being interviewed as jurors on a capital murder case where they might have to decide if someone lived or died.

To add to this responsibility, and to ensure that they had been thoroughly inconvenienced, each was assigned a date to come back so they could be grilled individually by the prosecutor and the defense attorney.

Both sides of the case were given a couple of days to pore over the surveys the potential jurors had filled out about themselves.

On the defense side, Deaton, Taylor, and Saenz went over the surveys and graded them, but they went further than that. Before jury selection began, the defense had brought in some people from the Texas Defender Service, a nonprofit organization that aims "to establish a fair and just criminal system in Texas." Deaton scanned the surveys and sent them to one of the people in the Defender Service, who graded them and sent them back. Deaton communicated back and forth with him by phone or text regarding the consultant's opinion on whether or not that juror was a good one.

On the date and time of the citizens' inquisition, they showed up and were put in a small room to await the summons to the courtroom. Sometimes the wait was long—well past their appointment time. They had an hour slotted in the schedule, but the wheels of justice are slow and seldom start on time. All they could do was wait. Of course, the longer they waited, the more nervous they became. What would the lawyers ask them? How should they answer questions? Most wanted to answer the questions truthfully, but they didn't want to sound stupid, or fumble their words and have the court misunderstand what they were trying to say.

When their time did come, the jurors entered the courtroom escorted by an armed bailiff.

As the prosecutor, Clyde Herrington started off the process. He first greeted each potential juror with an even, quiet voice that somehow seemed to relax the person on the witness stand, which indeed was his objective. In a way, Herrington was also training that juror as to how he conducted business, in jury selection and in the courtroom—professional, organized, courteous, and credible.

Herrington also put the jurors at ease by first telling them something about himself. He related how he, like them, was born and raised in East Texas. His parents worked there; his father had been an employee at Lufkin Industries for forty-two years. Several of the potential jurors also worked for Lufkin Industries, or had relatives or friends who did.

But more than that, Herrington was making a connection to all of them. This was the man whom they'd continuously reelected to the office to do the job he was going to talk to them about. However, in a show-and-tell world, he was showing them that he was like them. He grew up on a farm with a smell on his boots that most were familiar with. He had to work his way up the ladder. Nothing had been given to him. He was an East Texas country boy through and through, and few if any of the potential jurors would fault him for that.

Herrington chatted with each person on the stand for about five minutes. Some he talked to about a book they were reading or others about their favorite movie or TV show, and no matter the subject or content of the book, he seemed to know something about it. Others he spoke to about their jobs or hobbies, and most about their spouses, children, and family. He made sure that they realized that he was a normal family man like they were. Of course, he got all this from all those questions the potential jurors had to answer about themselves in that "survey."

As the jurors relaxed, they then got to tell Herrington about themselves. And why shouldn't they talk to him? He'd given them the blueprint. With his down-home way, quiet voice, and even-keeled temperament, he was more than just the DA to the potential jurors; he was someone they knew and respected, one of them. Before Herrington began the questioning process, he explained to them that the "survey" that they'd spent hours filling out was nothing more than their opinion, and no matter what they'd answered, they couldn't be wrong. All he asked of them was to be honest.

In truth: Herrington needed all of those down-home connections and more. He faced some serious challenges in the Saenz case, and most of them had nothing to do with guilt or innocence. The first major hurdle he had to overcome was the death penalty itself. The court initially sent out 400 jury summonses, but only about 150 people who received them actually showed up for selection, and of that, at least half of them tried to use an exemption to get out of the duty. But it really wasn't necessary. If a potential juror didn't want to serve on the jury, all they would have to say was they could never under any circumstances vote for the death penalty. That would be a strike for cause.

On paper, a vast majority of Texans—men and women—are in favor of the death penalty. In fact, Texas is known for executing people. Since 1982, Virginia has executed 107 people by lethal injection. This is the second highest total in the United States. Who leads? Texas's 472 executions since 1982 are more than four times the number of Virginia's.

Those numbers should say it all, but believing in the death penalty and being the one who imposed that penalty on someone else are two different things. And like it or not, another problem reared its head: in this case, the person facing death was a woman. Although it shouldn't make a difference if she was guilty of the crimes she was accused of, it mattered that the accused was female. Texas has no problem executing men, but women are another story. Of those 472 executions in Texas, only three had been women. Karla Faye Tucker, the first woman executed in Texas since 1863, was put to death in 1998; Betty Lou Beets in 2000; and Frances Newton in 2005.

But Herrington had an ace up his sleeve—one that few people knew, even Texans. It was that Texas jurors *don't* actually vote for or against the death penalty.

The truth is that district judges in Texas are the ones who impose the penalty in capital cases. In a capital case, the judge has the ability to issue either life in prison without the possibility of parole or the death penalty if that person is convicted.

In the second phase, called the punishment phase, the jury listens to evidence from both the prosecution and defense in order to help them decide whether the convicted person would be a future danger to society.

If they vote no, the punishment phase ends there. Their answer goes to the judge, who then imposes life in prison without the possibility of parole.

If the jurors vote yes, then the jury goes on to a second question, called the mitigating question, and votes on whether the defendant had an excuse for the crime they were convicted of; for example, a mitigating reason can be anything the jurors want it to be—anything from how the defendant was raised, abuse he or she had endured in the past, or their mental capacity.

If the jury finds that the person *did* have a mitigating reason to murder the person or persons they were convicted of killing, then the judge would issue life in prison. If not, the judge issues the death penalty.

The special circumstances questions give the prosecutor some help with potential jurors who don't want to, or won't, vote for death. The DA can honestly say that the juror will not vote to impose the death penalty, which is true, because the judge is the one who does that. But of course, the smart jurors Herrington needed would also understand the consequences of their vote.

Besides the death penalty, Herrington had some other problems he needed to deal with, and of course, *voir dire* was the perfect place to prep the potential jurors for these problems. First, the biggest obstacle was the question of motive. Why did Saenz do it? Most, if not all Angelina County residents—and a good part of the world—knew that the district attorney's office didn't have a motive. Deaton told the paper several times, "[Saenz] is a married mother of two and has no motive for the crimes she is accused of committing. She has no motive to kill anyone."

The general population believed that the DA couldn't convict Saenz without a motive. Most of the jurors didn't know until Herrington told them that in Texas (or for that matter, any state), proof of motive was not required to convict someone of murder. "Have you ever seen someone do something and think, why in the world did they do that?" Herrington asked them. Of course just about everyone has. Then he finished it. "You saw that person do it—you know they did it, but unless they tell you why, you won't know. Does that mean they aren't guilty? Of course not."

In order to prove motive, the accused person would first have to tell why he or she did it, and most people for obvious reasons don't like to admit to murder. If the judicial system was required to prove what was inside someone's head at the time of the murder, a perfect murder would be to do it and not tell anyone why. That would be a loophole few would appreciate.

Though Herrington didn't have to prove motive in order to convict, he still needed to combat the stumbling block of unsatisfied curiosity. It's human nature to want to know what caused a person to act in a certain way or do something—especially an act as heinous as killing people. What was their incentive? What was their goal?

With most homicides, the public understands the motive—they may not go along with it, but they can relate to it. Jealousy, greed, lust, and revenge all have been around since the beginning. These are the motives the public can understand. However, seldom are serial killings done for reasons as remotely pure as those listed above.

Herrington's problem going into *voir dire* wasn't proving or not proving a motive for someone to kill five people and basically attempt to kill five others by injecting them with bleach. His problem was to educate the potential jurors first that he didn't have to have a motive to convict Saenz, and second, that they may never know the true reason if she didn't tell anyone why.

Another one of Herrington's goals going into *voir dire* was to head off common misunderstandings concerning the evidence. He had a case that was 99 percent circumstantial, and he had to get the idea fostered by TV and movies that "circumstantial evidence" was a dirty word out of the potential jurors' minds. He started off telling them exactly what circumstantial evidence was. It's evidence that requires an inference to connect it to a fact. A suspect's fingerprint is found in a victim's home and the suspect shouldn't have been in that home. In this case, the fingerprint is circumstantial evidence—it infers that the suspect was, in fact, in the home, and any reasonable person would draw that conclusion from that piece of evidence.

All scientific evidence including DNA is considered circumstantial. Herrington told the individual jurors a story that a man kidnaps a woman, ties her up, and throws her in the trunk of his car, and no one sees him do it. He then drives that woman out into the woods, rapes her and murders her, and leaves her body at the scene, and still no one has seen him. The police find the murder weapon in his possession with the victim's blood on it, and they find his DNA all over the woman. Besides that, they have his footprints at the scene that match perfectly with the shoes he's wearing. They also have the rope he used to tie her up found in his possession as well as pictures he took of her after he killed her. They also find her blood in the trunk of his car.

Most of the jurors were shocked to hear that every bit of that evidence was circumstantial. Herrington basically shot down the perpetual belief that circumstantial evidence may not be used to convict someone. More often than not, circumstantial evidence is the only evidence linking an accused to a crime.

The importance of circumstantial evidence is backed up by the Supreme Court. It has ruled that this type of evidence is fundamentally no different than eyewitness testimony. Most people who are convicted of a crime and later exonerated are the ones who had eyewitnesses testifying against them.

That fingerprint in the house can't be swayed to change its testimony.

Of course, a lone piece of circumstantial evidence may not prove conclusive. Take that fingerprint in the house. The fingerprint only proves the suspect was in the house—not that he or she killed someone or committed a crime, and in most cases the fingerprint can probably be explained away. However, it's a start because in order for the suspect to kill someone in the house, he would have to be in it. The accumulation of circumstantial evidence like the example Herrington gave the jury is what makes cases in court.

In Saenz's *voir dire*, Herrington came away with a jury pool that was smart and would stand the rigors of a long trial—ones who would pay attention and follow the evidence—and keep themselves away from jury misconduct. Because of the long trial, this one started with fifteen jurors—twelve members plus three alternates. Even though it lasted so long, they never lost a juror for any reason. People commented on how attentive and diligent the jury was, how they continued to take notes until the last person testified. If justice and fairness were sought, neither side could complain about the jury.

People said, and observations tended to bear out this fact, that in addition to Herrington's stated objectives, he had an unstated objective in *voir dire* as well. It stood to reason that if an attorney can use the process to educate the jury and send them certain messages, then that same attorney can also convey messages to the opposing counsel. Which was what Herrington did, whether intentionally or not.

During the selection process, two defense attorneys opposed Herrington: Ryan Deaton and Steve Taylor. During the initial process with the entire jury pool in the courtroom, Deaton was the one who spoke to the jurors. In that phase, Deaton made sure to point out that he was one of them, an East Texas good ol' boy, while Herrington didn't mention where he was from. Was this a strategy on the part of Herrington? Did he know that in the individual process he would more often than not oppose Taylor rather than Deaton? Could it be a coincidence that Herrington brought out his own East Texas roots only when he opposed Taylor, the attorney from Conroe, and not East Texas?

In answer to this question, attorneys in Lufkin gave a little smile and said, "Yeah, right."

The three-week process to impanel the fifteen jurors saw some remarkable cooperation between Herrington and Taylor. Because this was a capital case, both sides had fifteen challenges to use, but seldom did. In fact, many of the potential jurors were dismissed on agreement from both sides. In this case, no challenges were required.

Taylor and Herrington worked well together, and both seemed to have the same objectives—find a jury pool that fit both their needs. The respect between the two attorneys seemed obvious. That same respect didn't seem to exist when Deaton was the one participating in the individual process. Judge Bryan gave a lot of latitude to both sides. However, there were four objections during *voir dire*, and all four of them from Herrington about Deaton. The judge upheld them all.

One thing was sure in the Saenz jury selection: the process was smooth and organized on Herrington's side. When both sides were through asking and talking to the potential juror, that person was asked to step out while the attorneys conferred. For the most part, Herrington had no one to confer with and had no problem making up his mind. He had an answer for the judge immediately. However, the other side was an entirely different story. Just who made the decisions on which jurors to select can be debated—maybe all three did. After each juror left, Taylor, Deaton, and Saenz huddled together and whispered as if they were about to call a football play. These conversations usually took a while.

At one point, Herrington informed the judge that a potential juror was acceptable to him. When this happened, the defense took to their huddle with all three of them having their say. After about five minutes, Herrington sat back down. Ten more minutes passed before the defense team asked the judge if they could give an answer after lunch.

At this point, a ticked-off Herrington stood and asked the judge to take back his recommendation. If the defense was going to get the lunch period to make up their minds, he should, too. Over the objection of the defense, the judge agreed.

Taylor said later that the defense had a checklist of everything they wanted to cover in *voir dire*. Along with that, they had the graded surveys. He also said that Deaton and Saenz had to sign a sheet saying they agreed to the selection of each juror chosen. Taylor said that they didn't choose anyone that Saenz didn't want. On one in particular, she just had a negative feeling about that person so they didn't choose him.

Potential jurors saw and interacted with only one person on the prosecution's side—Herrington. Every single one of the people who sat in the witness stand saw and spoke to the same prosecutor. This wasn't the case with the defense. Taylor handled a lot of the interviews, but Deaton took several himself. Taylor later said that Deaton or his father knew some of the jurors from the community. These were the ones Deaton chose to talk to.

David Bradford was one of the people whom Deaton questioned. Bradford was a local building contractor, but he also had the distinction of being the father of a former Lufkin quarterback who'd gone on to the University of Texas as a punter. Of course, Deaton talked to him about his son and let him know that he, too, had played football for Lufkin High School and gone to college on a football scholarship. Besides that, Bradford was friends with an elected official that Deaton had run against at one time. Deaton asked him if he held it against him for running against his friend. Bradford responded that he didn't even remember him running in any election.

Bradford was an ideal juror for both sides, and was put on the jury panel.

Because Taylor and Deaton were totally different in just about every way, what the potential jurors saw, heard, and experienced depended on whom they drew on the defense team. A couple of the people who sat on the stand for *voir dire* later aped Deaton, imploring them, "Do you promise me if you are chosen to be on the jury that you won't let the others sway you into a position you don't believe? Do you promise me you won't let the others bully you?"

All of the ones Taylor questioned in the process also remembered him, and one part that he prepped them for not only stuck in their minds, but also played a crucial role in the trial. Deaton's questions in *voir dire* largely centered on guilt or innocence. However, Taylor understood that there could possibly be two phases to the trial—guilt and punishment—and he was the one who introduced a concept in the jurors' minds that wouldn't go away.

Because the case involved the death penalty, a good part of the individual selection process involved issues with the death penalty and those special circumstances questions, especially that first one: If the jury couldn't get past that "future danger to society" question, there would be no death penalty. Common sense dictates that if someone is guilty of killing five people and trying to kill five others, they are going to be a danger to society. Who just starts killing people and then suddenly stops?

This was where Taylor's genius came in. He brought forth the question of exactly what society this question referred to. He went on to tell the potential jurors that if Saenz were found guilty, the least she could receive was life in prison without the possibility of parole. His words reverberated with them. "You won't see her at Walmart or Whataburger. She will only leave prison in a pine box." In other words, the only society that she would be in if found guilty was a prison society—one that is regimented and with armed guards. "It would be extremely difficult for her to commit future crimes in prison," he concluded.

Taylor had planted a seed in the potential jurors' minds just in case he needed it. But according to people close to the defense team, if his client had listened to Taylor, she would have pled to the charge.

And there was a deal on the table.

The plea called for Saenz to plead guilty and she would receive a substantial amount of jail time for each charge, and it would run consecutively, but she would avoid the death penalty. With the deal, she would have spent a lot of her life in prison but would eventually be eligible for parole. There was a catch, however. The deal was only good until the twelfth juror was selected. After that, the deal left and they went to trial.

Taylor looked at the charges, all the evidence against Saenz, and whom they were facing. He discussed the deal with Saenz and her family and advised them to take it, but Saenz refused. After all, she had one of her attorneys telling her he'd get her off, and that was better than prison.

During *voir dire*, someone close to the defense said, "Taylor handled the choosing of the jurors, Deaton will handle the trial, and when Saenz is convicted, Taylor will have to come in and save her life."

The mounting tension was obvious as the jury selection neared an end. Saenz and the defense attorneys were more on edge than usual. When the attorneys agreed on the twelfth juror, the deal on the table died. One of the most sensational and unique trials in East Texas history would actually take place.

CHAPTER 16

THE PARTY BEGINS

If Kimberly Clark Saenz had shone like a new penny at pretrial hearings, she was fairly luminous when the trial began on March 5, 2012. She was the center of attention in the trial of the century in East Texas. Writers, news reporters, and TV camera crews were everywhere to capture the moment. The courtroom was packed with potential witnesses waiting to be sworn in as well as spectators who were just there to witness the trial.

Saenz wasn't the only one enjoying the moment. Her defense attorney, Ryan Deaton, who sat on the right of the defense table, looked so pleased and so confident that he had an almost blissful expression on his face. Saenz sat close—really close—to Deaton's left, and then all the way on the other end of the table away from everyone was Steve Taylor. He wasn't needed anymore. He'd gotten Deaton to the big dance and now he was the ugly date who was dumped.

It wouldn't take long for Deaton's expression to change, or for him to get into trouble. As soon as the trial process began and before the jurors came in, Deaton confessed to the judge that he felt unprepared for the trial and wasn't prepared for opening statements. He then started telling the judge the importance of the opening and got admonished by Judge Bryan for lecturing him on opening statements.

It is seldom a good idea to tick the judge off in the first minutes of a trial. But that wasn't the last time Deaton would get under Judge Bryan's skin during trial, or the last time that day for that matter. Besides, with a jury waiting in the next room and with four years to get ready, there was no way this trial was going to be postponed.

Herrington's opening statement was delivered in the same way he had conducted the questions at jury selection. He began by telling the jury panel of ten women and five men, which included a black male and two black women, "The medical profession is an honorable one. We put our faith in them. We don't check on them—we trust that they are going to take care of us." That trust was something Saenz violated.

In his opening, which lasted about thirty minutes, Herrington said little that stuck with anyone, with one exception. He mentioned some Internet searches they'd found on Saenz's computers that would prove interesting.

When he was through, he turned the floor over to Deaton, who didn't waste any time trying to prove he wasn't ready for his opening and ticking off Herrington, the judge, and several of the jury members.

Ryan Deaton began, "DaVita is a puppet master—"

That's as far as he got before Herrington objected. Judge Bryan sustained the objection.

Deaton began again, still focused on blaming DaVita. He told the jury how DaVita was a Fortune 500 company who manipulated everyone and had their tentacles in everyone. Herrington again objected to hearsay, and again the judge sustained the objection.

Deaton made one statement that the jury members remembered: he promised that Saenz's husband would testify that he'd been the one who'd done the searches on the computer, and not Saenz. Since this was the first anyone had heard about these searches and they'd piqued everyone's interest, so did this promise.

Opening statements complete, Herrington opened the trial with guns blazing. His first witness was sixty-eight-year-old Linda Hall, the surviving eyewitness that claimed to have seen Saenz inject the patients with bleach. Ms. Hamilton, the second patient who'd claimed to see Saenz inject the patients on April 28, had died before the trial began.

The elderly black woman was obviously in bad health. She was rolled into the courtroom in a wheelchair, and had to be helped out of her chair and into the witness booth.

As they rolled her in, out of respect and courtroom etiquette, prosecutors Herrington, Tortorice, and defense attorney Taylor stood. Only Deaton continued to sit, and spit his dip in a Styrofoam cup.

Corporal Mike Shurley several years before had listened to Ms. Hall tell her story, and when she was finished, for the first time he had believed that Saenz was guilty of those two aggravated assaults. Ms. Hall had delivered his aha moment. He and Sergeant Abbott had no doubt about the credibility of this witness.

When Herrington was through taking her through the paces, neither did any of the unbiased people in the trial.

Ms. Hall was deadly to the defense. She would hurt the defense even more when Deaton began his cross-examination. In the process of questioning her, Deaton raised his voice, which brought not only an objection to the way he was treating her, but a murmur from the crowd. Several of the jurors' mouths fell wide open at the insolent manner in which Deaton spoke to Ms. Hall.

More than the disrespect he'd shown her, he simply could not shake her testimony.

After Ms. Hall left the stand, Herrington brought in relatives of the victims to describe their loved ones' conditions at the time of their incidents. First was Mr. James Rhone, the husband of Marva Rhone, one of the patients that the two witnesses claimed Saenz had injected with bleach. Although Ms. Rhone had survived the incident, she unfortunately hadn't lived to testify.

Mr. Garlin Kelley's widow followed, and then Herrington ended the day with the video deposition from Ms. Lurlene Hamilton. Early in the investigation, Herrington had anticipated that his witnesses might not make it to trial, and he'd deposed Ms. Hall and Ms. Hamilton just for that purpose.

Because he did, he was able to let the jury see and hear Ms. Hamilton's testimony.

Even so, in the long run, it wouldn't be Ms. Hamilton's

deposition that played a major role in the outcome of the trial—it would be Ms. Hall's deposition that turned out to provide one of the most critical pieces of evidence in the entire trial.

———

Day two started off with a second video deposition from Ms. Hamilton, and then Herrington brought in DaVita employees who'd worked at the Lufkin facility in April 2008—most of whom no longer worked for DaVita.

The first was Angie Rodriguez. She was the PCT teamed with Saenz on the morning of April 28, 2008. In fact, Ms. Rhone and Ms. Risinger were her patients. She left her patients in the care of Saenz, and when she retuned from break, she found Ms. Rhone in distress. She testified, "Kim wasn't happy—didn't like her job and complained often. I honestly thought she was going to leave."

Rodriguez was the first but not the last person to describe how Saenz waited to be the last person in the med room before drawing up her meds. She also stated that Saenz did not like patient care. She only wanted to be the med nurse.

Deaton's cross of Rodriguez left people in the courtroom shaking their heads in disbelief. In order to attempt to impeach her testimony, he picked up his laptop off his table, carried it to the witness stand, and spent quite a bit of time looking for videotape of Rodriguez's interview with the police. Once he found it, he showed it to her.

He asked her if she remembered saying something specific to the police four years before, and like most of the witnesses, she didn't have a clue what her exact words were. He then had to find it on the computer and show it to her. This went on for most of her testimony—him standing by the witness box with his laptop searching for video to show her.

This was not a one-time occurrence but happened with many of the DaVita witnesses. Steve Taylor said later that he'd never seen a witness impeached by having to watch a DVD on a laptop.

Herrington and the prosecution team had transcribed every one of those interviews—all Deaton had to do was ask, "Can you provide me with a copy of the transcripts so I don't waste my time and money doing it myself?" However, instead of doing so, Deaton had times written down based on the times on the computer.

Deaton's fumbling for video made him look like an unorganized goof not only to the spectators, but to the ones who counted the most in that courtroom—the jury.

The next witness was Arlene Gamble, one of the monitors brought in by Amy Clinton to help find the problems at DaVita in April. Not only was she an RN with the title of Clinical Service Specialist, but she had been one of the DaVita instructors from 2003 to 2008.

As Chris Tortorice took Gamble through her paces, she seemed like an excellent witness—knowledgeable, confident. One of her biggest statements was that the water was all on a loop. What one patient got, they all got. If something harmful were in the water, all of the patients would be affected, not just one or two. This was something that many people would say over the course of the trial. Although Deaton tried his best to dispute, gloss over, or hide this fact, the logic of this statement was too simple to miss.

Unfortunately for the prosecution, Gamble ended up being counterproductive under the cross-examination. Deaton not only rattled her, but made her look unprofessional. She became visibly angry and Judge Bryan had to urge her to answer Deaton's questions. She did, but snapped the answers.

As Tortorice watched his witness come apart on the stand—while Saenz and her supporters were all smiles, nods, and gleeful whisperings—he knew he had to do something. When Deaton finished with her, an idea came to Tortorice on the spur of the moment. As Gamble had testified, they'd entered one of the bleach buckets as evidence.

Tortorice also had a bottle of water on his table. He took the bleach bucket and set it on the floor, and squatted down next to it with the bottle of water. He pretended to pour bleach into the bucket and then use a syringe to draw it up. He showed the jury that to use this method— the one that Saenz claimed—he needed to squirt the bleach right back into the pan he'd just drawn it out of.

It was a physical demonstration of exactly what the witnesses had claimed Saenz did, and he had Gamble there to tell the jury how ridiculous it was. It made a lasting impression.

The talk in the hallways and courtroom was as much about Saenz and her actions in the courtroom as it was with what was happening in the trial. As she had in pretrial hearings, *voir dire*, and the first day of the trial, Saenz seemed to be enjoying herself immensely. People commented how on a number of occasions, Saenz seemed to act as if she were at a social event. She laughed, smiled, and carried on like anything but someone on trial for her life.

Her immediate family sat in the first row of pew seats directly behind her, and she was constantly turning to them, gesturing, mouthing words, and giving hand signs. At times she appeared almost giddy.

At one point during Cartwright's testimony, a debate had ensued between the defense and prosecution at the bench. Representing the state in the debate were Thompson, Tortorice, and Herrington. They were opposed by Deaton. Taylor had remained seated, leaned back, and relaxed at the defense table.

During the debate, Saenz turned to her family with that huge smile she often displayed, and held up three fingers to indicate the state and one for her attorney who was battling them all by himself.

Why this was so humorous was anyone's guess. Particularly since her attorney lost the argument.

But this was par for the course.

The general consensus was that either Saenz was supremely confident she was going to get off, or she didn't care. However, it wasn't just Saenz who exuded confidence to the point of smugness. Deaton; Lesa and Vann Kelley, Deaton's investigators; and most of Saenz's family all exuded the same attitude. The only exceptions were Saenz's father, Kent Fowler, and her court-appointed defense attorney, Steve Taylor.

Because the courtroom was on the second floor of the courthouse and there was only one way to access it—the main stairwell in front of the building—everyone, including jurors, got an opportunity to view the spectacle Kim Saenz put on. In addition to Saenz's supreme confidence, the other incongruous thing about her was that she didn't *look* like a serial killer. Not a single person in that courtroom could say what a serial killer was supposed to look like, but whatever it was, it wasn't Saenz.

Herrington told the E! Program after the trial, "One of the things about Kimberly Saenz that is scary, she isn't someone if you knew her or looked at her, you could tell that she would do something like this."

While the people in the courthouse—including the jury—couldn't imagine what a serial killer might look like, they were getting a good demonstration of how one might act. Saenz's lack of seriousness made an impression on them.

Day three began with the survivors. The prosecution had charged Saenz with five counts of aggravated assault, against Ms. Risinger, Ms. Rhone, Ms. Bradley, Ms. Oates, and Ms. Castaneda. They didn't get as much media attention as the patients whom Saenz was accused of having murdered, but although Ms. Risinger had died in a car accident and Ms. Rhone of natural causes before the trial began, the other three were very important to the trial, and they were on hand to tell their stories.

The prosecution led off with Ms. Bradley, a white female from Lufkin who appeared to be in her sixties. She was of average height and weight with light brown hair. She also walked into the courtroom and took a seat without assistance. For her age and health conditions, she was spry. No one looking at her in person would think she was a dialysis patient and had been one for several years—let alone a survivor of a bleach attack.

Ms. Bradley told the jury that on April 23, 2008, she'd driven herself to her dialysis treatments at DaVita in Lufkin, as she always did. At the time she was feeling fine, and had no problems as the treatments began and progressed. But she woke up in Memorial Hospital in Lufkin two and a half days later—a time that she had lost forever. She had no idea what happened or how she got to the hospital.

She stated that after she got out of the hospital, she would not go back to DaVita—she started treatments at Henderson Dialysis Clinic. When she talked about DaVita on the stand, she had nothing good to say about them. She said that DaVita didn't know how to set up the machines, and DaVita used more clamps on the lines than Henderson did.

Similarly, she said that Henderson handled the heparin, a blood-thinning drug, differently. She said that Henderson gave it at the beginning of the treatment, whereas DaVita had given it at intervals throughout the treatment.

She stated that she felt so much better after a treatment at Henderson than she did at DaVita that it was unreal.

As Ms. Bradley answered Herrington's questions, the spot on the back of Deaton's neck glowed red. When Herrington passed the witness to Deaton, it became obvious why. Deaton hadn't spoken to her before she took the stand. She had refused to talk to him or his investigators before the trial. She told him flat out, she didn't talk to them because she didn't want to. She wanted to forget all of it.

Her statement didn't seem to make Deaton any happier. Herrington ended up objecting to Deaton's badgering her.

After Ms. Bradley, Herrington called Ms. Graciela Castaneda to the stand. The differences between Ms. Castaneda and Ms. Bradley were immediately clear. Ms. Castaneda was in a wheelchair and her husband had to push her into the courtroom, then she had to be helped from the chair to the witness stand. Unlike Ms. Bradley, the Hispanic woman appeared frail. She had black hair and a dark complexion. She also didn't speak English, and the court needed a translator.

Via the translator, Ms. Castaneda told the jury that she'd been a dialysis patient for ten years in April 2008, and on the day of the alleged bleach attack, she'd felt fine—no different than the other days of her treatment.

When Herrington asked her if she'd had heart or breathing problems prior to April 16, 2008, the day EMTs rushed her to the hospital from DaVita, she said no. Since that date, however, she has had both.

Ms. Castaneda testified that she remembered talking to a lady who was doing something to her dialysis lines, and then she didn't remember anything else. A couple of months later, when her daughter was looking at a picture of a woman on the front page of a newspaper, Ms. Castaneda pointed to the photo and told her daughter that it was the same woman who'd been messing with her dialysis lines when she passed out. The picture on the newspaper's front page was of Kimberly Clark Saenz.

On cross-examination, Deaton didn't get much out of Ms. Castaneda, but he did ask her if she ever chewed gum when she took her treatments. Ms. Castaneda said no, but Deaton introduced a document into evidence that would become important down the line. What he introduced was Ms. Castaneda's medical records. On the bottom of the page, someone—neither side ever figured out who— had written that when treating Ms. Castaneda on April 16, 2008, they had to pry a piece of chewing gum out of her throat.

The third survivor called that day was Ms. Debra Oates. Unlike Ms. Bradley, Ms. Oates was a large woman—short and very squat with light brown hair, and perhaps the youngest of all the alleged victims. However, like Ms. Bradley, Ms. Oates walked herself into and out of the courtroom and the witness box with no problems or need for assistance. Also like Ms. Bradley, she'd driven herself to and from treatments at DaVita, and she was still driving herself.

If anyone ever considered this to be an "angel of mercy"–type action, whereby Saenz was putting severely ill patients "out of their misery," they'd only need to look at Ms. Bradley and Ms. Oates to knock down that theory.

When Ms. Oates took the stand, she did something no other witness at the trial, past or future, prosecution or defense, did—she looked at Saenz and said, "Hi, Kim."

Under examination by Herrington, Ms. Oates testified that she was extremely familiar with the dialysis process, so much so that she knew the tastes of all the meds given to her while undergoing treatment. She explained that the meds were given through the IV port and patients could taste them. After a while, they learned to differentiate the meds by their taste.

She testified that as she underwent her treatments, she felt some strange sensations followed by chest pains. She said she couldn't breathe, and it felt like every bone in her body was being crushed and her site wouldn't stop bleeding.

Ms. Oates went on to say that she had a funny taste in her mouth, one that she never tasted with any of the drugs she was given, and she asked, "What did you give me?"

Deaton, who'd actually been the one asking the questions when she said this, asked her, "Who did you say this to?"

Ms. Oates replied, "I said it to Kim. She was the one giving me my meds."

Most attorneys say that they shouldn't ask questions they don't know the answer to, or there are some questions best left unasked. This might have been an example of both those cases.

When Ms. Oates had greeted Saenz from the stand, the former nurse didn't say anything back, but she did flash a big smile for Ms. Oates. However, that smile vanished when the witness made this statement—one that another employee would later back up. With her face scrunched up and brow wrinkled, Saenz leaned over and whispered to Deaton. He then asked Ms. Oates if she was talking about the medications given at 8:30 that morning.

These were the kinds of things that went on with Deaton and Saenz during the entire trial as Taylor, the experienced attorney and death penalty specialist, sat far to the left of them, and led everyone, including the jury, to wonder just who was assisting Deaton.

As the day continued, Sharon Smith, an RN with DaVita in 2008 and a charge nurse, took the stand. She was one of the most important witnesses for the prosecution—so important she'd ultimately have to testify several times.

Sharon Smith reiterated what other DaVita employees had said, especially that syringes weren't used to measure bleach. But she was important for other reasons, too. Ms. Debra Oates had testified that after Saenz gave her the medication, it had tasted funny and she'd asked Saenz what she'd given her. Smith had come up just as Ms. Oates had asked that question—right before she became extremely ill. Smith heard and testified to that.

However, another huge part of Smith's testimony was crucial to the prosecution and deadly for the defense. She had been the charge nurse when Ms. Few coded and died. After Ms. Few was transported away from DaVita, Dr. Nazeer had asked Smith what meds Ms. Few was given. When Smith looked in the computer, she didn't see the meds documented, so she asked Saenz if she'd given Ms. Few her meds. When Saenz said yes, Smith told her to document it. Saenz then went on the computer and put in a time she'd given the meds.

The 3ml syringe Saenz had used to give Ms. Few's meds that day, clearly marked with her name and information, had been dropped into a sharps container. This was the syringe that Christy Pate found—the one that tested positive for bleach and started the murder investigation.

When Smith finished testifying, that spot on the back

left of Ryan Deaton's head that turned red when he was angry, upset, or things weren't going his way was glowing like Rudolph's nose.

Smith had done well with her testimony while Herrington questioned her—very well, in fact. But like Arlene Gamble, Sharon Smith had a temper on the stand when Deaton questioned her. It is entirely possible that Deaton was counting on this when he opened his cross-examination by asking her, "Why did DaVita fire you?"

The question brought an immediate objection from Herrington, which was sustained by the judge. The question was improper. There was no evidence that Smith had been fired by DaVita, and never would be. She'd gotten a good recommendation from them when she left, and her present employers had nothing but good things to say about her.

However, the damage was done. Smith was livid and showed it. After that, Deaton made his jaunt to the witness stand with the laptop, leaned on the rail close to her, and Smith asked the judge to get him away from her. She didn't want him close to her. As he asked her questions, the judge had to order her to answer the questions several times.

She was the first witness that had a little talk with Herrington or the judge after she testified about her conduct on the stand, but she wouldn't be the last.

PART IV

THE STORM BLOWS

They call this war a cloud over the land.
But they made the weather and then they
stand in the rain and say "Shit, it's
raining!"

—CHARLES FRAZIER, *COLD MOUNTAIN*

CHAPTER 17

THE GATHERING CLOUDS

There's a saying in East Texas: "You can't ride a dead horse." No one seemed to have told Ryan Deaton, however, because he kept putting the saddle on and hoping his horse would move. From the time he'd taken over the Saenz defense, he'd laid claim to the scapegoat theory. He pronounced it in the papers leading up to the trial and he'd boldly said in his opening that his client was innocent, and she was being used as DaVita's scapegoat.

Deaton's manner might give one the impression that he never had a guilty client.

In his theory, the real guilty party was DaVita, who would then also be responsible for one of the greatest and most complex cover-ups in history. But that didn't daunt Deaton.

One DaVita employee after another heard the same thing from him. "You still work for DaVita, don't you?"

His question to the employees was laced with as much

disdain for the witness as could possibly be put into seven words. No one doubted the disrespect he heaped on them and the implication that because they wouldn't say what he wanted them to say, therefore they were liars and a part of the conspiracy against his client.

Deaton also seemed to take issue with the DaVita attorneys and almost came to blows with one of them, Joel Sprott. As a big, rich, Fortune 500 company, DaVita had attorneys there to represent their employees, and during the trial, Sprott had lodged a complaint that Deaton constantly tried to talk to his clients when he wasn't present— even after he'd told him not to do it several times.

After the trial, when asked what was the biggest obstacle the defense had to overcome, Steve Taylor replied, "Deaton's arrogance. You can only beat up on someone so much and then you start losing points. Defense attorneys should try to negate testimony that has already come in or give a different light on it to help soften it, but when you get up there and call him a lying sucker to his own face in front of twelve people . . . Jurors use their eyes, their ears, and their noses. They know when something stinks. If a skunk walked through the room, they'd remember it and would ask themselves later if the skunk was still around."

Juror David Bradford was tall, solid, had white hair, and stood out in a crowd. He was also a juror that Deaton had wanted. During *voir dire*, Taylor had questioned most of the potential jurors and Deaton questioned one every now and then. Bradford was one that Deaton took— maybe because he thought they could relate. Bradford had not starred on the Lufkin football team as Deaton had, but his son, the starting quarterback, and later punter for the University of Texas, did. But if Deaton thought he had an ally on the jury, he was sorely mistaken.

David Bradford said after the trial, "About the third day of the trial, I was so tired of Deaton beating us over the heads like dumbasses. I said to myself, lay it out and let it go but don't beat us to death with it."

Bradford was referring to that dead horse—the alleged conspiracy and that question dripping with sarcasm, scorn, and loathing for each of the DaVita employees.

———

Wanda Hillyer, another DaVita employee, followed Sharon Smith, and her testimony repeated what all the others, including the ex-employees, had said. But Herrington took her into another area, the cleaning of the dialysis machines.

In 2008, the routine was that on every Thursday, after all the patients were out of the clinic, the staff cleaned all the dialysis machines. This included running bleach through them. When they were finished, the machines were supposed to be thoroughly rinsed so no bleach remained. They were tested to make sure.

Since, as previously stated, the water in DaVita was on one continual loop, it meant that every machine got the same water and bleach when cleaned and rinsed.

Hillyer took the jury through the cleaning process. It was abundantly clear that if DaVita was responsible for bleach being in the bloodlines and harming patients, this was the best opportunity for it to get there. However, Herrington took her through every one of the incidents where patients were harmed and died, and not one incident occurred on a Friday after a Thursday night cleaning, as would have been expected. And again, one fact kept popping up with every witness: if the water was bad, every patient being dialysized that day would've been affected, not only one or two.

Deaton asked Hillyer the same question he'd asked the other DaVita employees. He asked if she'd ever seen or heard of other DaVita employees using another's password to get into the computers. None of the others had.

When Deaton asked Hillyer the question, the attorneys met at the bench for a few moments, then the judge sent the jury out of the courtroom, and they *voir dired* Wanda Hillyer on this question. In answer, she said that she'd heard of it once. When Herrington asked her what happened to the person who used another's password, she responded that DaVita had fired the employee.

Herrington told the judge that he was okay with the jury hearing this testimony.

Deaton, however, must not have been because when the jury returned, he didn't continue to pursue that line of questioning.

The next-to-last witness Herrington called on day three was a young black man named Werlan Guillory, who projected an aura of intelligence and honesty. He was dressed nicely, but not flashily. He also appeared totally credible.

In April 2008, Guillory was a PCT at DaVita and a friend of Kimberly Saenz's. He was also aquatinted with Ryan Deaton, having played basketball with him.

Prior to the trial, Guillory said, he'd spoken to Deaton once for about ten minutes when he ran into him at the grocery store. Although on the stand Deaton attempted to insinuate that Guillory's friendship with Saenz was more than it was, Guillory did admit to caring for Saenz as a friend. But there were things about her that really disturbed him.

He related the story on the stand about how he'd called Saenz after she'd been sent home on April 28, and asked her if she was going to be at the meeting the next day. He said that she told him that she wasn't, she was going to her daughter's field day at the Expo Center in Lufkin instead.

When Saenz really didn't show up for the meeting, Guillory drove to the Expo Center to check on her. To him it was nothing that a friend wouldn't do for another. Saenz's appearance shocked him—she was crying, her eyes were swollen, and her hair was disheveled. Not only that, although they'd worked together for eight months and he considered her a friend, she acted at first like she didn't even know him. While they were talking, Saenz, an emotional wreck, told him that her husband had accused her of harming the patients.

This in itself was damning, but Guillory was about to stick a dagger into the heart of Saenz's defense.

He told the jury that when Ms. Strange coded on April 1, Kim had acted like she didn't care. Then on April 26, when Ms. Few coded, he ran outside to get Kim, who was smoking a cigarette, but she didn't respond or come in.

This little tidbit got a reaction out of the jury and Deaton. The red spot on his head was flashing like a neon sign.

Who would want their health care provider to choose to continue to smoke a cigarette instead of attempting to save his or her life? It was something the jury never forgot, nor did they forget Guillory's answer when Deaton asked him why he ran outside to get Kim.

He said, "I just felt that I needed to get Kim off break to save a life."

Herrington's last witness was also devastating. It was Kimberly Saenz herself.

Herrington played the tape of her police interview, and all twelve members of the jury sat forward on the edge of their seats, as did the spectators.

Meanwhile, Saenz turned in her seat and was laughing, smiling, and mouthing words to her family. Most people in the court, including the jury, couldn't understand what was so amusing about what was being shown.

Everyone in the courtroom heard Saenz tell the police that she thought the problems with the patients in April had to do with blood pressure, and she said she'd never researched bleach on the Internet. This raised some eyebrows from the jury because from Herrington's opening they knew that Internet searches on bleach had been found on Saenz's computer, and from Deaton's opening, they knew her husband was going to discount this evidence. Whatever was coming with those computer searches, they knew it would be important.

In the interview, Saenz couldn't remember when her last day at work for DaVita was or who her patients were, even though the interview took place on April 29, the day after she was sent home. This left everyone wondering about her mental state.

From Herrington's point of view, it was the absolute best time to play Saenz's interview. The jury had sat and listened to a long line of DaVita employees who testified that Saenz not only hated her job, but hated a bunch of the patients. Whether coincidental or not, the patients they named that she hated just happened to be the ones she was accused of harming or killing.

Now on the tape Saenz was telling police how much she loved her job.

But that wouldn't be all she said in that interview as she rambled on. Saenz told them that she was supposed to use a measuring cup to measure bleach, but used a syringe when she didn't have a cup. She said that when she used a syringe, she'd pour the bleach into a measuring cup—the one she supposedly didn't have—and then draw the bleach into a syringe from that.

One other thing she said also didn't make any sense: Saenz said all she'd injected into Ms. Rhone's line was saline. Now the jurors looked at the dialysis machine that stayed in the courtroom as a prop. Both sides had used it numerous times. The jurors could easily see the saline bag hanging over the machine with a line leading down from it. Attached to that line was a clamp. Loosening that clamp allowed the saline to be released into the patient's lines.

In other words, why inject saline into a bag full of saline?

Other witnesses came and went, and then RN and DaVita monitor Amy Clinton took the stand. When the jury was asked after the trial which witness was the most impressive, most said Amy Clinton right off.

The jury had watched Arlene Gamble and Sharon Smith lose their cool on the stand, and might have expected the same from Clinton. If Deaton did, he would be sorely disappointed. Clinton's temperament never changed. It was obvious that Amy Clinton was the regional director of DaVita for a reason, and it had nothing to do with her good looks. She ended up testifying four times, but each time the court saw the exact same thing from her: intelligence, professionalism, and deportment. She could not be shaken. Her voice didn't change from the questions Herrington asked to the grilling she got from Deaton—nor did her body language.

Deaton wasn't able to break the next witness either, arguably the most important person in the entire case—Sergeant Stephen Abbott.

Sergeant Abbott took the jury through the entire case from day one. He never showed emotion. It was the facts, just the facts, and like Clinton, he couldn't be intimidated or swayed. In fact, Deaton lost a point with the jury whenever he said Sergeant Abbott's name—or rather, mis-said it, since he insisted on verbally demoting.

He never referred to him as Sergeant Abbott, and it became a point of total disrespect. He called him *Officer* Abbott. The way Deaton said it, the jury could hear and almost see the disdain dripping off the word.

In any case, Abbott could add his name to the long list of witnesses Deaton had harassed on the stand. He'd badgered Ms. Hall and Ms. Bradley while they testified and had had objections sustained on both of them. When people talk about Judge Bryan, they invariably mention how patient he is, but Deaton was trying that patience already. So far Deaton had just irked him, but that was soon to change. Deaton soon stepped in it with both feet.

CHAPTER 18

THE STORM

In the courtroom, no one saw the explosion about to happen with the judge. Prosecutor Chris Tortorice had called to the stand Dr. Imran Nazeer, a man with impeccable credentials, but he was also the medical administrator for DaVita in April 2008, and therefore in defense attorney Ryan Deaton's crosshairs.

After Tortorice passed the witness to Deaton, the trouble began.

It began with Deaton asking Dr. Nazeer a question. "Okay. And back in April of 2008, administration had told you and your facility that y'all would have an order that all adverse occurrences—"

Tortorice objected on the grounds that the question was hearsay and assuming facts not in evidence.

Although Deaton said he would rephrase the question, the judge called them to the bench anyway. This wasn't anything unusual. This trial had to set a record for bench conferences. Unfortunately, this one was off the record, and exact words in that conference are not known.

When the trial resumed, Deaton asked the same question that Tortorice had just objected to. Tortorice objected again.

The judge, obviously irritated, said, "Come up. That's what we just talked about."

People described Judge Bryan as a duck in the trial. Cool, calm, and collected on the surface, but feet pedaling furiously underneath. The court had only seen the surface half of the judge—now they were about to see what lay beneath.

The conversation at the bench was again off the record, but it didn't stay that way long. Judge Bryan's face turned the color of a ripe tomato. Furious, he hustled the jury out of the courtroom. When the jury left the room, the rest was said in open court and for the record.

Tortorice told the court that the prosecution had an issue with a secret recording done by Deaton of Dr. Nazeer.

Deaton responded as Judge Bryan simmered. "First, the recording was not done by me. Secondly, whatever agreement I had with [DaVita lawyer] Mr. Sprott, he's a civil lawyer. He's not part of this case. Okay?"

When Judge Bryan said, "So . . ." through clenched teeth, Deaton continued.

"I had no agreement with the district attorney's office. And I only intended to use [the recording] if the man lies. That's it—or misstates what he told me."

Judge Bryan then asked Deaton, "So how many other ones did *you* record?"

Deaton responded, "Just one. We've only been allowed to talk with one witness, that being Mr. Nazeer."

The disrespect of not calling him doctor was nothing new for Deaton.

Judge Bryan then asked Deaton, "So did you know it was being recorded?"

It was hard to believe the judge's face could turn even redder but it did when Deaton replied, "I did not. I didn't." Deaton went on to tell him that his investigator had recorded Dr. Nazeer, not him.

However, Judge Bryan wasn't buying what Deaton was trying to sell. He asked, "The person under your control and direction was there at the meeting, was present, that you're responsible for his actions?"

Tortorice started to join the conversation. "Your Honor, the information that—"

Deaton didn't give him a chance to finish. "Your Honor, it's not an issue if the man just tells the truth. It sounds like he wasn't going to tell the truth."

The judge's words seemed to bounce off the walls in the deathly silent courtroom. "It's an issue when all counsel are responsible to the Court for being honest in their dealings between each other," Bryan said. "That makes it an issue."

As the judge simmered, Tortorice, who'd waited in the wings for this moment, knowing it was coming, spoke up. He told the judge about the DaVita attorney having come to him and telling him that even though they'd asked Deaton not to record the conversation and Deaton had agreed not to, at the time the DaVita attorney believed he had recorded it.

Everyone understood that Deaton's investigator, Vann Kelley, in the presence of Deaton, had secretly recorded a conversation with Dr. Nazeer, even though he had agreed not to.

Deaton had attempted to crawfish his way out of it before, but he was really scooting backward now. He said, "I'm not even sure it was intentional. In other words, we did go in with the idea of recording the statements. I don't think there's anything wrong with that. I don't—I mean, those—how that happened, I'm not exactly for sure, but the bottom line is, is that it's—I don't care. I don't want to bring it up. I have no desire to—"

Judge Bryan cut him off. "Then why are you bringing it up?"

Almost in a whine, Deaton told the judge, "I want to ask this man questions. That's all I want to do, and I want him to be truthful."

At that time, it was decided by all parties that Clyde Herrington and Chris Tortorice would get to hear the recording, and the court took a break. Of course, the jury had heard none of this. Groups of spectators gathered in the halls to whisper about what was happening.

When the court resumed still without the jury present, spectators realized the fireworks were only starting.

As soon as everyone in the courtroom sat, Tortorice asked to approach the bench, and the judge motioned them forward. Deaton, Herrington, and Tortorice made the trek. Steve Taylor remained in his seat and leaned back, almost as if to say, "You told me to keep my mouth shut. Dig your own way out of the mess you created." As Herrington commented after the trial, "Steve Taylor's honest, and that was probably the reason Deaton left him out of the defense—he wouldn't have put up with some of that stuff."

Tortorice began by saying that Deaton hadn't allowed them to listen to the beginning of the tape. He'd requested a copy of the tape but had been denied.

Deaton told the judge, "I let them listen to the part where we walk in the room. The discussion has not been had at any point prior to that whether or not there's going to be a recording. We walk in the room, and Mr. Sprott says, 'Let's get some ground rules. Do you want—or no recording.' I said okay. And that was it."

Herrington then told Judge Bryan, "Judge, if you listen to the beginning of it, there's a clear indication it was going to be recorded, I think. That's the way I interpret it."

Tortorice reiterated what Herrington had said. "They were joking, 'we're about to be on the record,' then what appeared to be sounds like getting out of the car."

Judge Bryan looked at Deaton and his words sliced to the bone. "What you asked me, 'what does this have to do with anything?' When an attorney consistently misdirects the Court and engages in dishonesty, then it makes the Court's job doubly hard, because a judge does not know when to believe a lawyer or when not to. And that's where I find myself at. So anything you tell me, I have to scrutinize twice because I can't rely on what you tell me. That's the real problem."

Deaton looked like a whipped dog. Perhaps if he had left it right then, he wouldn't have gotten both barrels, but it just wasn't his style to leave things alone. He said, "I haven't been dishonest with this Court."

Judge Bryan glared at him. "Well, when you say things like, 'well, the evidence is,' and then I ask you what is the evidence on a certain issue, you say, 'well, it's what I believe.' And then I ask you what is the evidence, though? 'Well, there isn't any.' That's not exactly being straight. When you misquote witnesses in questions saying, 'well, if so-and-so said,' and that wasn't what was said—and some of it's been objected to and some of it hasn't—that's not exactly being straight."

Deaton still pushed the issue. "In a normal situation, Your Honor, the only thing I would say is that people, lawyers who are investigating cases, investigators who are investigating cases, record conversations all the time—without a person's knowledge."

Judge Bryan responded, "But there's not an affirmative comment that, 'I'm not recording it.' And it's a little different when you're dealing with an attorney than when you're dealing with a citizen. You don't have to tell—there's some dispute whether you do or don't. I think there have been some ethics opinions or comment to ethics opinion that a person shouldn't record anybody if they don't—a lawyer shouldn't, but there's obviously certain protections that come with doing that, with recording them without telling them to preserve what they said. But when you have an attorney that you're dealing with, and if there was an affirmative statement that, 'we're not going to record it' or an agreement that it's not to be recorded, then that's a little different because of ethics and other issues."

It's not often that spectators in a criminal trial get to hear the judge call the defense attorney dishonest.

Tortorice commented after the trial that what Deaton

had done was a violation of the rules of professional conduct. It's not a violation for citizens in Texas to record others, but attorneys and their representatives are different. However, this was even worse than that. It also violated a specific agreement that the attorneys would not record the interview.

After the trial, the prosecution team said that they respected Deaton's stamina. His psyche took some dents from the judge's tongue-lashing, but it didn't take long for the armor surrounding his personality to pop right back in place, and the judge's admonitions never seemed to bother Saenz at all.

The defense party continued like nothing had happened even as Herrington turned up the heat. At the heart of the prosecution's case was a long and difficult word to spell, "3-chlorotyrosine," and Herrington called Dr. Mark Sochaski, director of analytical chemistry at the Hammer Institute for Health Research, as an expert witness to explain this word and what part it played in the case. Interestingly enough, this was the expert witness that Deaton attempted to exclude before the trial—the one that he said used bad science.

Officially, 3-chlorotyrosine is a marker of protein damage in the body, and many experts believed that bleach in the blood would not only destroy tissue, but also protein, and because of this, the aftereffect of the protein damage was 3-chlorotyrosine. They believed that the presence of 3-chlorotyrosine was an indicator of the effects of bleach on a person's blood. Dr. Sochaski had spent years studying the effects of chlorine on rats.

Proteins are composed of chains of amino acids linked

together like beads on a large necklace, and were at the heart of his research and the reason that he believed that the effects of chlorine on rats would be the same as on humans. Rats have the exact same amino acids as humans do.

However, 3-chlorotyrosine, amino acids, chlorine, and rats were only part of what Dr. Sochaski traveled all the way to Lufkin, Texas, to testify to, and maybe not even the most important. The last part of his testimony, and probably the reason Deaton tried to get him excluded, would be huge in this case, and something the jury would talk about after the trial ended.

Early on in Abbott's investigation, after he discovered that the FDA and CDC could examine the syringes and bloodlines, he sent away fifty-one samples in what they called a blind study. Intermingled in those fifty-one random samples was the evidence. All the group receiving those samples knew about them were their identifying numbers, from 1 to 51. They had no idea which if any of the samples contained the evidence. As it happened, it was Dr. Sochaski who conducted the tests on those blind samples. The problem for the defense was that every single sample that Dr. Sochaski said contained bleach was an evidence sample, and every one that he said didn't, wasn't.

The next expert that Tortorice called was David Jackson, a forensic chemist with the U.S. Food and Drug Administration. His testimony was vital to the state's case. He was the person who'd tested all those bloodlines and syringes that Sergeant Steve Abbott had collected from DaVita. Using color charts, Jackson showed the jury exactly where he'd been able to find bleach and bleach residue in the evidence.

The expert witnesses for the state had all been interesting and appeared to be professional and competent. However, none would capture the attention of the spectators and jury like the next two. Leading off in what could best be described as a true *CSI* moment was a scientist from the FDA's Forensic Chemistry Center. Stanley Frank Platek had worked with the FDA for twenty-one years, and he worked in the trace evidence section.

When asked what he did, he stated, "Anything left behind. My specialty is small particle analysis."

However, as it turned out, Mr. Platek had another specialty—puncture analysis, and this was the reason he was in Lufkin to testify. He would say, "Puncture marks in bloodline ports are very distinctive." But that wasn't all; he also testified that syringe needles left a very distinctive mark and he could identify the exact needle that made the mark.

One of the lines he examined was that of Ms. Opal Few. She was the patient who'd died on April 26, 2008. A week after Ms. Few's death, Christy Pate from the Lufkin Police Department had discovered Ms. Few's labeled 3ml syringe in one of the confiscated sharps containers. This syringe undercut Saenz's argument that she used a syringe to measure bleach, because it was too small by far for that purpose. It was when Christy Pate discovered that bleach-laden syringe that the police investigation went from aggravated assault to murder.

Now, Mr. Platek testified with absolute certainty that the puncture wound in Ms. Few's line had been made by a 3ml syringe—the one that had Ms. Few's name on it.

Then on day ten of the trial, the mysterious computer

searches were finally addressed. Mario Mares, a forensic computer specialist for the Office of the Inspector General, was scheduled to testify. But right before Mares was to take the stand, Deaton surprised the court. Though he'd had three years to prepare his defense, Deaton made a motion to suppress evidence found on the computers because of the search warrant.

In most trials, this is something done in pretrial hearings—not the last second before an expert witness testifies.

After the trial was over, when asked about this motion, Taylor said, "Who knows. Maybe he just woke up and thought he had to object to it."

After a break for the judge to examine the search warrants, the objection was overruled, the trial resumed, and Mares took the stand.

Mares explained the process he went through to search a computer, and informed the court how data deleted from a computer never really leaves it. It can be found using software on the unallocated portions of the hard drive.

Another aspect of what Mares did was look through all the files and attempt to identify all users on Saenz's parents' computer. On that one, he found Kimberly Saenz's 2007 H&R Block tax return with her name, date of birth, and social security number. Along with that, he also found e-mails with her name on them. Both activities led him to believe that Saenz was one of the users on that computer.

Before Mares began his search, he received key words from the police to look for. In this case, he didn't know that it was Kimberly Clark Saenz's own husband, Kevin Saenz, who'd given the police those key words.

At 4:14 in the morning of April 2, 2008, Mares found that someone did a Yahoo! search on the computer for bleach poisoning. The date was significant. It was the morning after Ms. Strange and Ms. Metcalf had coded and died. It was their deaths that prompted DaVita to investigate their own facility. However, this search also flew into the face of Saenz's statement to the police that she thought the problem was with blood pressure, and she'd never searched the computer for the cause, a claim she later did a one-eighty on when she testified in front of the grand jury. The time also seemed significant: Kim Saenz was regularly up at this hour in order to get ready for work.

When Mares finished his testimony, the court broke for lunch, but an air of anticipation buzzed through the courtroom. Everyone had already got a glimpse of the next witness sitting in the front row ready to testify.

———

Dr. Michael Schwartz was the medical officer for the Centers for Disease Control. The CDC is a part of the national government—a part of the United States Public Health Service Commissioned Corps (PHSCC), to be exact. Because the PHSCC is one of the seven uniformed services that includes the Army, Navy, and Air Force, the officers must hold a military rank. Although the Surgeon General holds an Army rank, the others hold Navy ranks. Schwartz, who held the rank of naval commander, was tall, handsome, and solidly built. He made an imposing sight as he came into the courtroom dressed in his naval uniform, and marched up to the witness stand. His military bearing gave him credit in this part of the country before a word was even uttered.

However, this was a man who didn't need any help with credits. He was a graduate of Cornell University, and from there had gone to Oxford Medical School in England, and then back to Cornell for his Ph.D. A two-year fellowship at Emory in medical toxicology followed, where he did significant work on antifreeze poisoning in dogs. He now trained toxicology students at Emory University, and volunteered on the weekends for ER shifts at the Atlanta hospitals.

In fact, Schwartz's list of credentials was a lot longer—so long it brought on an objection from Deaton when Tortorice was halfway through reading them. However, the judge let Tortorice keep listing them. People's estimation of Schwartz grew with each successive accomplishment.

Because Dr. Schwartz was a medical doctor as well as a board-certified forensic toxicologist, he was perhaps the best person in the country to examine all the evidence the state had and render an opinion.

Unlike some of the other experts, Dr. Schwartz hadn't merely spent just a couple of weeks with the case and evidence. He'd spent a couple of years. In fact, he spent one entire month doing nothing but reading all the literature available on bleach poisoning.

Deaton tried to discredit him, trip him up, or make him look wrong, but it was a fool's mission. Dr. Schwartz's military bearing wasn't just surface image. The man was a consummate professional.

When Dr. Schwartz left the stand, Taylor, who had a son in the Navy, approached the man to apologize. Taylor believed Deaton had been rude and disrespectful during his testimony. Dr. Schwartz told Taylor he hadn't taken offense, that he understood the stakes.

But it seemed to be a big deal to Deaton's mother. Taylor said, "She climbed all over my butt. 'How—what are you doing—don't apologize, you're supposed to be a part of our team!' "

However, to Taylor it was a matter of respect no matter what side the person was on. Just because an expert's testimony went against his client didn't make the person a mortal enemy. Taylor believed that respect can be given to a person's deeds without total reliance on his words.

Although Dr. Schwartz wasn't Taylor's enemy, his last words were devastating to the defense's case. He made it clear that, in his medical opinion, the victims had all died or been injured as a result of injections of sodium hypochlorite—bleach—into the dialysis lines or bloodstream. The jury left with those last words ringing inside their heads.

In order to convict someone of murder, the prosecution had to prove that the victim was actually murdered. In most murder cases, this was easy and seldom challenged by the defense in court. But because the alleged weapon, bleach, was so difficult to detect in the bloodstream, the Saenz prosecution was especially difficult. If the jury believed Dr. Schwartz, however, Herrington had just proven a major part of the case.

CHAPTER 19

TROUBLED WATERS

At nine in the morning of March 19, 2012, the Kimberly Clark Saenz trial began its third week and most expected the state to rest. If so, the people who followed the trial would finally get to see just why the defense were so sure of themselves.

As the trial wore on and the evidence began to pile up, Saenz's frequent laughter and smiles, and her seeming imperviousness to the gravity of the charges against her, grated on the victims' family members' nerves. Even worse, they felt, was Saenz's habit of turning slightly and looking back at the victims' families. Several of the family members said that she turned and smiled at them or had a smirk on her face—as one family member said, it looked like "she really thought she was going to get away with it."

Once prosecutor Clyde Herrington rested his case, defense attorney Ryan Deaton made a motion for the judge to dismiss the case because the state hadn't proven his client was guilty. It was a normal defense tactic, but Judge Bryan dismissed the motion. No way would Saenz get off that easy.

As the defense began, Saenz's supporters, mostly from her church, showed up in court en masse. From their smiles and cheerful attitudes, it was clear that the Saenz camp believed Deaton was about to destroy Herrington's case.

However, as Deaton had done from the moment he became Saenz's attorney, he either overestimated himself or underestimated the prosecution team. Now the prosecutors had some surprises in store for Deaton. They'd objected numerous times during Deaton's cross of state witnesses—mostly for misrepresenting facts—but the defense attorney hadn't seen anything yet. Attorneys who are cross-examining witnesses as Deaton had as the prosecution put on their case can do so with leading questions, but not when conducting direct examination. Before, the state was putting on its witnesses and the defense cross-examined. However, now the defense would be putting on the witnesses and would have to ask non-leading questions.

At one point, Herrington rose from his seat and objected to one of Deaton's leading questions. When the judge sustained the objection, Herrington didn't even sit down. Instead he remained standing, waiting on the next question so he could object to that, too. Which he did, and the judge had no choice but to sustain the second objection, too.

Deaton's first witness was Jim Risinger, husband of

Carolyn Risinger, one of the alleged victims whom Ms. Hall and Ms. Hamilton had witnessed Saenz inject with bleach. Unfortunately, Ms. Risinger had been killed in an automobile accident, so she wasn't there to speak for herself. Jim Risinger wanted to tell the jury that his wife had told him that Saenz hadn't done anything to her. But Herrington was ready for that—even novices to the courtroom know that hearsay isn't allowed in a trial. Why Deaton thought he could slip that by was anyone's guess.

Mr. Risinger's testimony did nothing to help the defense, but as it turned out, Herrington had a few questions for him. Under Herrington's questioning, Risinger went on to testify that he'd never seen the techs mix the bleach at the machines, that they always did that before the patients arrived, which contradicted what Saenz had said and reinforced what every other DaVita employee had testified to.

After Risinger, Deaton called Gail Owens to the stand. Ms. Owens was an LVN for eighteen years, but had been a dialysis patient since 2002. Deaton asked Ms. Owens if she'd ever seen Saenz do anything wrong, and she responded that she hadn't. But after several similar questions, she said something that left people shaking or scratching their heads:

The witness told Deaton that she was legally blind.

Deaton did better with Kenny Graham, another DaVita patient, although Mr. Graham admitted that he had tunnel vision without being able to see anything in his peripherals. At least Deaton had known this. Graham also claimed that he was Carolyn Risinger's friend, and had had his head turned in her direction the entire time she was undergoing treatment and he never saw anyone do anything to her.

Deaton next called Giselle Frenette, one of the monitors who came to DaVita with Amy Clinton in April. She was the employee who'd assisted Clinton in opening the two sharps containers and testing the syringes when bleach was found. Frenette turned into a really strong witness—for the prosecution.

Deaton ended with his sarcastic "You work for DaVita, don't you?" question. This was a question he reserved just for the employees who still worked for DaVita and didn't answer the questions the way he wanted them to, but this was his own witness. He even asked her, "You were told how to testify, weren't you?" She responded that she was: she was told to tell the truth.

On day thirteen of the trial, the jury spent most of the day out of the courtroom, and then the judge sent them home early. A witness by the name of Catherine Denese Pickens had come forward to claim that another DaVita employee could have killed the patients. Since Pickens wasn't on the witness list, they *voir dired* her testimony on the stand without the jury present.

Pickens, who was no stranger to the courtroom (she'd been arrested on several occasions for possession of a controlled substance), told a story that involved a love triangle between herself, her husband, and Sharon Smith, the DaVita RN whose testimony was so damaging to the defense. Pickens claimed that Smith had been having an affair with her husband, and alleged that after the affair ended, Smith had threatened the couple with a knife.

Pickens went on to claim that she'd also received an

anonymous package containing a 10cc syringe loaded with a mysterious clear liquid and a letter that said something to the effect of "Bang. Get your high on." Pickens said that instinct dictated she hold on to the syringe, but after a couple of months, she threw it away.

This brought on a debate between opposing attorneys on whether the testimony should be allowed in court. Deaton opened by calling Sharon Smith "aggressive and violent" and saying, "If there is anybody here that is a killer, I would have to say that is her."

Herrington quickly shot back that Pickens's story was "nothing more than a love triangle with no bearing on this case. Nothing but anonymous innuendos connected with a boyfriend/girlfriend situation. It's irrelevant and prejudicial."

Why Deaton thought he'd be able to use Pickens's testimony is unclear. First, witnesses can't testify about things that aren't in evidence. The alleged letter and the syringe with that mysterious clear liquid weren't in evidence, and never would be because Pickens said she'd thrown them away. Therefore, she couldn't testify to the items' existence.

The other issue with Pickens's testimony that Deaton evidently hadn't considered was raised by Judge Bryan when he asked, "Are you accepting the fact that people at DaVita were killed by syringes filled with bleach?"

That was definitely a slippery slope. If the judge let that testimony in, which he wasn't about to do, Deaton was virtually admitting that the patients had died from injections of bleach. However, no one had ever come forward and said Sharon Smith was injecting patients with bleach. That was reserved only for Deaton's client.

Obviously the judge's question had merit. Just as obvious, the jury never heard this testimony. What it turned out to be was a waste of time. In any event, Smith later disputed some of Pickens's story.

While the jury was gone, Deaton had one more witness he wanted to put on the stand—for the record in case there was an appeal, but not for the jury to hear. It was Kevin Saenz.

In his opening statement, Deaton had promised the jury that Kevin Saenz would testify to disprove the theory that it was his wife Kimberly who'd done those computer searches. But Deaton could not put Kevin Saenz in the witness box in front of a jury. That alone would have been enough to prove ineffective counsel, and it would have doomed Kimberly Saenz. Tortorice was licking his chops waiting on this one.

After all, it was Kevin Saenz who had led the police to that computer in the first place. It was he who had given the police the key words the forensic computer specialist used to find the information searched for on the computer.

At the time he was cooperating with police, Saenz had filed for divorce, had a restraining order in place against his wife, and had every intention of retaining custody of their daughter. However, if anyone was going to defend Kimberly Saenz, that divorce had to disappear. After all, the Constitution clearly states that a spouse cannot be compelled to testify against the other spouse. As Saenz's husband, he could not be made to testify by the prosecution. Obviously, Deaton didn't think his testimony would help her. With Saenz testifying for the record but out of the presence of the jury, the defense could control what the prosecution could ask him.

As the ex-husband, Kevin Saenz could and would have been subpoenaed by Herrington to testify. There would be no way that he could get out of his sworn testimony for the protective order that declared Kimberly Saenz to be addicted to drugs and violent at times. He'd also sworn in that affidavit that he thought she was a danger to their daughter.

The prosecution could force him to testify to the reason he told others that he thought Kimberly Saenz had injured the patients. The only way any attorney had to prevent this testimony would be to stop the divorce.

Also, forensic computer expert Mario Mares had given the prosecution a detailed report on what he'd done to examine the computer and everything he'd found. With Judge Bryan's approval, the prosecution had given Deaton a summary of that report. Had Deaton elected to put Kevin Saenz on the stand in front of the jury, the prosecution knew, based on search histories, that they could prove it was actually Kimberly Saenz doing those searches and not Kevin, her parents, or her children.

The prosecution even had Robert Flournoy listed as a witness. Flournoy was Kevin Saenz's attorney and the one who'd called the police on Kevin Saenz's behalf. He had also been present when Kevin Saenz had first talked with Corporal Mike Shurley.

The jury didn't hear the testimony of Catherine

Denese Pickens or Kevin Saenz, and if they had, more than likely the testimony of these two would have helped the prosecution more than hurt it. However, the jury did hear from an expert witness for the defense—one that they would not forget. He was a nephrologist from Boston, Massachusetts, by the name of Dr. Michael Germain.

Sixty-year-old Dr. Germain was short and stocky with brown hair styled professionally, as were his clothes. But his appearance and professionalism had more to do with his bearing and speech, than his clothes.

On the stand he seemed to understand the gravity of the situation and presented himself as a consummate professional in every way. Which his credentials backed up. After graduating from the University of Calgary Faculty of Medicine in 1976, Dr. Germain became board certified in internal medicine as well as nephrology. At the time of his testimony, he had thirty-six years experience as a kidney doctor and had authored over twelve articles in professional medical journals. He'd also been named as one of America's leading experts on kidney disease.

Besides his affiliation with a dozen hospitals, he was also the medical administrator of a dialysis clinic, and the perfect person to speak about dialysis. He was critical of how Dr. Nazeer, the medical administrator, and DaVita handled the situation on April 28, 2008. That was the morning that Ms. Hall and Ms. Hamilton had allegedly witnessed Kimberly Saenz inject two patients with bleach.

His criticism came about the handling of the two injected patients—one that was controversial. Both Ms. Rhone and Ms. Risinger, the two patients allegedly injected by Saenz, had adverse medical occurrences while at DaVita. Both were at the end of their treatment and both got over their problems quickly. At the time of the incident, Dr. Nazeer had not been present at DaVita. He returned when the staff called him and told him that Ms. Risinger was having a problem.

When Dr. Nazeer returned, Amy Clinton informed him of the allegation against Saenz and the fact that she'd sent the nurse home for the day. At that moment, all they had was the allegation of the two witnesses. Amy Clinton had not opened the sharps containers then or tested the syringes.

Dr. Nazeer advised both patients, Ms. Risinger and Ms. Rhone, that they needed to go to the hospital, get checked out, and get blood work done. At that time he didn't tell them about the allegation that Saenz had injected them with bleach. Maybe because he didn't tell them, no one will ever know, both patients refused to go to the hospital. They were feeling better.

This was the morning of April 28, and it wasn't until around four that afternoon that DaVita called the two patients and informed them that they might have been injected with bleach and needed to go to the hospital for blood work—which both patients did.

On the stand, Dr. Nazeer had testified that when he was informed of the alleged incident, he was shocked and had never heard of anything like that before. He went on to say that although he was shocked, he also felt a sense of relief. It gave them an explanation of the problems and the reason they couldn't find out what was causing the patients' deaths and injuries.

In regard to why he didn't initially tell the two patients

that they might have been injected by bleach, he said that he had urged them both to go to the emergency room, but at the time, he didn't think he had enough facts. All he had was an allegation against an employee.

Dr. Germain had another take on this controversy. Unequivocally, he stated that he didn't agree with the way the facility handled the situation. When asked about Dr. Nazeer's decision not to tell the patients on the morning of the twenty-eighth that they might have been injected with bleach, he said, "I never believe in keeping anything from patients. I always tell them what I know. The truth is the best policy."

Like the Texas Department of Health and Human Services, who investigated DaVita and issued a scathing report on them in May 2008, after DaVita had shut down, Dr. Germain had a lot of uncomplimentary things to say about how the DaVita Lufkin clinic operated. Like the Texas DHHS, he also faulted DaVita for patient care, and said that this could have ultimately caused the five deaths. He said he wasn't surprised that six of the patients went into cardiac arrest when their blood was returned to them. He attributed this to DaVita's poor supervision and the alleged victims' frail health.

He told the jury that dialysis patients were the most vulnerable at the end of the dialysis process because of excess fluids being pulled from their bodies causing a drop in blood pressure—sometimes too much of a drop. This normally isn't a problem unless they aren't monitored properly, which he didn't believe the DaVita patients were.

He went on to tell the jury that the hardest thing he

could ever do was decide how a patient had died—
especially considering that he'd never seen the patient in
person and all he had to go on was their patient charts.
However, after he reviewed the records here, he said that
the patients were frail and near death. Among the patients
that he highlighted was Ms. Metcalf, one of two patients
who died on April 1, 2008, leading to the mass investigation by DaVita. "This was not an atypical death. It's what
you see in a sick elderly dialysis patient," he said of Ms.
Metcalf. "Her blood pressure was stable until the end of
her treatment, then she became unresponsive. I would
have to say it was the dialysis treatment that led to her
cardiac arrest. It was just too much for her body to
handle."

In addition to Ms. Metcalf, Dr. Germain weighed in
on the death of Mr. Kelley, saying he also believed the
dialysis process had been too much for Kelley's body to
handle.

As the doctor went through each of the victims' charts,
he indicated that the patients were frail and close to death,
and that it was the dialysis process, as well as the poorly
supervised treatments they received, that had caused their
deaths.

If Dr. Germain knew about, saw, or even heard the
rumblings, mumblings, and shaking of heads, or the outright glares from the side of the courtroom behind the
prosecution table, he didn't let on. For the most part, the
loved ones of the victims had sat and listened to testimony
stoically, but Dr. Germain testimony was one of the few
times that rattled them.

Among the spectators behind the prosecutor's table was Wanda Hollingsworth, the daughter of Ms. Metcalf, along with her brother and sister-in-law. Dr. Germain didn't know that Ms. Hollingsworth had testified earlier to how spunky and energetic—not frail—her mother had been.

Also listening were friends and family members of Mr. Kelley, whom no one had ever described as frail, sick, or near death. Nor did Dr. Germain know about all the past and present DaVita employees who had testified about the favorable condition Mr. Kelley was in at the time he coded at DaVita.

In truth, Dr. Germain had never seen or treated any of the patients, and all he had to go on was records he was given to view by the defense.

He was definitely a witness the jury would remember— mainly because of his professionalism, but also because they felt he was honest—especially when Herrington cross-examined him. Herrington's last question to him would stick in the jury's mind.

Dr. Germain had been critical of DaVita and Dr. Nazeer, but also attributed the patients' deaths to natural causes. But when the defense passed the witness, Herrington asked him, "Can you say that all these things could not have been caused by the bleach injections?"

Dr. Germain may have been an ideal witness for the defense, but even so, he still had to answer "no" to Herrington's question.

The jury would eventually get to hear another witness after she was *voir dired* out of their presence. Connie

Baker, the witness, seemed to pop out of nowhere. She'd very recently contacted Deaton and told him her story. After hearing it, Deaton was all too glad to let her testify. She was an ex-DaVita employee who had worked in Lufkin in April 2008, but had resigned.

Deaton led her through her testimony, and Baker backed up Kimberly Saenz's version of events, agreeing that she and other employees had all used syringes to measure bleach, and so forth. In fact, Baker testified to every single thing Deaton needed her to. She even recalled a meeting in early April in which Amy Clinton had told all the employees that she knew there was something going on. Baker claimed that Clinton had pointed her finger at them, saying, "I will not go down for this. I will take someone with me."

Baker told the jury that she'd felt threatened by Clinton and so scared that she decided at that moment to quit. She handed in her two-week notice the next day, and stated that she left DaVita because she believed someone was going to be blamed for the problems that happened in April 2008.

The Lufkin News led off with the headlines in bold black print, WITNESS SAYS CLINIC SEEKING SCAPEGOAT. Along with that headline, they had a picture of Saenz with a smug smile on her face—one that she had displayed throughout the trial. The article described Baker's testimony, what Baker claimed Clinton had said and how she'd felt threatened. However, despite the headline, Baker never used the term "scapegoat."

Then it was Herrington's turn to ask questions. He began by asking Baker who else at DaVita besides Saenz and herself had used a syringe to measure bleach, but Baker couldn't recall any names. He also asked her who else besides Saenz and herself had heard Amy Clinton make that statement. Baker couldn't name any individuals.

Finally, Herrington produced a piece of paper and, before asking to have it admitted to the record, showed it to Baker, who testified that it was her letter of resignation, and then handed it to Deaton. Deaton read it and in a small voice said he had no objection to having it admitted into evidence.

Herrington never told the courtroom what was in the letter, but he posted it to the jury so they could read it. Everyone in the courtroom knew that letter had to be important and was curious to know what was in it. According to jurors who spoke after the trial, the letter of resignation did not back up Baker's story of a scared employee just wanting to get out so she wouldn't be blamed for anything. In fact, in the letter she asked DaVita if she could be eligible for "PRN" duty, which means as needed. In other words, she wanted to work when they needed her to fill in for someone and not on a schedule. For one thing, PRN employees usually make more. Also, former coworkers said Connie Baker told them she was quitting because the amount she was paying for gas was eating her paychecks up—not to mention the hours. She was working ten-hour shifts on top of a two-hour commute each way to get to and from work.

After the defense rested, Herrington called several rebuttal witnesses—either DaVita employees or past employees. Some of the ones he called were defense witnesses, and all of them had been present at that meeting in which Clinton had supposedly threatened the staff. However, not a single one of them heard Clinton say anything remotely close to what Baker had reported. None of them even remembered Amy Clinton speaking at all during that meeting, which was supported by documentation. DaVita meetings had sign-in sheets and agendas of who spoke and on what topic. At that particular meeting, Clinton wasn't scheduled to speak.

Most said that they would have remembered something that sounded so threatening.

Only one employee said she wouldn't have considered them threatening. When asked why, she said, "I was doing my job correctly. Why would I feel threatened?"

Peter Cartwright was president at Cartwright Consulting Co. He possessed a bachelor's degree in chemical engineering from the University of Minnesota and was a registered engineer in several states. He also specialized in marketing and technical consulting for water purification—especially in dialysis clinics.

Cartwright was in Lufkin as one of Deaton's expert witnesses because when Deaton wasn't blaming DaVita for the cause of the injuries and deaths, he was blaming the water.

As Deaton questioned Cartwright, the expert told the jury that Lufkin DaVita was the most poorly run and operated system in hemodialysis he'd ever seen. The truth was, DaVita had some problems in the way it was run. There was no doubt about that.

At the heart of the water argument was how the water was treated. Municipal water plants in the United States use either chlorine or chloramine (a combination of ammonia and chlorine) to treat water before it is sent to people to drink. However, the water used in dialysis centers has to be pure, free of everything, including either chlorine or chloramine, and chlorine is easier to remove than chloramine, and fortunately for DaVita Lufkin, they had to deal with chlorine.

In Cartwright's testimony, he said that he didn't believe that DaVita's carbon tanks had been filtering the chlorine properly in April 2008. He criticized DaVita for not dating water logs, and several other things.

There was no question that DaVita had not handled this process well. The damage done by Cartwright fell to prosecutor Layne Thompson to clean up. During Deaton's direct examination of Cartwright, Thompson had spent a good deal of the time objecting to Deaton's questions—either on the basis that they were leading, or that Deaton was misrepresenting facts—most of which were sustained by Judge Bryan.

From Cartwright's apprehensive expression, he expected Thompson to come out on the attack. Instead, Thompson surprised everyone. He asked Cartwright how much he was being paid. Some eyebrows rose when the expert said $300 an hour, and that included the time to testify. This was the first time in the trial the question had come up. All the other experts for the state were government employees, and not paid by the county.

The key to Thompson's questions wasn't just what he

asked, but how he asked it. His words and sentences were clipped and delivered with a snap. He took Cartwright through the process by which carbon tanks were used to take the chlorine and chloramine out of the water.

Then he got to the meat of his cross-examination:

In that snappish manner, Thompson asked, "You understand that Lufkin uses free chlorine to disinfect their water, correct?"

Cartwright answered, "That's my understanding."

However, the expert witness's attitude, maybe because of the way Thompson popped the questions at him, or the fact that Thompson had spent so much time objecting during Deaton's examination, was less than stellar. Compared to the performance of the witnesses put on by the state, he was lacking. As one juror said later, everything seemed beneath him.

Thompson, the prosecutor with all that medical and scientific experience, the one who had spent years defending medical malpractice, knew exactly what he was doing and where he was going. In fact, he didn't believe that the defense had made everything available to the expert and he was on the stand blind in certain regards.

Thompson led the expert through a series of questions. At one point Thompson objected because the witness was nonresponsive—meaning he wasn't answering the question. Judge Bryan sustaining the objection and ordering Cartwright to answer the question didn't do much for the expert's attitude.

In that biting tone, Thompson asked, "The question, *sir*, is, isn't it true that chloramine takes longer to be taken out of the water by granulated activated charcoal?"

Cartwright replied, "*NO!*"

If the Saenz trial had a dumb jury, this would have flown right past them, but since they didn't, it didn't. Was this a mistake on the expert's part? Everyone who followed the trial knew the answer was yes.

Thompson: *Chloramine isn't instantly taken out of water by charcoal, true? Or even very quickly?*

Cartwright: *You're asking for a conclusion that is difficult to give a yes or no answer to.*

Most people in the courtroom believed that Thompson was asking for a conclusion that Cartwright just didn't want to answer. This doesn't help the credibility of an expert witness.

Thompson: *Were you aware that just a week before the first two patients had cardiac arrests on April 1 that DaVita put four brand new 3.6 square foot granulated activated carbons tanks in place of four tanks that had been there previously?*

Cartwright: *I didn't relate it to the deaths but I do recall a document saying they were installed on March 25th.*

Thompson: *Let's do the math, Doctor, or Mr. Cartwright, four 3.6 cubic feet of carbon tanks, how many cubic feet does that constitute?*

(This was not a slip of the tongue on Thompson's part. He was simply reminding the jury that Cartwright didn't hold a doctoral degree in the subject he was speaking on.)

> Cartwright: *If my math is correct, that's 14.4 cubic feet.*
>
> Thompson: *March 25th 2008, less than a week before two patients arresting at DaVita, 14.2 cubic feet of new granulated activated carbon was put into the water system at DaVita, correct?*
>
> Cartwright: *Apparently, yes.*
>
> Thompson: *It would be fair to say that it would be really unusual for 14 cubic feet of new activated granulated carbon put in place on March 25th 2008 would no longer be effective of filtering tap water five weeks later on May 3rd when the CDC took the water samples from the treatment center, true? That would be odd that they weren't still working, true?*
>
> Cartwright: *Yes.*

This question was important for several reasons and would be remembered by the jury. Thompson referred to this water that they'd been talking about all trial as tap water, the same water most of the jury got at their houses.

> Thompson: *You wouldn't expect minor variations in the amount of chlorine Lufkin was using in their city water in that 5-week period in the exhaustion of 14 cubic feet of granulated activated carbon, would you?*
>
> Cartwright: *Not minor variations, no.*

In other words, whatever caused the injuries and deaths to the patients, it wasn't the water. The only person who clung to this theory after this point was Deaton, who told the E! Program a month after the trial, "One of the possibilities of why these people were hurt was the water was bad. If their filters aren't working properly that chlorine or chloramine can get into the water and therefore into the system of the patients and can cause them to die or get very, very sick."

But according to Deaton's own expert, 14 cubic feet of new granulated activated carbon was more than enough to properly filter the DaVita water, and besides, every patient received the exact same water. The jury never seriously considered the water the problem. If there was enough chlorine in the water to kill one, it would have killed or injured them all.

While watching Thompson cross-examine Cartwright, an eighteen-year-old high school senior who was there just to watch a portion of the trial admiringly compared Thompson to Joe Pesci's role in the movie *My Cousin Vinny*, where Pesci demolishes the other side's case point by point.

Thompson was tickled by the young man's comment. Not only that, he said—he and his family went out and rented the movie afterward.

CHAPTER 20

MAGIC BULLETS

What does a savior look like? Kimberly Clark Saenz's defense had a couple of them planned, and defense attorney Ryan Deaton had saved them for the end of the trial. These were his magic bullets meant to destroy the state's case, the people who'd put the smiles on Saenz's face and the reason she treated the trial as a social event.

The first of these was Nick Luker. Taylor said in an interview after the trial, "It was my understanding from the beginning that Luker was going to save them."

After he was sworn in, Luker sat in the witness box as if he were relaxed at home in front of his TV. Dressed in a short-sleeved, faded scrub shirt and well-worn jeans, and sporting a condescending smirk, he didn't look like much of a savior.

When the jury entered, everyone in the courtroom stood except Luker. For a jury who had entered and left the courtroom a hundred times with everyone, including witnesses, standing for them, one that didn't stood out. The fact that the witness box was located right in front of the jury box didn't help.

David Bradford, one of the jurors, later said about Luker, "I pegged him when he got up there. He's screwy. He was just too slick."

Deaton, however, believed in Luker so much that he tried to get the court to declare Luker an expert medical witness, but Herrington and Judge Bryan disagreed.

However, during his testimony, like Connie Baker, Luker declared he'd seen things that no one else had seen. He had nothing good to say about DaVita, their practices, the people he'd worked with, and even the water and the water process system.

Before Deaton turned the questioning over to Prosecutor Clyde Herrington, he headed the DA off from his first questions by having Luker explain his criminal history, which, leaving off traffic violations, was still peppered with DWIs. The first mark on Luker's criminal adult record in Angelina County was on December 31, 1984, at the age of twenty-one. On that date, law enforcement charged him with misdemeanor driving while intoxicated. On March 19, 1985, law enforcement again charged him with misdemeanor DWI. Luker upgraded those charges to a felony DWI in 1988, and then another felony DWI in 1996. On December 8, 2005, law enforcement charged him with felony failure to stop and render aid.

Deaton then asked Luker why DaVita had fired him. Luker told the jury that DaVita had fired him because he didn't shave.

Deaton's last question was if Luker had any reason for

hard feelings against DaVita. Luker answered, "I don't work for them anymore, so why would I have any hard feelings?"

Most people in the courtroom, however, understood that being fired from a job just might cause some hard feelings.

At that point in the trial, Herrington had not attacked any witnesses. He'd treated them all the same—whether their testimony helped or hurt his case. Connie Baker, for instance: her testimony wasn't consistent with anything the other witnesses had said, even defense witnesses, yet Herrington had treated her just like the others. He never raised his voice, and he didn't even read her resignation letter out loud in the courtroom. He simply gave it to the jury to read.

Luker was the exception. While Herrington thought Baker was mistaken, he didn't think she was lying, and that was the difference between her and Luker. Also, Baker had been a surprise to the prosecution, but they'd been waiting for Luker.

Herrington's first question was, "Did you tell this court you were fired for not shaving?"

As Luker started to explain, Herrington snapped, "Answer yes or no."

This was the first time he'd been curt with any witness during the trial, and the jury didn't fail to notice it.

When Luker answered yes, Herrington produced his file. It seemed that Luker had actually been fired for some of the things he'd accused other employees of doing, including almost hooking a patient up to the wrong machine and, according to Herrington, refusing to wash his hands.

The prosecution was ready for Luker because Detective Steve Abbott had gone the extra mile in the investigation and interviewed him four months after Saenz was accused of injecting the two patients with bleach. His testimony at the trial contradicted much of what he'd told the police in the interview, but Luker actually claimed that he remembered everything better four years later than he had four months after the accusation.

Taylor put Luker's testimony in perspective. He said simply, "Luker was a disaster."

After Herrington's cross of Luker, some of the swagger left the defense, but the party still continued. Throughout the trial, the defendant, her family, and Deaton had acted like they had a secret that no one else had—one that would free Kimberly Saenz from that GPS ankle bracelet. On Friday, the courthouse found out that the big gun was Dr. Amy Gruszecki.

Friday after lunch, Deaton called Dr. Gruszecki to the stand. In many ways, Saenz's defense rested on Dr. Gruszecki's testimony, and they believed she was up to the challenge. The prosecution, however, had no idea what she was going to say.

When Dr. Gruszecki took the stand, Tortorice had asked several people in the audience to take down every word she said so he would have some ideas of how to challenge her testimony.

She appeared to be in her forties, about five-six and a hundred and forty pounds, with mousy brown hair and conservatively dressed. But her attitude was anything but conservative—despite the seriousness of the trial, Dr. Gruszecki's attitude was so bubbly and cheerful, one spectator commented on whether next she would break out her pom-poms. And her exuberance seemed to infect the demeanor of the defendant, defense attorney, and Saenz's family, whose smiles and laughter were even more pronounced than normal. She even chuckled several times while delivering her opinion on the cause of death of the victims.

Dr. Gruszecki seemed so confident not only in herself but the information that she possessed that at times she acted like anything but a medical expert and someone testifying in a capital murder case involving five dead people, and with the death penalty on the line. She giggled, and answered questions with an incessant chatter. At one point, the defense attorney, needing to tell her something, approached her without asking the judge's permission because she wouldn't be quiet long enough for him to ask permission. He stood behind her as she talked and finally leaned down and whispered something in her ear. Whatever he said, she nodded.

However, Chris Tortorice didn't have time to worry about Gruszecki's courtroom demeanor. As Friday wore on, it was obvious to spectators that this witness was indeed damaging the state's case against Saenz.

Dr. Gruszecki's credentials were daunting: She was a forensic pathologist—she conducted autopsies to determine the cause of all manners of death. She had a bachelor of science degree from the University of Trenton in Trenton, Pennsylvania; a master of science degree in forensic science from the University of Alabama at Birmingham; then did medical school and osteopathic medicine in Pennsylvania, and followed that up with a one-year internship as an internal medicine doctor. She added pathology residency after that for four years at the University of Alabama at Birmingham, and did a one-year fellowship in forensic pathology.

She had medical licenses in four states—Texas, Alabama, Pennsylvania, and Mississippi—and was board certified in anatomical and forensic pathology. She was an adjunct professor at the University of North Texas, and had worked as a medical examiner at Southwestern Medical Center in Dallas.

Dr. Gruszecki was critical of the police, DaVita, the medical examiner who'd looked at the patients, and the state's experts. She testified that every one of the DaVita victims had died of natural causes. And if they'd died of natural causes, then there was no murder.

But it seemed Dr. Gruszecki wasn't satisfied with answering questions briefly.

She went on and on in her replies, and the more she talked, the closer the little hand of the clock continued to move toward five—the time Judge Bryan would end the trial for that day.

Dr. Gruszecki was the big gun designed to rip the state's evidence to shreds, and it had appeared that she'd done just that. Of the prosecution team's three attorneys, two had vast experience in the courtroom and in capital murder cases. They'd both cross-examined many medical experts in their careers. But the cross of Dr. Gruszecki, and all likelihood the saving of the state's case against Saenz, fell not to the two experienced attorneys, but to Christopher T. Tortorice, the young assistant U.S. Attorney prosecuting his first capital murder.

When Deaton finally passed the witness, the judge looked at the clock and announced that they would resume Monday morning at nine. Chris Tortorice closed his eyes and let out a huge sigh of relief.

He now had the whole weekend to prepare for cross.

Tension threatened to choke the packed courtroom on a wet Monday morning. The capital murder trial for Kimberly Clark Saenz was reaching its conclusion, and the Friday before, the defense had put on its last and by far most important witness—Dr. Amy Gruszecki, commonly referred to as the M.E.

Tortorice now had a confident Dr. Amy Gruszecki on the stand awaiting him. He'd realized that her testimony had hurt, but he'd felt she'd made some mistakes. And since, unlike normal witnesses, the testimony of experts was taped, Tortorice had spent the entire weekend studying Dr. Gruszecki's testimony.

The young, mild-mannered, geeky-looking attorney's first question knocked the smile off Dr. Gruszecki's face, and it wouldn't be seen again in this trial. He asked, "You're not board certified in clinical pathology, correct?"

Dr. Gruszecki replied, "Correct."

"Have you taken those boards?" Tortorice asked.

"I took them, yes," she admitted.

Tortorice zeroed in. "Did you pass them?"

Instead of replying yes or no, Dr. Gruszecki deflected. "I decided not to pursue it. I don't need them to practice pathology," was her reply.

It didn't take a genius to guess why she decided not to pursue clinical pathology after she went to the trouble of paying for and taking the test.

Tortorice's next question and Gruszecki's answer also lodged in the jurors' minds. He asked her if she'd resigned from the Dallas County medical examiner's office after a controversy. She replied that she had submitted her resignation and they'd accepted it. If that was a controversy, so be it.

Tortorice never pursued it any further than that, but he didn't need to. He had a smart jury who could read between the lines. When Tortorice asked this question, several jurors recalled reading about the controversy in the medical examiner's office, and now they had a face to go with it.

Tortorice had gone into the cross knowing that Dr. Gruszecki's testimony had hurt them on Friday, but now he was about to pull the rug out from under some of her statements.

For example, Dr. Gruszecki had been critical in her testimony of the police for not exhuming Ms. Thelma Metcalf and doing an autopsy. She'd made this statement confidently—but evidently without ever taking a close look at Ms. Metcalf's death certificate.

After Tortorice handed her the death certificate, he asked, "Does it say on there whether or not Ms. Metcalf was cremated?" The question brought gasps from the audience and embarrassment to the defense.

Dr. Gruszecki was forced to concede that Ms. Metcalf had indeed been cremated. Tortorice asked, "Would that make an autopsy more difficult?"

Although everyone in the courtroom knew the answer, Dr. Gruszecki was forced to concede again, and it was obvious she didn't want to. No one at this point believed she was going to break out any pom-poms. Unfortunately for her and the defense, this was just the beginning.

There was one point Tortorice had waited anxiously to attack because he knew the doctor was dead wrong on it. On Friday, Dr. Gruszecki had testified that there was only one lab in the whole world doing research on 3-chlorotyrosine, a marker for chlorine exposure in blood. Tortorice had played back the tape of her testimony several times just to make sure she'd really made a mistake like that. He knew for a fact there were several labs doing research on it.

She'd clearly had time to reconsider as well, for when Tortorice asked her about that previous statement, Dr. Gruszecki denied having made it. He said, "Okay, Doctor! The jury will remember that." He was right. They did.

However, the worst was yet to come. She'd testified Friday that injections of bleach would cause redness and even stated where she found that in literature on bleach injections. Yet when Tortorice handed Dr. Gruszecki a copy of the article from which she'd claimed to have obtained the information, she was forced to admit that it didn't say anything about redness.

Throughout the trial, Kimberly Saenz had appeared happy, engaged in the process. Saenz would smile at Deaton, whisper to him, or turn and laugh or smile at her family and friends behind her. That is, when she wasn't smirking at the families of the victims. Herrington said that she enjoyed the process and she showed that she did.

Spectators and jury members alike couldn't understand what made her so supremely confident that she would get off. However, halfway through Tortorice's cross of Gruszecki, Saenz began to cry.

Her crying at this point left people shaking their heads. Had she only just woken up and realized that she was on trial for killing five people and facing the death penalty? Or had she just discovered that it wasn't going all that well?

The party was without a doubt over, but Tortorice wasn't close to turning out the lights yet. He took Dr. Gruszecki through mistakes she'd made on hemolysis, or cell damage. He questioned her about a phantom article she'd quoted from but couldn't recall anything substantial about—like who wrote or who published it.

Up to that point Tortorice had made Dr. Gruszecki look foolish, but now he was about to totally discredit this medical professional and the hopes of the defense. He focused on two huge statements that she'd said on Friday.

"Let's talk about Ms. Clara Strange," he began. "You testified on Friday—very confidently, I might add, three or four times—that you didn't see anything abnormal in Clara Strange's lab values. Is that correct?"

Dr. Gruszecki looked at her notes, and glanced up. "Nothing to do with hemolysis, correct."

Tortorice asked the judge for permission to approach, and when the judge gave him permission, he strode to the witness stand and handed her Ms. Strange's medical records. "Please find Ms. Strange's lab values."

Dr. Gruszecki began leafing through them one by one

until she reached the end and began to flip through them again.

Tortorice had stood with his arms crossed, waiting, but finally said, "Doctor, maybe it will save you some time if you recall from her medical records that she was dead on arrival at the hospital and didn't have blood drawn. Is that correct?"

A resounding gasp swept through the courtroom, and then the room fell deathly quiet except for Saenz's sobs.

Dr. Gruszecki paused for a while. What was going through her head then was anyone's guess. Finally she said, "That's correct."

Tortorice went in for the kill. "So when you told this jury you didn't see anything abnormal in her lab values, that was probably because she didn't have any blood drawn, right?"

Now with a permanent frown, she said, "Um, it could be."

Still standing, Tortorice asked, "Could be?"

Dr. Gruszecki didn't bother to answer, but again, she really didn't need to.

Tortorice twisted the knife. "You said of Ms. Strange, you would expect her to be in pain and have massive hemolysis. Would you agree with me that she probably didn't complain about pain because her heart wasn't beating, correct?"

Sheepishly she said, "That would be true."

"And you'll agree with me that your statement that you would expect to see massive hemolysis was misguided because there were no lab values?"

Dr. Gruszecki responded the only way she could. "It was an error on my part."

Without a doubt that was the biggest understatement in the trial.

Dr. Gruszecki also tried to convince the jurors that Mr. Garlin Kelley had died from what the spectators termed "five-minute pneumonia." He'd gone from resting comfortably and watching TV with no symptoms of pneumonia, or anything else for that matter, to five minutes later unresponsive. When pressed on the matter, Dr. Gruszecki would not agree with Tortorice that Mr. Kelley's cause of death might be attributed to the bleach found in his bloodlines and in the syringe still hanging from them, and she placed no importance on the extremely high 3-chlorotyrosine levels in his blood.

But by this point, no one was listening to her anyway. The youngest member of the prosecution team, the one who didn't have the experience the other two did, had effectively killed her testimony and discredited her.

In an interview after the trial, Herrington smiled and said, "That Gruszecki cross was good, wasn't it."

The boy had turned into Superman in front of everyone's eyes.

CHAPTER 21

THE VERDICT

The party attitude that Saenz and the defense had exhibited throughout the trial didn't return after prosecutor Chris Tortorice discredited their expert witness, Dr. Gruszecki. It was as if only now, four weeks into the trial, the defense team and the defendant had suddenly realized that the trial was about murder and the death penalty—not a misdemeanor.

After Deaton rested, Herington called several witnesses as rebuttals, but in effect, the trial was over. Wednesday, March 28, 2012, after the owl's pronouncement and Herrington's powerful closing argument, the jury retired to find justice.

With the announcement of a pending verdict from the jury, for the first time during the trial, Kimberly Clark Saenz, her family, and her attorneys entered the courthouse and the second floor by the back way, evidently keeping away from the media and the hallway packed with spectators.

The people who gathered in the courthouse all had different opinions and came by them by different means. But none of those would be the ones who had to make the decision. That fell on the shoulders of twelve people. Both sides had participated in the process of picking the jurors, all, including Saenz, had signed off that those twelve were unbiased strangers with no preconceived ideas of guilt or innocence, who would listen to all the evidence and make an honest and fair decision.

When whispers began flying around the hallway that the jury had a verdict, Deaton for the first time hustled the family into a County Court at Law room down the hall from the district courtroom. The door had a combination lock on it and guaranteed privacy. The last thing the spectators saw as the group disappeared into the room was Saenz's young daughter, her first appearance at the trial, almost inconsolable, being helped into the room.

Some believed that Herrington was responsible for this. He was the one who had persecuted an innocent Christian woman—threatened to take her from her family.

The sight of Saenz's daughter was sobering to everyone in the hallway who witnessed her grief. It was a reminder of how many victims there were in this case, and not only the ones who had died.

Kimberly Saenz, flanked by both of her attorneys, stood as Judge Bryan held the charge sheet to announce the jury's verdict. No place on earth could have been quieter than the courtroom. The hundreds of people packed in simply didn't move or breathe.

The judge's voice cracked with tension as he read the verdict aloud. "On count one, aggravated assault with a deadly weapon"—this was Ms. Marva Rhone's—"the jury finds Kimberly Saenz guilty as charged."

A shudder visibly sped through Saenz's family in the front row. Saenz's knees wobbled as if she was having trouble standing.

The judge continued, "On count two, aggravated assault with a deadly weapon"—this was Ms. Carolyn Risinger—"the jury finds Kimberly Saenz not guilty."

Still no words were uttered but hope seemed to buoy one side of the courtroom.

"On count three, aggravated assault with a deadly weapon"—this was Ms. Graciela Castaneda—"the jury finds Kimberly Saenz not guilty."

As optimism swept through the Saenz side, the judge continued to announce the verdicts without glancing up. His gaze remained riveted on the charge sheet.

Inside the courtroom, the tension was almost unbearable.

"On count four, aggravated assault with a deadly weapon"—this was Ms. Marie Bradley—"the jury finds Kimberly Saenz guilty as charged."

"On count five, aggravated assault with a deadly weapon"—this was Ms. Debra Oates—"the jury finds Kimberly Saenz guilty as charged."

With three guilty verdicts on the aggravated assaults, Kimberly Saenz would most likely go to jail for a long time. The maximum the jury could give her was twenty years each, but on the other hand, they could opt to only give her probation.

Still, those first five charges were comparatively insignificant to everyone but the victims. It was the sixth charge that everyone waited to hear. Herrington had combined Ms. Clara Strange, Ms. Thelma Metcalf, Mr. Garlin Kelley, Ms. Cora Bryant, and Ms. Opal Few's murders into a single capital murder charge. Capital murder is regular murder plus something extra. In this case, the extra was intentionally or knowingly murdering more than one person during the same criminal episode or pursuant to the same scheme or course of conduct. This meant that the jury only had to find Kimberly Saenz guilty of two of those murders in order to find her guilty of capital murder because two would constitute more than one person during the same criminal episode or pursuant to the same scheme or course of conduct.

If she was found guilty of capital murder, then the least she could get was life in prison without the possibility of parole. The maximum sentence was the death penalty.

Before the judge announced the last and most important verdict, the law enforcement officers standing against the walls and surrounding the spectators eased forward a half step, almost as if they'd rehearsed it.

For the first time since he began reading the charges, Judge Bryan looked up at the defendant. "On count six, capital murder, the jury finds Kimberly Saenz . . . guilty as charged."

For several seconds the entire courtroom stood in frozen, stunned silence. Then as one a collective breath whooshed from everyone—a long pent-up breath of relief from the prosecution and the victims and their loved ones, and an agonized, visceral deflating one from the defense and the Saenz supporters. If there were wails of anguish or cries of joy, they were drowned out by the mad stampeding of feet as the media rushed outside getting into position to interview the spectators.

Before the judge announced the verdict, the spectators centered their attention either on Saenz and her attorneys, on the judge, or on the jury. Four deputy sheriffs standing in the court section close to the defense table went unnoticed.

Outside the double doors of the courtroom, *The Lufkin News* photographer had been poised to capture the reaction of the family as the last charge was announced. He wasn't disappointed. He clicked just as Saenz's father buried his face in his hands. Although Kent Fowler's face isn't shown, the picture succeeds in capturing the total anguish of a father.

The photographer's next shot captured Saenz herself, heavyset, face constricted, eyes swollen from crying, and her right hand in the process of covering her face as she turned to face her family.

That was when the four deputies came into play. For the first time in four years, they placed Saenz in custody.

On the other side of the courtroom in the trial area, DA Clyde Herrington and Sergeant Stephen Abbott, two men who had put their reputations on the line for something they deeply believed, came together in a giant bear hug.

Initially, neither Abbott nor Herrington had believed what they'd heard about Saenz. Even when they'd started to change their minds about her guilt, they had doubts about getting a conviction. It was a case like no other.

Never in the history of the United States had anyone been accused of and gone on trial for killing people with bleach.

Defense attorney Ryan Deaton sat slumped in his seat, as if he'd taken a giant blow to the stomach.

Some other spectators were simply too stunned to move. Quite a few of them had come out expecting to help Saenz and Deaton celebrate a great victory.

The news of the verdict swept through Angelina County as it did the entire country. However, only the citizens of Angelina County, many of whom had been basing their opinions on hearsay and the limited information they were getting from the media, seemed stunned by the verdict. A vast majority of locals believe that Saenz was going to be found not guilty.

As the courtroom emptied Friday evening, a realization hit. The jury had only given their verdict. The second phase of the trial was still to come on Monday morning, when the jury would gather to decide Saenz's punishment. The world had to wait to hear her fate, but the owl had already announced it.

Either way, Saenz's life as she knew it had ended.

CHAPTER 22

THE JURY

When the Kimberly Clark Saenz trial went to deliberations, the jurors had unanimously elected Larry Walker foreman of the jury. Many said later that this was the smartest decision that they made. His objective was to make sure the ones who talked the most didn't, and the ones who talked the least had their say.

Many in the audience said afterward that they'd assumed the jurors' minds had already been made up. People in the defense group claimed that they'd made a deal on guilt in the first phase, that all twelve couldn't be convinced of Saenz's guilt, so they said they wouldn't give her death if everyone voted guilty. Others said that they couldn't have been too sure of the witnesses if they hadn't found Saenz guilty on all of the aggravated assaults—especially Ms. Risinger.

The truth, however, was, there was no deal in the jury room. They hadn't made up their minds, and they all believed that Saenz was guilty of all of the murders, and all of the assaults, but unlike the murders, they didn't think the prosecution proved guilt beyond a reasonable doubt in the two assaults. After all, that was their charge to begin with. Hold the state accountable to proving beyond a reasonable doubt the allegations it had brought.

If there was a question or confusion, they stopped and discussed it or found the evidence to clear up what was bothering that juror. Walker later said that the jury had worked hard. They'd taken a few breaks but mostly they stayed on task.

The jury was not only intelligent, but extremely attentive. They took notes and were mentally engaged with every witness and every single piece of evidence. For the most part, they were fifteen strangers, five men and ten women—three of the men worked at Lufkin Industries, but not with one another.

During the trial, the jurors had come and gone from the jury room on the second floor, positioned down a small hallway behind the courtroom. (They were even able to problem-solve one issue early on; in the jury room, the men's restroom had three stalls, but the women's only one. To keep the peace, they ended up switching the names on the bathroom doors.) The jury room's location made it easy for the jurors to enter and leave the courtroom without encountering anyone else.

But once the trial portion ended, the court moved the jury up to the third floor. Perhaps the move was made for security measures. If so, it worked, because most people didn't realize the jury wasn't in their normal place.

The jurors were extremely emotional about the

decisions they had to make. Martha Moffett said, "More than once we all held hands and prayed about this." In fact, none of the jurors wanted to find Saenz guilty.

Larry Walker said, "We were really searching for the truth. But also there was three, four, or five—maybe all of us actually, that were really trying to find her not guilty."

Walker also said, "They'd moved us up to the third floor and when we took a break we had to go out on the roof. I was afraid that someone might jump. There was some, several times we had to have a break because people were very emotional. I was worried someone was going to go overboard."

He also said he found that when one female started crying, several joined in.

After they elected Walker as foreman, the jury's next decision was where to start? Should they begin by considering the five aggravated assaults or the five murders? They decided to start with the most important ones, the deaths.

First they called for a secret vote. The options were guilty, not guilty, or unsure, and the ballots came in split at six guilty, two not guilty, and four question marks.

In his closing, Herrington had said he thought Deaton would have stopped blaming the water by then. Deaton should have, because the jury had. That was the very first argument they dismissed. Once they decided the water hadn't been the problem, that took away at least a fourth of the ton of evidence they had to plow through.

Steve Taylor in an interview after the trial said, "Deaton spent most of the time chasing rabbit trails. Stuff that wasn't going to sell." Rabbits protect their homes by leaving many different paths, but the jurors didn't follow them. They stayed with the evidence: the bloodlines and syringes. David Bradford became the jury's expert on this. As a contractor who'd started out as a plumber, he was very familiar with how liquids flowed through pipes and lines. He, like the other jurors, believed in this evidence, and would for the entire duration of the deliberation.

There was no doubt in any of the jurors' minds that there was bleach in those bloodlines and syringes, and not accidentally; it had been put there by someone. But who? That was the big question they had to answer.

Kimberly Flores said, "The jurors wrote on the chalkboard the names of the victims and put a plus if they had a positive bloodline or syringe or minus by their name if they didn't—it kind of guided them and what they were looking for—it helped with the guilty or not guilty."

The jury never bought the DaVita conspiracy theory either. Larry Walker said, "We looked at it and quite frankly unless the DaVita people were experts there was no way they could have put the bleach in, stopped the blood flow at the points they did, done the things they did, I mean in the time that they had and given that they weren't prepared to do that sort of thing. So, that put us at a point that conspiracy was pretty much out the window."

Kristine Bailey, the first alternate, who didn't participate in the deliberation process, said after the trial, "If it was a big conspiracy why here—why Lufkin? One thing Ryan said in his opening statement was DaVita was a big huge cooperation and had dialysis centers all over the world all using the same policy. Why was Lufkin the only one having issues? That didn't make any sense."

She wasn't the only one who weighed in on the

conspiracy theory. Deaton's rabbit trails didn't lead the jury away from the nest, but right to it. David Bradford said that whenever "Deaton made a big deal over how shoddy things were done and how could [Saenz] have done all of this with all these people not knowing, it was obvious. There was enough stupidity going on for her to get away easily with that kind of stuff."

One of the problems that Bradford and the jury saw was each patient care person at DaVita, whether it was a nurse or PCT, cared for four patients at a time. There is a lot to do for the patients, and the health care professional needed to monitor the patients constantly. In April 2008, the state required end-stage renal disease facilities to have a patient-nurse/technician ratio of 4 to 1. Obviously DaVita met those guidelines. However, at DaVita, the nurses and PCTs worked with a "teammate." When one went on break or lunch, the teammate took care of that one's patients. During those times, each one looked after eight patients.

It wasn't hard for the jury to see the pattern. Most of the ten incidents Saenz was accused of committing had happened during those break or lunch times.

Deaton inadvertently kept reminding the jury of this. He asked every DaVita employee, whether they still worked there or not, if they'd ever seen Kim do anything. Of course their answer was they hadn't. If they had, they would have said something. However, these questions always brought a redirect from Herrington. First he would ask them if they were paying attention to any other employee, and all of them responded, no, they were concentrating on their own patients.

Herrington's second question also helped the jury understand how this could happen under the employees' noses. "Was it unusual to see a DaVita nurse go around to the patient stations and help the patients?"

The obvious answer was of course not. That is what nurses do.

The jurors later talked about how Deaton had tried to claim that witnesses whose testimony didn't agree with another witness's must have been conspiring, but the jurors saw that differently. If there *had* been a conspiracy, with the employees using a script, then surely the witnesses' stories would have agreed. The same went for the employees whom Deaton had ridiculed for having so-called convenient memory losses; again, the jury saw those lapses as more signs that there *wasn't* a conspiracy. It had been four years, after all, and they thought it was normal for the employees to have had some memory discrepancies. Again, if there was the great conspiracy that Deaton tried to sell, the employees would have gone by the script.

In attempting to insinuate a conspiracy, Deaton had only managed to convince the jury that there wasn't one.

David Bradford said, "If Deaton had kept it on one level, he would have had better chance than beating them over the heads like dumbasses. When every guy that comes on the stand, he goes, 'Do you know Joe Blow, he's on Fortune 500.' No, I haven't had lunch with him."

Bradford was referring to an exchange that occurred when the first witness from the CDC testified. In Deaton's cross, he brought up the fact that a past CDC director was now on the DaVita board of directors. The witness had heard of the man, but didn't know him.

Deaton would ride that same dead horse with every CDC employee who followed—the insinuation in his question that their testimony was somehow linked to an ex-CDC director they didn't even know.

In his attempt to convince the jury about the big, money-grubbing Fortune 500 Company, Deaton forgot one aspect of that, but the jury didn't. Laura Bush, no relationship to the former president, said, "When you are talking about real time folks and locals, they're just trying to do their jobs." The jury recognized those employees he ridiculed, many of whom no longer worked for DaVita by the time the trial came around, as honest, hardworking East Texans just trying to do their jobs and take care of their patients.

Deaton's aggressive style with witnesses also backfired in a concrete way with the jury. The jurors said that they were given everything they asked for, with one exception: when they asked for the transcript of Ms. Hall's testimony in the trial, the judge sent a note back that said he would give them a part of the transcript but not the whole transcript because there was a dispute with the attorneys. Ms. Linda Hall had been the first witness called by Herrington. She was also the one whom Deaton had attacked on the stand and drew reactions not only from the spectators but the jurors, too. Walker said that Ms. Hall's testimony in court was pretty compelling. "That was the only time I got choked up during the entire trial."

But then one of the jurors remembered that while they were missing the court transcript of Ms. Hall's testimony, they actually already had the transcript of her deposition.

Since Ms. Hall had testified in person, there had been

no need to watch her video deposition as they had Ms. Hamilton's, who had unfortunately not lived long enough to make it to trial. But several years before the trial took place, Herrington had taken video depositions of both women, and Herrington had placed the transcript of Ms. Hall's deposition into evidence and the jury had that.

So, instead of using her court testimony, they used her testimony in her deposition. Juror Caren Brooks read Ms. Hall's deposition aloud as foreman Larry Walker read the questions asked of her by Herrington and Scott Tatum, Saenz's previous attorney.

Kimberly Flores said, "The defense attorney tried to portray Ms. Hamilton and Ms. Hall, the two witnesses, as being weak and sick. That wasn't an issue to me. They saw what they saw. They'd been in dialysis for years and they saw something that wasn't right. To me, the eyewitnesses deserve a lot of credit."

―――――

At the end of Thursday, the day the jury began deliberating, they held another silent vote, but this time Walker asked if they had a question mark last time, go ahead and put guilty or not guilty—whichever way they were leaning just so they could get a feel. He thought that would help them out but actually those question marks were split. They were now eight guilty and four not guilty.

In an interview after the trial, juror Daniel Phipps related how difficult the trial and the deliberation were for him. He said, "I wanted [Saenz] to be innocent so bad. You just don't know it. That Thursday night I might have slept maybe an hour to an hour and a half. I cried,

I tossed, I turned. As a matter of fact, after it was all over, my wife told me, she said, 'I'm so glad that this is over because I thought our marriage was going to break up because you were about to burst.' " Phipps said he pushed everyone away. "I couldn't even deal with my family."

Like Daniel Phipps, all the other jurors' emotions were tearing them apart. But all of them had another issue to face besides the enormous weight on their shoulders. They were scared to death of jury misconduct. Every one of them was always very careful about it. All of them told about hearing rumors in the courthouse that Deaton's investigators were following the jurors around.

Walker said, "I think they were trying for jury misconduct, because when you go to the appeal you don't want to go before this three-judge panel. You want a new trial, and the best way to get that is with jury misconduct."

––––––

On Friday morning, the second day of deliberations, Walker took another vote. This time, they had ten jurors who believed Saenz was guilty of the murders, and two who didn't.

At the beginning of *voir dire*, the objective on both sides was to find intelligent jurors. They succeeded. That morning the jury began what they called probabilities study. Every single juror agreed that a DaVita employee had injected the patients with bleach. The bleach was in those bloodlines and syringes. The water didn't do it and there was never a big conspiracy to blame everything on Kimberly Saenz. As Herrington had said in his closing, "Deaton wants you to think that DaVita waited around for twenty-eight days on the off-chance that someone would see and report something so they could blame that person." But none of the jurors believed that.

The question with all of the jurors wasn't if an employee injected bleach into the patients, but *which* employee did it. The jurors had the calendar that the state presented that had all the days that Saenz worked, which was only twelve days out of the twenty-eight that month. There were ten events on six different days.

The odds that Saenz would have been at any of those events were 40 percent.

Juror Karla Myers said, "Yeah, but how many other DaVita employees were also there on all of those days?"

They went through every time sheet on every DaVita employee.

Kimberly Saenz was the *only* employee who had worked on every day there was an event.

Juror Kimberly Flores, a math teacher, was the perfect one to help the jury conduct a probability study. The list of probabilities included: the probability of someone dying on the dialysis machine; the probability that Saenz was the only one working on every single day; and the probability of Saenz being the only name on any of the syringes shown to contain bleach. Add up the odds of all of those and multiply it out, and the odds are approximately 1 in 640,000,000.

And that didn't even take into account the two eyewitnesses who saw Saenz inject patients with bleach.

Another crucial element for the jury was the computer search, specifically the search, "Can bleach be detected in bloodlines?" The search with that phrase had been run in the early morning, the time Saenz normally got up to go to work, on April 2, 2008, the day after the first two patients died.

This raised the question in the jurors' minds: how could anyone using that computer have known about bleach in the bloodlines on April 2, 2008? The police would not be involved or collect the bloodlines for twenty-six days after that search was conducted. Not to mention, Saenz had herself told police, unprompted, that she hadn't conducted any computer searches on the topic. Deaton had promised the jury that Kevin Saenz would testify to explain away those searches on the computer, but though the jury had waited for him to do so, he never did.

The computer searches and the probability study were what won over the remaining jurors who'd still been leaning toward not guilty.

It became emotional in the jury room once they'd decided Saenz was guilty of the murders. Juror Martha Moffett said, "I really wanted her to be not guilty, but she's not," and then she started crying.

Caren Brooks echoed what Moffett said. "I thought the evidence was just so compelling against Kim. She's a mom with kids and I kind of wanted to feel sorry for her. I wanted her not to be guilty, but after we got started, the evidence just showed otherwise."

Kimberly Flores was another one who voiced that she wanted Saenz to be innocent. "We all wanted her to be innocent. My job every day is to pull for the underdog— I'm a teacher. I mean I wanted her to be innocent, she just wasn't."

After the jurors found Saenz guilty of the murders,

they still had those five aggravated assaults to consider, although some jurors now thought of them as nit-picking, when compared to murder. They didn't see the difference in life without parole and twenty years, or life without parole and a hundred and twenty years.

Daniel Phipps wasn't one of the jurors who felt the assaults didn't matter. He brought up the fact that there was family out there of victims not on the capital murder count, and they, too, wanted closure. Some patients in the audience were themselves victims of these assaults.

After the trial, Phipps said, "I was real strong on this, and I am glad I was."

One of the other jurors who took the assault charges seriously was David Bradford.

Bradford said, "One of the funny dynamics that happened was the two jurors who were the most outspoken for the defense and not guilty, when we flipped over to the nit-picking, the two that were the strongest for innocent, once they saw the truth for what it was, they turned like they'd had a lover cheat on them."

The jurors said it was 11–1, with the 1 being Bradford, for a long time on the five aggravated assaults. The eleven wanted guilty on all five. However, Bradford wanted the same evidence to apply to the assaults that applied to the murders. He said, "I was determined that the criteria they used for the murders should also be used for the assaults."

He made a statement, "I can hold out till hell freezes over."

In the end, the jury found Saenz guilty of the aggravated assaults of Ms. Marva Rhone, Ms. Marie Bradley, and Ms. Debra Oates. The two assaults they found Saenz not guilty of were Ms. Castaneda and Ms. Risinger. They gave Deaton credit for creating doubt with Ms. Castaneda. During the trial, he'd raised a question about whether she had actually choked on a piece of gum she was chewing, causing the onset of her problems.

Besides that, neither Ms. Castaneda nor Ms. Risinger had had bloodlines submitted for testing. Debra Oates's bloodlines weren't submitted either, but she was there to testify for herself.

At the end, they went around the table to get each juror's vote. Larry Walker told them that they all needed to say it loud so that everyone could hear one another. "It was guilty all the way to the last person, who was Daniel Phipps," recalled Walker. "All of a sudden he kind of choked up like we all did from time to time, and this was on Friday right before four forty."

Daniel Phipps said, "She's guilty, I know she's guilty, but can we have the weekend to pray about it?"

Larry Walker didn't know what to say, but then someone spoke up and reminded them that they still had to do the punishment deal Monday. Daniel Phipps said, "Then she's guilty." They'd been at it so long, most of the jurors had completely forgotten that there was a punishment phase to follow.

Larry Walker said, "I'm not normally an emotional person, but after the guilty verdict, I'd almost made it home—right as I got in the driveway, it all came to a head. I couldn't get out of my truck. I had to sit in the truck five minutes. I had an emotional breakdown."

CHAPTER 23

⋀

STRETCH MARKS ON THE SOUL

On Monday morning, April 2, 2012, four years and one day after Ms. Clara Strange and Ms. Thelma Metcalf died at DaVita, and exactly four years to the day of Kimberly Clark Saenz's fateful computer search, the jury filed back into the courtroom for the punishment phase.

The punishment phase in a trial is sometimes called the second trial, but the objective is different for both sides. The first phase is about guilt or innocence only. The second phase is about punishment, but now the fact that the person was convicted can also be used.

Otherwise, the second phase is exactly like the first. The prosecution puts on evidence and witnesses, usually in an attempt to get the maximum punishment, and the defense does the same, but to attempt to get the least punishment. Then the jury deliberates again to answer the question of what sort of sentence the guilty party will receive.

As the crowd filed in Monday morning for the

punishment phase of the Kimberly Clark Saenz trial, her
defense attorney Ryan Deaton, all the swagger and cockiness knocked out of him, sat slumped in his chair much
as he had after hearing the guilty verdict. The big smile
he'd worn throughout most of the trial had disappeared
from his face. He sat without uttering a word for the
entire process.

The reason for Deaton's silence was because of something that took place behind the scenes. Co-defense lawyer Steve Taylor had approached DA Herrington and
asked him to waive the death penalty and give Saenz life.

Herrington told Taylor that he would only agree to
waive the death penalty if Saenz changed her plea to guilty
and waived her appeal options. If not, he was inclined to
let the jury decide her punishment.

Taylor told him that Saenz wouldn't go for that, but
then asked Herrington not to hammer on the death penalty in his closing. Herrington's response was that if Deaton
was involved in the punishment phase, he had no choice
but to seek the death penalty with everything he had.

But that wasn't all that was at stake. Saenz had two
children, and neither Taylor nor Herrington wanted to
cause them any more pain than they were already experiencing. Taylor later said, "Herrington knew what we
were going to try to do in the punishment phase. I didn't
want to destroy the young man [Jacob Hopper], a good-
looking, hardworking, nice young man. Didn't want to
put him through that."

The problem was that hearsay isn't allowed in any
phase of a trial, and people aren't allowed to tell what
someone else told them. This was the reason that Jim

Risinger wasn't allowed to tell what his wife had told him. Because of that, character witnesses would not be able to talk about or tell what the children had told them. The children themselves would have to be put on the stand to do that.

"If *you* want to ask witnesses what the kids said or things about them, then I'm okay with that," Herrington told Taylor but, still seething from Deaton's closing the previous Thursday, also said, "If Deaton is involved, I can't do that. Deaton isn't trustworthy."

What went on behind the scenes between Herrington and Taylor was unknown to most, but Monday morning, Taylor was the only attorney who spoke for the defense, and because of the agreement, Saenz's two children did not have to testify.

Kim Saenz had been escorted back to the courthouse in chains Monday morning for the sentencing hearing. During the trial, she'd worn makeup and dressed fairly nicely, but that wouldn't be the case for the hearing. Her face, devoid of makeup, showed that she appeared to have spent the entire weekend crying. Her eyes were puffy, and her face was red. After the jury had found Saenz guilty of four of the six charges, sheriff's deputies took her to the Angelina County Jail, where she was placed on a ten-minute interval suicide watch. Normally, the county had prisoners they suspected of suicidal tendencies on a thirty-minute watch.

Saenz sat between a totally dejected Deaton, and Taylor, who for the first time was actually sitting close, not pushed away from the table. Her attitude was also in stark contrast to what it had been most of the time during the trial. Without a doubt, she was no longer enjoying the process going on around her. The only person on the defense side who showed any signs of life was Taylor, and he had a job to do—attempt to save her life. From the beginning, he'd been the only one who'd taken a realistic approach to the trial, the only one who'd attempted to prepare for this eventuality.

Prosecutor Clyde Herrington began the punishment phase by calling two Lufkin police officers, both of whom had arrested Saenz before for domestic problems with her husband. Then he called Sergeant Steve Abbott to testify. Abbott testified about a few of the jobs Saenz had, including the firing at Woodland Heights, but Herrington didn't ask him to go into detail. He then passed the punishment phase to Taylor.

It soon became clear that the defense had real problems with this phase of the trial. They were severely lacking in character witnesses for Saenz—not because no one would have spoken for her, but because all of her supporters had been with her in court and so weren't allowed to testify on her behalf now.

This was the reason attorneys plan for this stage even if they don't think they may need it. Without prior planning, they only had from Friday evening to Monday morning to get this together. And Saenz's life was at stake.

Cheryl Pettry, the mitigation specialist, said that she only spoke to Deaton twice: once when he wanted her to sign an affidavit to get a continuance, and after the trial when he called her at her hotel room because someone told him she'd said something bad about him. She fully admitted she had said a lot of bad things about him.

Vann Kelley, the investigator, hadn't helped matters either, because he, too, had apparently assumed that this phase of the trial would never take place. And Saenz had insisted that all of her family members sit in the courtroom. Now that they were needed, they couldn't testify on her behalf.

Pettry had been able to find some people to come in and testify, including a couple of people from Fleetwood Transportation, the place that had employed Kimberly Saenz before she married Kevin and went to nursing school. Pettry also found a couple from the Central School in Pollok, a man who coached her daughter's softball team, and the preacher from Saenz's church. Even though he could have objected to some of the testimony, Herrington let it go. In fact, throughout the entire process, there was not one single objection from either side.

The last witness Taylor called was Frank Aubuchon, an expert with the Texas Department of Corrections. Aubuchon told the jury that life in prison is extremely structured. While violent incidents happened in the male prisons, there were hardly ever any incidents in the women's prisons.

He told the jury that at the present time, there were twenty-seven women serving sentences of life without parole, and if sentenced to life, Saenz would share a cell with one other woman, who also would have to have a sentence of sixty years or more.

The last fact he told the jury gave them a little pause. The only jobs Saenz qualified for were in the kitchen or the laundry. These two jobs would give her access to bleach.

When Taylor was through, Herrington gave his closing remarks, but they were nowhere close to what he'd done at the end of the trial phase because his emotions were different. When he delivered his devastating closing in the trial phase, he had been furious with Deaton and the misrepresentations. In the punishment phase, Deaton wasn't involved and therefore couldn't fan those flames that still smoldered in Herrington.

When he sat and gave the floor to Taylor, he did so without asking the jury for the death penalty. It was still on the table, but he didn't ask them to choose it outright. He'd told Taylor he wouldn't push the issue if Deaton didn't speak, and he was a man of his word.

But it wasn't Herrington's closing that stood out in the punishment phase—it was Steve Taylor's. He'd already prepped the jurors in *voir dire* for this eventuality. They already knew about the society that Saenz would enter, and it wouldn't be the same one as the jurors or their loved ones. She would never be a danger to their society again. She would only leave prison in a pine box. They knew this, but he also reminded them.

The audience sat spellbound as Taylor told them about "stretch marks on the soul."

"Each of us goes through life experiences that make us who we are," he said. "Sometimes there is a fine line of something we'll always remember and something we'll never forget. Sometimes that line is kind of wavy and things cross over.

"Capital cases aren't just tough on the families of the victims or the accused. It's very tough on the twelve people sitting in the box. You are also innocent participants in the trial. You were asked to dedicate your time to serve your community to be impartial jurors.

"In making decisions we go back to our roots, our parents, grandparents, and the life changes that make us who we are. Life-changing experiences leave stretch marks on the soul."

————

If Deaton had looked like he'd taken a giant punch in the stomach that morning, the twelve jurors, men and women alike, had filed in looking like they'd gone three rounds with Mike Tyson. The tremendous burden they'd been placed under showed in their faces and posture. The members of the jury were all mentally and physically exhausted, and they still had to deal with the punishment phase, and then decide whether they would vote to have Saenz executed—not an easy topic to rest on someone's mind and shoulders for an entire weekend.

During the trial they had been alert and followed every word. They had taken notes and been engaged in every facet, even the boring stuff. Now, their eyes almost looked glassy. The enormity of what they had to decide seemed to turn their personalities inside out.

In his closing, Taylor had talked about the burden placed on the jurors, and it was indeed daunting. In the end, every one of them had not only stretch marks on their souls, but scars. Since the death penalty had been a major topic in *voir dire* that began at the end of January, they'd had it on their minds for over two months. Without a doubt, Steve Taylor left a lasting impression on them. They slept with his words, "If she's found guilty, she will only come out of prison in a pine box." In his closing, they'd heard it again.

After the trial was over, several jurors quoted Taylor saying, "You won't find her in Walmart or Whataburger." The seeds he'd planted about the society that Saenz would be in, and the fact it wasn't the one they'd gone in expecting, also left a lasting impression.

There were some other things that these jurors came out of *voir dire* with. Most simply didn't believe Herrington was truly pushing for the death penalty.

These feelings were magnified later in the punishment phase. It seemed like Herrington only put on a token case for the death penalty. He never challenged Taylor, and even the jurors saw places where Herrington could have easily done so.

Then there was the fact that Herrington did not even ask for the death penalty.

After the trial was over and punishment meted out, the question was, just who had saved Saenz's life? It's not a simple matter to sit in judgment and say someone should die. Death penalty cases are complex and require the jury to make decisions about life and death that are far beyond the usual juror decision of guilt or innocence.

It's also extremely confusing. The people who construct the laws and procedures use language typically foreign to the people whose understanding of it is the most crucial—the jurors.

To wit: "In death penalty cases, mitigating factors do not have to be proven beyond a reasonable doubt, and jurors do not have to agree on the existence of a particular mitigating factor or on how much weight it should be given. However, jurors must find that at least one aggravating factor has been proven by the prosecution beyond a reasonable doubt in order to find the defendant is eligible for the death penalty."

This is not the language that most people use every day, and it even confuses people who do use legal language. Even Taylor and Herrington got befuddled while trying to explain it to the jurors in *voir dire*.

The jurors left the courtroom to deliberate, in effect, whether Saenz lived or died. (Although technically speaking, the jury doesn't make that decision—the judge does. The judge makes his decision based on the jury's answer to one, and maybe two, special circumstance questions. However, every juror in that room knew what the effects of their answers would be.)

Of course that first question was the vital one because it was really the only one the jury had to answer. They would only go to the second one based on answers to the first. The first question is often called the "future danger" question. *Whether there is a probability that the defendant would commit criminal acts of violence that would constitute a continuing threat to society.*

Was Saenz a future danger? The jurors heard from Herrington in *voir dire* that the best way to predict future actions was look at what that person did in the past, the way an employer might look at an applicant's grades in school. If that person had worked hard to achieve good grades, he or she would probably work hard at their job.

Both sides presented past actions by Saenz. However, the jury had one past action that weighed heavily on them: they'd just convicted her of capital murder and aggravated assault. If she was capable of doing it in the past, she could do it in the future. The question of whether she was a future danger to society was still an extremely difficult one to answer, and the jury's decision had to be unanimous.

If no, she wasn't a future danger, then they would submit that to the judge, and he would issue life without the possibility of parole.

If the jury answered yes, they did find her a future danger, they would go to question two, the "mitigation" question.

Described thus, it seems like a simple process. But that is the language of one society, the one who didn't construct the law. Here is how that other society says it:

> *(2) it may not answer any issue submitted under Subsection (b) of this article "yes" unless it agrees unanimously and it may not answer any issue "no" unless 10 or more jurors agree; and*

> *(3) members of the jury need not agree on what particular evidence supports a negative answer to any issue submitted under Subsection (b) of this article.*

Huh? What happens if ten of the jurors vote she would be a future danger? This is an important question because that is exactly what happened inside that jury room. The jurors were confused by this going in and they were confused by this coming out. A month after the trial was over, they were still confused over it.

Larry Walker, the foreman, said, "We didn't ever get

to question two. We had to have ten or more jurors to go to number two, and we had exactly ten—actually I was one of those who wanted to take it to two. Juror Regina McAvoy was so shaken up, she got confused, she said, 'What do I put down if I don't want to give her the death penalty?'"

Ms. McAvoy later confirmed that she was one of the two who'd voted no. She honestly didn't think Saenz would be a future danger, and she didn't want to give her the death penalty.

In fact, they were all confused. They couldn't vote yes, because they didn't have a unanimous vote. Could they say no, she wasn't a future danger? They didn't have ten or more say no. They only had two.

Under normal circumstances, the ten might have been able to convince the two that she would be a future danger. After all, they did have some ammunition to use in order to convince them, and if they hadn't been so confused about the ten or more, they might have tried. In this case they didn't. Once they had the 10–2 vote, Larry Walker asked them, "Do we need to discuss this?"

They did have a unanimous vote on that—no.

After that, they had no problem agreeing on giving Saenz the maximum sentence for the three aggravated assaults.

Forty-five minutes after beginning their deliberations, the jury returned with their verdict.

Kimberly Saenz had told people that she would rather get death if she was found guilty. Somewhere along the process she must have changed her mind. She mouthed "thank you" to the jury when the judge issued the sentence of life in prison without the possibility of parole, plus sixty years.

The day after Judge Bryan announced Saenz's punishment, *The Lufkin News* led off with a quote from the daughter of one of the victims in big, bold headlines: I HOPE YOU BURN IN HELL.

After the jury had returned with Saenz's punishment, the judge had thanked and dismissed them, but the court process wasn't finished. What remained were the gut-wrenching victim impact statements.

Many of Cora Bryant's, Opal Few's, Thelma Metcalf's, Clara Strange's, and in a limited way, Garlin Kelley Jr.'s family members had attended most of the trial. With them was Ms. Marie Bradley, who had survived the bleach injection, and Mr. James Rhone, husband of Marva Rhone, another survivor who'd later passed away from natural causes.

The families had simmered with rage when Saenz turned around and smirked and smiled at them during trial. Their family members were dead, taken away from them, and here their accused killer was walking around laughing, giggling, and carrying on as if it didn't matter. As a matter of fact, many of the people watching her came away with the feeling that she was taunting them with her guilt, and her confidence that she was going to get away with it.

The feelings they'd suppressed erupted in the impact statements. With the exception of Garlin Kelley's relatives, who did not participate in the statements, the families of the murder victims all now addressed Saenz directly.

In fact, it was Wanda Hollingsworth, daughter of Thelma Metcalf, who'd uttered those words plastered across the headlines: "I hope you burn in hell." She'd gone on to say to Saenz, "You are nothing more than a psychopathic serial killer."

Marisa Fernandez, granddaughter of Clara Strange, took the podium, but was often too distraught to speak. At times she broke down and had to take a few moments before she could continue. She told about how her grandmother had raised her from the age of seven, after her mother died.

Her most heartbreaking words came when she related how she still kept her grandmother's number in her cell phone wishing she could call her. "Now I have my own children," she said, "and I have no one to call. No one to ask questions only a mother could answer."

Then, perhaps in a jab at Saenz for the torment she'd put the family through during the trial, Fernandez said, "When I go home I'll get to spend time with my children. You will not."

Linda Few James followed. She was the daughter of ninety-one-year-old Opal Few, who even in her advanced age, was perhaps the victim in the best health. All signs had pointed to her having many years left—in fact, Linda Few James mentioned that her mother's oldest sister was about to turn one hundred years old. Linda Few James told Saenz how she'd robbed her mother of the benefit of dying at home surrounded by her family—which had been Ms. Few's wish.

The last person to take the stand to address Saenz was Angela Scott, daughter of Ms. Cora Bryant. She addressed some of her comments to Kimberly Saenz, but some she addressed instead to Bennie Fowler, Kimberly Saenz's mother, who sat in the first row behind the defense table. In one of the oddest quirks of the trial, Angela Scott, the daughter of one of the victims, and Bennie Fowler, mother of the convicted killer, worked together at Walmart. As Scott told KTRE-TV after the sentencing, "The sentencing was fair. [Saenz] got what was due to her. She's of age and she's held accountable for what she does."

Kimberly Clark Saenz never expressed any emotion during the reading of the impact statements. She sat at the table, looking down and writing on a legal pad. But even her lack of reaction to the statements said a lot about her.

As the day ended, many questions remained unanswered, most notably the big one, the same one that had baffled people from day one: the one that even kept law enforcement detectives, federal agents, CSU people, and yes, even Herrington from believing Saenz initially guilty—why did she do it?

Although Herrington wasn't required to prove motive to convict Kimberly Saenz, he understood that people wanted to know. He'd taken extra steps to try to find out what might have spurred this young East Texas woman to kill the patients in her charge.

He contacted Professor Beatrice Yonkers, an RN and Director of Nursing at California State University, considered the foremost authority in the country on motives for criminal acts involving medical professionals.

In an article by *USA Today* writer Rick Hampson, Yonkers explained, "Fearing lawsuits, many hospitals will confirm only the dates of employment for a former worker and make no positive or negative recommendation to another hospital thinking about hiring the ex-employee. The problem has been exacerbated by a nursing shortage. Some hospitals just want a warm body with a nursing license and a CPR card who can be on the floor the next day."

This was what had happened with Saenz. DaVita and the other places she'd worked had checked references, or as much as was provided, and they had no other means to get information. When DaVita hired Saenz, there was a serious allegation against her from Woodland Heights Hospital, but at the time, they didn't have access to that information.

In truth, DaVita had needed nurses badly, but whether they would have hired her even if they'd known the problems she'd had at other jobs, no one will ever know.

As for the reasons medical professionals kill patients, Yonkers's answer in the article was spine-chilling. She said: "Nurses who kill patients do so for a variety of reasons. Orville Majors, convicted of six counts of murder in Indiana in 1999, was sick of complaining patients. Genene Jones, a pediatric nurse convicted of murder in Texas in 1984, apparently enjoyed watching babies go into cardiac arrest."

She went on to say, "Some are motivated by Munchausen syndrome by proxy," a psychological disorder attributed to those who create medical emergencies in those under their care to draw attention to themselves.

Her last answer was the most chilling of all. She said, "Possibly the biggest reason that some nurses kill is that they can."

Speaking with Yonkers was what had led Herrington to say in his closing, "Why do mothers sometimes scald their babies, why does it happen?"

In effect what he was saying was that sometimes we don't know the reason, and even if we did, we wouldn't understand it. Sometimes it's best not to know.

When Sergeant Abbott initially told Herrington about the case, the DA's first coherent utterance had been, "Holy cow, that can't be true." After a few minutes, Herrington had then realized that if it was true, he still might not manage a conviction, which was the reason he contacted Yonkers and others.

Before this came up in Lufkin, Herrington had not realized how prevalent these kinds of accusations against medical personnel were, and his first impression about the difficulty proving them was correct. All across the world, similar accusations are brought forth, but they are extremely difficult to prove. The public simply doesn't want to believe such things can happen.

The public has a tendency to hold certain professionals to a higher standard—the policeman, the judge, the district attorney, and member of the clergy. These people are trained to help and serve the public. Held to an even higher standard are medical professionals. The last thing the public wants to think is that the person they trust to heal them could, in fact, be attempting to kill them.

The American public has a tendency to categorize such crimes as "angel of mercy" killings—an attempt to rationalize how health care professionals, although wrong to kill, might've had a good motive for doing it. When Nancy Grace profiled the Kimberly Clark Saenz case on her March 7, 2012, show, she even referred to Saenz as an "angel of mercy."

Ron Panzer, president of Hospice Patients Alliance and the author of *Stealth Euthanasia: Health Care Tyranny in America*, states, "Most medical serial killings, or to use a more politically correct term—Health Care Serial Killings are not the work of madmen, alone. Nor are they the work of a person with compassionate characteristics. For the most part that is a fallacy. Those that are killing are doing so because: they can and/or because they are being rewarded financially, but very rarely is anyone killed to end anyone's suffering, out of a claim of compassion by the murderer, and all the other flowery excuses that are tossed about."

Exactly what does a health care serial killer, or for that matter, any killer look like? This was one of Herrington's big concerns before and during the trial. Most murderers don't have beady eyes and aren't outwardly cruel. Nor do they have SERIAL KILLER written on their foreheads. Neither did Kimberly Saenz, and hence Herrington's worry. People didn't look at her and automatically see a serial killer. Even after she was fired from DaVita and the police arrested her for aggravated assault against Ms. Risinger and Ms. Rhone, and her name was splashed across the news in East Texas as well as the world, not only was Saenz still able to walk into the Lufkin Dermatology Clinic and apply for a job—they hired her! Of course she lied on the application, but not about her name. And mostly: she didn't look like a serial killer.

Besides all that, health care professionals work with patients who are very sick—some are old and some young, but it wouldn't surprise many people if they died. In Saenz's case, she worked with elderly patients who had kidney disease; many of them, as Dr. Germain stated, were frail and sick. She also had access to drugs, syringes, IV tubing, all the things that science provides to help with the healing process. And all of which could also be used to end the patient's life.

After Ms. Metcalf and Ms. Strange died on April 1, 2008, DaVita knew something was wrong. They spent a lot of time and money investigating the problem, and they knew one existed. However, they never looked at the employees.

Because of Herrington's talks with Yonkers and others, he knew that, for the most part, the medical professionals who were eventually convicted were typically because of a confession rather than a trial. He found out that, on average, prosecutors were able to convict only around 50 percent of the health care professionals charged with killing or harming patients. Medical professionals are trained in science, kill with science, and it is extremely difficult to convict them with science, and in most cases, that is the only way.

When the Lufkin police arrested Saenz the first time for the two aggravated assaults, the hope was to get a confession out of her, but that didn't work, and without that confession, all that is left are educated guesses. Herrington, for instance, believed that Saenz was just what Wanda Hollingsworth called her, a sociopathic serial killer.

"I think her whole life was coming apart," he said. "She had marital and other personal problems. She was addicted to drugs, severely depressed, and hated her job." He also said, "Talking to some of the folks who worked with her at DaVita, it sounded to me like her husband was forcing her to continue to work there. She was frustrated and took it out on the people who were helpless to her."

Chris Tortorice, Layne Thompson, and Sergeant Abbott agreed with Herrington's assessment. However, mitigation specialist Cheryl Pettry had another theory. She believed that Saenz wanted DaVita to hire more employees and they wouldn't, so she took it upon herself to show them.

The jury also agreed with these professionals on the motive of Saenz, but they took it a step further, all on their own, in their probability study that no one else did— no one had access to the DaVita work calendar because Herrington didn't present it in trial, just placed it into evidence. In the twenty-eight days of April that DaVita employed Saenz, she worked twelve of those days. There were ten events on six days—all days that Saenz worked, and she was the only one to work all those days.

If a person closely took a realistic look at Kimberly Clark Saenz's life, put certain events from her personal life down on paper, and then overlaid that with the DaVita patients' deaths or injuries in April 2008, the ones Herrington charged her with, the correlation would be frightening and illuminating.

For instance, on February 15, 2008, Capital One Bank had filed a civil suit against Kimberly Saenz. The papers were delivered to her on April 14, 2008. Kimberly Saenz did not work on April 15, but she did on April 16, and that was the day Mr. Kelley coded, went into a coma, and eventually died. However, it was also the day Ms. Castaneda coded while on the dialysis machines.

Another example would be the day leading up to April 26. Friends and some family members say that just prior to this date, Kimberly and Kevin had a huge fight that ultimately led to him filing for divorce. The next day, the twenty-sixth, Kimberly Saenz worked. On that day she encountered Ms. Debra Oates, Ms. Cora Bryant, and Ms. Opal Few. Two of these patients died, and the other, Ms. Oates, came close.

There is some validity in what the friends and family members say because on April 29, the day DaVita fired Kimberly Saenz, Detective Mike Shurley met with Kevin Saenz in his attorney's office, where he was in the process of filing for divorce.

This also doesn't account for April 28, 2008. That was the day that the two witnesses observed Saenz injecting Ms. Risinger and Ms. Rhone with bleach. No one who ever looked at those two accusations in detail doubted what those two women saw. Everything they told Amy Clinton and the police proved true, and was backed up with science.

However, sometimes people lose sight of what had happened before Saenz injected the two patients. That morning she was scheduled to be the med nurse—a job she loved, but was switched from the duty back to patient care—something she hated. She was so upset by the switch in duty that Amy Clinton had to coax her into going back to work.

Just thinking of how many people could have died on April 28, 2008, or the days after, if these two patients hadn't seen her, or told anyone what they'd seen, is chilling.

Looking at this, it is easy to conclude that Saenz was indeed taking her frustrations out on people who were powerless to do anything about it—people who trusted her to care for them.

However, to take it a step further, there's also the specific people whom Saenz actually killed or injured to take into account. It wasn't a question of race, ethnicity, or sex: Ms. Metcalf, Ms. Strange, Ms. Few, Ms. Risinger, Ms. Bradley, and Ms. Oates were white. Ms. Bryant and Ms. Rhone were black as was Mr. Kelley, the only male, and Ms. Castaneda was Hispanic.

As stated earlier, for the most part, dialysis patients are sick, old, cranky, and difficult to deal with. But not Ms. Opal Few or Mr. Garlin Kelley Jr. Not a single employee had a bad word about either of those two—they were two of the most beloved patients at DaVita. Both had buoyant, warm personalities and made it a point to do things on their own so they wouldn't be a burden to others.

Employees of DaVita, past and at the time of trial, went out of their way to say good things about these two patients. Even the other patients had good things to say about these two.

Ms. Cora Bryant and Ms. Clara Strange had also been well thought of, and while Ms. Thelma Metcalf had been harder to care for than the others, because she had to be lifted in and out of her wheelchair and, in some cases, gurney, no one had a word to say against her.

When Ms. Debra Oates took the stand to testify, she'd looked at Saenz and said, "Hi, Kim." She'd considered

Saenz a friend. She told people that Kimberly Saenz had helped her pass the long dreary hours by telling her jokes while she was hooked up to the machine.

Although Ms. Risinger didn't live to see the trial, her husband, Jim Risinger, swore that his wife told him that Kim didn't do anything to her. She even credited Kim with saving her life once. Jim Risinger believed this so much that he testified at trial for Kimberly Saenz twice and even went on the E! Program to declare her innocence.

Obviously these were not difficult patients or even contrary to Saenz.

However, like all dialysis centers that treat older, extremely sick patients, DaVita Lufkin, according to employees past and present, did have quite a few difficult, hard to get along with, patients. As it happens, Saenz did not harm any that exhibited frustration or anger like she had. It's obvious to see that Saenz was taking her personal problem out on the patients—but not the ones who were weak or unhappy or unkind. It was as if she'd targeted the ones who *weren't* as miserable as she was.

Another huge question on people's minds before and after the Saenz trial was why the defense didn't ask for a change of venue from Angelina County.

This was a question broached to Steve Taylor, the experienced defense attorney and the death penalty specialist for the Saenz defense. In answer, he said that a change of venue was a lot harder to obtain than most people think. First, the defense would have to find three people from Angelina County—three who had nothing to do with the case or the defendant—who would swear in an affidavit that the defendant couldn't receive a fair trial in the county.

Then the prosecution would submit three affidavits from three unbiased people that the defendant could receive a fair trial. For the most part, this is usually easier for the prosecutor then the defense.

If all the affidavits are presented, the judge usually says, "Let's wait and see what the prospective jurors say. Wait for *voir dire*."

The judge will base his decision on whether the potential jurors can be objective—something all potential jurors are asked anyway.

Taylor said that one of the hardest parts of the process for the defense is to show the judge that the jury has been poisoned—something both Herrington and the police department had gone out of their way not to do.

Also, Taylor said to transfer a case to an adjacent county in the same jurisdiction or other nearby county is expensive—something that is taken into account.

However, when looking into a change of venue for this case, there were some major differences in this one and others, and a little had to do with that expense Taylor talked about. In most cases, to change to another county, there are either transfer costs of taking the prisoner back and forth for trial, or for another jurisdiction to house and transfer the prisoner.

The difference: in this case there was no prisoner to transport. Unlike most murder suspects, especially ones suspected and charged with serial killings, Saenz was free on bail. However, as a stipulation to that bail, she was not allowed to leave the county. She had a GPS ankle bracelet on to ensure that she didn't. A change of venue would mean the judge either had to revise the bail set or allow Saenz free movement, something Herrington was sure to fight, or revoke it, which Saenz most likely wouldn't have liked.

Of course, this brings in another factor that may or may not have played a part in this decision. Saenz was out of jail on an attorney bond. This is a practice accepted in Texas, but most if not all other states won't allow it, and the American Bar Association is totally against it. In this case, if Saenz decided to skip, then Deaton would be the one liable for paying the entire bond that guaranteed her release from jail.

Of course there are other factors. If the case had been moved out of Lufkin and East Texas, then Deaton could not have played the sympathy card he did in closing about the huge Fortune 500 company taking this East Texas girl out of her home.

That card didn't work with an East Texas jury, but it sure wouldn't have worked if the trial had not been held in East Texas.

CHAPTER 24

THE POSTSCRIPT

Not everyone believed the jury got the verdict right. Brian Thigpen, one of Kimberly Clark Saenz's relatives, said simply, "She is not guilty and the courts got it wrong."

Several from the Saenz camp said that Kimberly Saenz was a good Christian woman who wouldn't have done what she was accused of doing.

Saenz's close family had sat through the entire trial and heard all the evidence, but barring a confession, they would never believe what they'd heard, and they heard only what they wanted to believe.

However, the judge, and the prosecution team all believed the jury had done a fantastic job from start to finish.

Would the prosecution have said the jury did a great job if the jury had found Saenz innocent? There's reason to believe that they would. The three prosecutors were the type of people who would have said, "It was my job to prove the case and I didn't do it well enough."

Defense attorney Steve Taylor said of the DA, "Herrington wanted the same thing I did—a fair and impartial jury, and he was satisfied when the twelfth was chosen. In my heart I was satisfied that they wouldn't kill her, and it would have been so easy for them to have done so."

Even *The Lufkin News* complimented the jury. In their "Toast and Roast" section after the trial, they commented, "A toast, first and foremost, to the 12 jurors and three alternates who heard every minute of evidence. It is hard enough for anyone to pay attention to a preacher's entire lesson on Sunday morning, but it was obvious that this group was going to listen to every witness' every word, as if someone's life depended on it—because it did."

They went on to say, "Attorneys from both sides did a good job of selecting what we thought was a fair representation of Saenz's peers."

As the spectators watched the jurors over the course of the trial, it became clear that the jury was extremely cohesive. Several people made comments during the trial that they didn't know what verdict the jury would come back with, but they would come back with one. That group would not be hung. They simply got along too well.

A month after the trial, ten of the jurors came together as a group to talk about the Saenz trial. The other two were out of town. To a person, they were proud that they'd served on the jury, and every one of them was equally convinced they'd come to the right decisions. They were also unanimous in their beliefs about the key players in the trial and the witnesses.

The jury had paid attention to what was going on during the trial. They watched everybody, especially the attorneys. They saw the professional demeanor from the three prosecutors and compared them to a defense attorney who sat in the courtroom and ate candy bars or spit his dip into a cup during trial.

The entire group agreed that the prosecution team of Herrington, Tortorice, and Thompson had done a great job throughout the trial. One juror said, and the others all agreed, "We were impressed with their professionalism and organization, their demeanor throughout the trial." There were never any issues with their credibility either.

They also paid special note to how well the prosecution team had worked together.

Larry Walker said, "Clyde Herrington is great but he knows his limitations and that scientific stuff—he turned it over to Chris Tortorice," who had also impressed Walker. "I thought the world of him," the foreman said of the young lawyer.

Their reaction would not be the same for the defense. As far as credibility went, Deaton's was less than zero with most of the jurors. They believed that he continuously attempted to deceive them. He didn't give them facts, he attempted to hide the facts from them, and he wasn't that good at it.

After the trial was over, the prosecution team met with the jurors. During that conversation, Kimberly Flores said she asked, "Being new to the judicial system, the other side that we saw, is that how a defense attorney is supposed to behave?"

She said that the prosecution team's answer was no, but it was a question many of the jurors wanted answered.

Kristene Bailey said simply, "The whole defense in my opinion was a joke." She was the first alternate and didn't get a vote on guilt or innocence, life or death, but she wasn't the only one who'd felt that way. "I'll be completely honest," Bailey said of Deaton, "as soon as he opened his mouth and said DaVita was a puppet master—that got objected to and it should have—that put me off right from the beginning."

In other words, from the moment Deaton opened his mouth at the trial, he began to lose jurors.

Most of the jurors thought Deaton treated them, as David Bradford said, "like dumbasses."

In their opinion, Deaton had been rude and disrespectful to the witnesses, to the court, and yes, to the jury, too.

But Deaton wasn't the only one they watched, and the jurors had also been appalled at Kimberly Clark Saenz's behavior. The smiling and laughing wasn't something that just went on before or after the trial. It took place while the trial was in progress in front of the jury.

As a matter of fact, Saenz often leaned close to Deaton and whispered, or passed little smiles back and forth—not what people expected in a trial where someone was accused of murdering five people and faced the death penalty.

As the trial progressed, this became one of the most talked-about topics by spectators in the hallways, how much Saenz appeared to enjoy the process all the way from the pretrial hearings to the trial, and the jurors were amazed at how she was walking around intermingling with everyone—just having a good old time.

Another element of the Deaton and Saenz dynamic that surprised the jurors was how poorly Saenz and Deaton treated Steve Taylor, the experienced attorney and death penalty specialist. Taylor sat way to the left and away from Saenz and Deaton, while Saenz appeared to be the one assisting Deaton, handing him things he needed, whispering, or passing him notes. It got to the point that people wondered: was this nurse who hadn't graduated from high school and possessed two years of junior college credits actually telling her defense attorney what questions to ask?

As one of the jurors also said, "Her carrying on with Ryan [Deaton], rubbing against him, bothered us. This went on in the courtroom and it didn't seem appropriate."

However, the jury's big question was: how could the defense attorney let his client act this way in a trial for her life?

Juror David Bradford said, "One of the things that impressed everyone, too, when they said Opal Few coded and she was on break out there, the employee ran out to her and says you need to get back in and she said, 'I'm finishing my break—I'm finishing my cigarette.'"

Bradford said, "When you heard that, you just went, I mean you know her mind-set because I don't care how frustrated you were, if you had any concerns you wouldn't have done that."

This was huge to the jury. Kimberly Flores said, "I wrote this in my notes. I know it doesn't make her guilty but what kind of health provider wants to finish her cigarette before helping a patient who's coding?"

Along these lines, she said, "That's like a kid dying in the hallway of my school and I won't go out and help him until I finish assigning homework."

The jurors also weighed in with their opinions on some of the witnesses. The ones who impressed them the most were Amy Clinton for the prosecution, and Candace Lackey for the defense. In regards to Lackey, several of the jurors said, "She was called by the defense but she wanted to tell the truth." They'd felt sorry for her. She had been shaking during her testimony, her foot was tapping. Several put it in their notes—"she is telling the truth."

Another defense witness who impressed the jury was nephrologist Dr. Michael Germain from Massachusetts. Bradford said, "He by far was the best, most polished witness to me. What I really liked about him was he seemed honest. At the end when Clyde [Herrington] said, 'Can you say that all these things could not have been caused by the bleach injections,' and he said no."

The witnesses the jurors had liked the most, no matter which side called them, were the ones they perceived as honest. The jurors didn't perceive Dr. Gruszecki as dishonest, but thought she was mistaken quite a bit. Larry Walker said, "Her opinion came right before the trial, and it seemed like she was not very familiar with all the witness statements or the FDA report, and she didn't review the victims' records thoroughly. Tortorice seemed to know more about 3-chlorotyrosine and the sciences than she did."

Even after the trial was over, the jury had trouble getting away from Deaton. One of the first was Walker, the foreman of the jury. Walker said, "Deaton called me and we got in an argument after he accused me of strong-arming the other jurors." Walker said he told him, "I didn't railroad anyone. You need to talk to them." He gave Deaton the names of the jurors who'd originally voted not guilty or who'd been on the fence.

Larry said as soon as he'd given Deaton the names, he felt awful, as if he'd betrayed them.

Deaton or his investigator did contact those jurors, including Gail Brasuell. She said that when Deaton's private investigator came to her house on Friday afternoon, she invited him in and they talked for about an hour, and he said something to the effect that he'd heard that the foreman had strong-armed her. She told him that wasn't true, and echoed what everyone else said: Larry was a great foreman.

Deaton or his investigator tried to talk to every one of the jurors who'd been undecided, even one who had told Deaton on the phone that she didn't want to talk. Despite that, Deaton's investigator showed up at her front door. She said he tried to get her to look at a bunch of papers. He asked her if she'd have known about what the papers said, would it have made any difference. She told him that she was through with that trial and didn't want to look at anything.

The jurors whom the defense contacted said they were never asked why they thought Saenz was guilty, what the defense could have done better, or why the other jurors had changed their minds about Saenz's guilt. Several of the jurors believed that Deaton's purpose was just to get the others to say Walker made them vote the way they did so he could get a reversal of the decision.

Gail Brasuell said no emphatically to the strong-arming. "[Walker] was excellent. He said my job is to make sure everybody speaks even those who are very quiet. Those who speak too much need to not speak as much."

Bradford said, "One of the things that Larry did good, when someone didn't know something, the approach that he took was, he'd say, 'Okay, explain to me the part that you are unsettled with. Give me the parts that really bother you,' and those were the parts that they delved into and tried to dig up the evidence to see where it would go and we didn't stop until everybody had every point that bothered them settled."

The jurors also credited Walker's organizational skills. They had gone around the table, talking about what they wanted to go over, and Larry made an agenda. Before they left that first day, he set the agenda for what they needed to discuss the next day.

One of the jurors commented, "Instead of Deaton trying to accuse Larry of strong-arming us, he should be asking him about how he was so organized."

CHAPTER 25

THE REAL CONSPIRACY

Kimberly Clark Saenz had a documented history of depression and had already undergone treatment at Brentwood Hospital in Shreveport, Louisiana. At the time of her initial interview with the police, she told them she was under a doctor's care and taking medication for depression. After the jury convicted her, the sheriff's department placed her on a suicide watch in the county jail. Perhaps because of all of this, from the Angelina County Jail, Kimberly Clark Saenz was transported to Jester IV. This is a Texas Department of Criminal Justice facility located at Richmond in Fort Bend County. The TDC unit, which is located southwest of Houston and around three hours from Lufkin, is actually listed as a male facility, but it is also a maximum-security psychiatric facility, which was the reason Saenz was transported there for evaluation.

After a stay at Jester IV, she was transported to the

Murray unit at Gatesville, a maximum-security prison for female offenders four hours directly west of Lufkin. Gatesville, in Coryell County, is forty-five minutes west of Waco in Central Texas.

Before she was shipped off to prison, she appeared one more time in Judge Bryan's court. Dressed now in the trademark orange jumpsuit and sandals with white socks, she appeared larger than she had during her trial. Chained hand and foot, she shuffled as she made her way in a line with other prisoners who were also appearing before the judge.

With her was Deaton, who told *The Lufkin News* that he intended to be involved in Saenz's appeal process. Deaton began the process in front of Judge Bryan by asking the court to waive the cost and give them a copy of the court transcript because his client was indigent. The transcript cost in the neighborhood of $30,000.

Deaton went on to tell the judge that the family planned to hire an attorney, meaning himself, to handle the appeal. The judge told Deaton it was all or nothing, meaning if they hired an attorney, they paid for the court transcript. If an attorney was assigned to handle the appeal, then the county would provide the appointed attorney the transcript.

Once Deaton heard this, he told the judge that the county would need to provide her with an attorney for the appeal and the transcript. Several said that Deaton wanted the judge to appoint him to handle her appeal, but that wasn't going to happen.

Judge Bryan instead appointed Robert A. Morrow III, an attorney from The Woodlands, a suburb of Houston and a thirty-four-year veteran of criminal defense, as Saenz's appeals attorney.

However, Lufkin is small and so is the courthouse, and rumors run as fast as East Texas rivers in flood. One that continuously made the circuit was that Bennie Fowler, Saenz's mother, cashed in her retirement at Walmart, and Kent Fowler, her father, cashed in his 401K from Peterbilt, planning to use the funds to rehire Deaton as soon as Morrow got the transcript from the court for the appeal.

One thing is for certain: Deaton wasn't about to do the appeal for free, and the court wasn't about to appoint him and pay him. People close to Saenz's parents said they were dead broke. The cost of the trial had already drained them of every cent they had. For sure, attorneys in a capital murder case don't come cheap.

Many of the Saenz supporters have the wrong idea about the appeals process. Several have said that the appeals court will look and see that there wasn't enough evidence to take Saenz to trial and release her. Unfortunately, that isn't what they do. The first appeal is before a panel of three judges. They look to see simply that the defendant received a fair trial. Her supporters were adamant that Saenz was going to get a new trial on appeal, and then be freed. They were as adamant about that as they were during the trial. Steve Taylor attempted to explain to Saenz and her family the long odds of winning that trial. Before the trial, he even brought in an expert to talk to them about realities, but they didn't buy it then, and they still weren't.

The success rate of direct appeals, the first appeal

process, is slightly less than 3 percent. But this statistic doesn't deal with cases involving multiple victims. Statistically, Saenz has a better chance of winning the lottery than winning an appeal.

The next step in the appeal process is the Court of Criminal Appeals. However, that court is a discretionary one. They choose which cases they are going to hear. There is less than 3 percent of the cases this court even hears, let alone overturns.

Taylor, one of the first attorneys in Texas to be certified in criminal appellate law, said, "Do you think they are going to give anybody any slack who was found guilty of killing five people, and committing aggravated assault on three others?"

Family and friends took to Facebook to right the wrong they thought was done to Saenz. They created a Facebook page called "Release Kim."

The Facebook page included a large picture titled "Shredded Justice," showing a man from the neck down, standing in the middle of a pile of shredded paper. Big red letters proclaimed "DaVita."

This image pointed to the heart of the reason Deaton and the family believed Kimberly Saenz was convicted: the court wouldn't allow the defense to present certain things as evidence.

During the trial, Deaton had attempted to bring in a couple of janitors who'd helped clean up the DaVita clinic after it closed down after April 28, 2008. Both janitors were *voir dired* outside the jury's presence. They testified that after the clinic closed, they'd carried out a lot of closed garbage bags of trash. The bags were very light, as if full of shredded paper. One of the janitors said that she'd seen paper shredders inside with paper dust on them.

However, the judge ruled the jury couldn't hear the testimony. Even if those bags had been full of shredded paper, it didn't mean anything. Saenz was on trial for killing and injuring patients with bleach. No one was accused of using paper.

Deaton had wanted this testimony in to help him prove his conspiracy theory, but even if the judge had let it in, it likely would have only hurt Deaton's case further. DaVita was a computer facility. They had no paper records on hand. When they needed a copy of a patient's file, they had to go to the computer and print that file out.

When DaVita reported what the witnesses had said on April 28, they were descended on by several organizations, including the Lufkin Police Department. Sergeant Steve Abbott alone examined over 16,000 documents, all of which DaVita had to print off for him.

What the defense attorney and the family members didn't seem to consider was that, by federal law, medical facilities are required to shred any documents they print. Evidence of paper shredding wouldn't have pointed to conspiracy; it would only have shown that DaVita was following federal law.

The document that Deaton and his investigator had attempted to get some of the jurors to look at after the trial was something else the judge had not allowed in. It was a Texas Department of Health and Human Services report that the agency did in May 2008, after DaVita had shut down.

In that report, the agency was very critical of DaVita

and its procedures. Among other things, the report stated that DaVita wasn't following their own procedures as far as reporting of incidents, paperwork, and other things like that. The agency concluded that it was possible that if DaVita had done all their paperwork correctly, a pattern might have been noticed prior to April.

Herrington explained why the court did not allow the document in. He said, "If a restaurant is using bad mayonnaise and it is causing illness and deaths to the customers, and investigators go in and find an open jar of tainted mayonnaise, that relates to the crime and is admissible.

"However, if they find a sealed jar of mayonnaise on the shelf that has been recalled, that can't be used because it hadn't even been opened. It wasn't the cause of the illnesses and deaths."

The report was critical to DaVita practices but nothing in it indicated that DaVita was responsible for the things that were injuring and killing patients. Therefore it was not admissible in a court of law.

These were the sorts of things the defense attorney and family had had all their hopes pinned on.

In addition to the Facebook page, Saenz supporters also created a website also under the "Release Kim" URL. Both the Facebook page and the website had a faith-based angle, though at the bottom of the website home page was a "Donate" link, allowing donors to send money to Saenz's supporters via any major credit card, and a "Get Involved" link offering suggestions of ways that her supporters could help, including donating monthly to help Kim's defense fund.

Kimberly Saenz eventually took to the Internet herself, though seemingly for different reasons. The Texas prison system allows its inmates to troll the internet for pen pals and such, and inmates can post personal ads, along with pictures of themselves and contact information. Saenz posted an ad calling herself "a cool mix of girlie and tough," and a "sexy, fun, devoted, social, open minded female seeking a pen pal for friendship." She listed her interests as including "reading, playing with animals, interior decorating, sports, traveling, and listening to music (mostly rap and country)," "keeping up with the latest gadgets, latest news, and scientific studies," plus "taking guitar lessons or learning French," and boasted "my intuition is spot on, trivia night is a jam, my shoe collection is fabulous." "Life is too short!" she also proclaims at one point, ignoring her role in having helped shorten any lives.

The ad read like an exercise in wish fulfillment—the photo she posted of herself wasn't a recent one, and most people who'd viewed her in the courtroom or the booking pictures wouldn't have recognized her from it. Saenz also claimed a release date of 3-31-2022, but the Department of Corrections doesn't agree. They simply list it as life without parole.

Ryan Deaton told *The Lufkin News* that he hoped Saenz got a new trial from the appeal. But even if she did, there was no guarantee that a new trial would find her innocent; and if she was convicted again, she'd again be in danger of getting the death penalty, which she'd missed by only two votes the first time around. The old saying to be careful of what you wish for was definitely in effect.

————————

After the trial was over, Clyde Herrington let the East Texas public in on a little piece of information that was even scarier than what had come out at the trial. Early on in the investigation, he contacted an epidemiologist at the CDC by the name of Dr. Melissa Schaeffer. Her study of the adverse occurrences at DaVita and the days Saenz worked and the way they matched up helped convince Herrington that he was on the right track with the investigation, and went a long way in convincing him that Saenz was guilty.

But there was actually more to Dr. Schaeffer's study: her study suggested that there may have been many more than only ten victims. Schaeffer had looked at all the adverse occurrences at DaVita, not just the ones that Saenz was accused of committing. As it turned out, Saenz was the only employee working on *all* the days that a patient had experienced unexplained health complications or death. But barring a confession, no one but Kimberly Saenz will ever know for sure, and there's no evidence to prove it. DaVita had created a policy in September 2007 of keeping the bloodlines and other equipment of patients who suffered cardiac problems at DaVita clinics, but DaVita Lufkin had begun following the policy only after Ms. Clara Strange and Ms. Thelma Metcalf died on April 1, 2008.

All the bloodlines that were so important to the jury as well as the syringes of the other patients before April 1, 2008, DaVita has discarded.

And there was another chilling little postscript to this

macabre story that had not come out during the trial. The searches on the effects of bleach poisoning and detecting bleach in bloodlines weren't the only suspicious things found on Kimberly Saenz's computer. Investigators also discovered searches for "cooking for diseased families" and "how to sniff Xanax." And among her files was a song titled: "I Got Away with Murder."

On Monday, April 9, 2012, nearly four years after the investigation into the suspicious deaths at the DaVita clinic began, the city of Lufkin had a visitor to pay homage to the people responsible for Kimberly Clark Saenz's conviction.

U.S. Attorney John Malcolm Bales held a press conference to acknowledge the "excellent example of the cooperation of multiple agencies of federal, state, and local law enforcement and prosecution teams in bringing justice to the Lufkin community."

When he was through talking, others who were involved in the case spoke to the gathered media. In his speech, Prosecutor Clyde Herrington credited Bales himself for responding to Herrington's call for help. Not only had Bales's influence helped get all the CDC and FDA employees to Lufkin to testify, but Bales had sent them Chris Tortorice, who turned out to be a Godsend to the case himself.

Last, Herrington credited one man in particular above all the others: Sergeant Stephen Abbott of the Lufkin Police Department.

On Tuesday, June 5, 2012, there was a real conspiracy

carried out in Lufkin. The week before, Herrington had been informed that the city was going to give Sergeant Abbott an award for his role in the Saenz investigation. Herrington never doubted that he deserved it. When they asked him if he would be there, he told them he wouldn't miss it.

When Herrington arrived, somebody congratulated him and he became suspicious, but after looking at the program that only listed Abbott, he relaxed—until he looked around and noticed his wife. At that moment, he realized that he'd been duped.

He wasn't the only one. It seemed that Abbott had shown up to support Herrington.

However, once there, the two men had no choice but to sit and take their medicine, as Mayor Bob Brown awarded them both Lufkin's meritorious service award.